_Deconstructing
Brad Pitt

_Deconstructing Brad Pitt

EDITED BY
CHRISTOPHER SCHABERG
AND ROBERT BENNETT

B L O O M S B U R Y
NEW YORK · LONDON · NEW DELHI · SYDNEY

Bloomsbury Academic
An imprint of Bloomsbury Publishing Inc

1385 Broadway	50 Bedford Square
New York	London
NY 10018	WC1B 3DP
USA	UK

www.bloomsbury.com

Bloomsbury is a registered trade mark of Bloomsbury Publishing Plc

First published 2014

Library of Congress Cataloging-in-Publication Data
Deconstructing Brad Pitt / edited by Christopher Schaberg and Robert Bennett.
pages cm
Includes bibliographical references and index.
ISBN 978-1-62356-946-4 (hardback : alk. paper) — ISBN 978-1-62356-179-6 (pbk. : alk.
paper) 1. Pitt, Brad, 1963—Criticism and interpretation. I. Schaberg, Christopher,
editor of compilation. II. Bennett, Robert, 1967- editor of compilation.
PN2287.P54D44 2014
791.4302'8092—dc23
2014010311

ISBN:	HB:	978-1-6235-6946-4
	PB:	978-1-6235-6179-6
	ePub:	978-1-6235-6193-2
	ePDF:	978-1-6235-6396-7

Typeset by RefineCatch Limited, Bungay, Suffolk
Printed and bound in the United States of America

For Lara and Chris
And for Julien, Camille, Theo, Sage, and Nina

CONTENTS

LIST OF FIGURES

Every exit from the book is made within the book.

—JACQUES DERRIDA, "EDMOND JABÈS AND
THE QUESTION OF THE BOOK"

PRELUDE

Bryan Batt

Bryan Batt is an American actor, author, designer, and philanthropist, known for his multiple roles on Broadway, in film, and as Salvatore Romano in the acclaimed AMC drama Mad Men (2007–2009).

When I was asked to write an introductory note for a book entitled _Deconstructing Brad Pitt, to be completely candid, I was a bit reluctant. The title was somewhat reminiscent of those skewering tabloid trash-rag headlines that surely Mr Pitt must be thoroughly disgusted with. However, knowing one of the editors as a kind and honorable gentleman, husband, and father, I gave it a read, and was thoroughly entertained.

I have never met Mr Pitt, although he and Angelina have shopped on Magazine Street for their children just steps away from our shop Hazlenut, causing quite a stir. Customers clamored to get a glimpse of the A-stars while they raved, "She's so gorgeous. . . ." She's gorgeous? Look at him!

I was hoping to meet Brad when I worked on the film *12 Years a Slave*, but alas, his car was racing away from the plantation as I was pulling in. Once again, I was hoping to make his acquaintance at his Make It Right Foundation Gala, but unfortunately work took me out of town.

So now, I am taking this time to tell you what I would tell him. As a New Orleanian and as a person that supports equal rights for all, thank you, Mr Pitt, for doing what you do. It's one thing to talk about it, but it's a completely different thing to put your money and time where your mouth and heart are and make a difference. His helping to rebuild New Orleans and producing such socially important films as the Oscar-winning *12 Years A Slave* and the brilliant *The Normal Heart* just demonstrate his commitment to making things right. Bravo!

FOREWORD

Robert Bennett

The first rule of Brad Pitt Studies is you do NOT talk about Brad Pitt.

I should know. I learned the hard way. I was a young, idealistic professor fresh out of graduate school when my first graduate student, Chris, suggested that we present papers about Brad Pitt at an academic conference. The suggestion immediately intrigued me. After all, the field of cultural studies continually explores new lines of critical inquiry, and Pitt seemed almost too obvious a choice. At the time Pitt's films were both critically acclaimed and widely popular, and he even vaguely resembled other Hollywood icons like Robert Redford. Beyond their obvious co-involvement in *A River Runs Through It*, both were good-looking, talented actors who first established their careers with a few significant Western films before branching out to explore a wider range of roles. More importantly, both had early performances that many considered to be generation-defining roles—most notably in *Fight Club* and *All the President's Men*—and yet, both actors also share the curious distinction of never having won an Oscar for their acting. From this perspective, the real question seemed less whether or not we should study Brad Pitt than why hadn't someone else already done it?

Boy, were we wrong. As soon as we issued our call for conference papers, the mere suggestion that we might tentatively explore Pitt's films struck a raw nerve among other academics.[1] *The Chronicle of Higher Education* quickly picked up our call, and—with an openly sneering grin—reprinted it as proof that the cultural studies lunatic fringe had once again gone off the rails.[2] Soon thereafter, *The Chronicle*'s derision went viral, circulating among bloggers and online pundits who, with less nuance and reserve, outright ridiculed our project. While one blogger insinuated that I must be a reliable source for pot, another suggested that Brad Pitt Studies shared a natural intellectual alliance with studies on the gendering of public toilets.[3] Calling our interest in Pitt "roba da pazzi" ("crazy stuff"), an Italian blogger suggested that our project would likely lead to future explorations of "Fat Studies, The Cultural Production of Ignorance, Medieval Video Gaming, Filthy Ideas and Indecent Expressions."[4] (Never mind that, nine years later, most of those things have indeed become valid fields of study.) We even "bristle[d]" the blogger at Acephalous—though I'm not exactly sure why, since it was he, not us, who used the insult "jackasses"—while an "annoyed" respondent to that post called us "nut-jobs" who had chosen to explore "some totally shitty topic."[5] Unbristled ourselves, we persisted, not realizing that the worst was yet to come.

The most impassioned and vitriolic responses would soon come in a barrage of personal hate e-mails, mostly from scholars in the Humanities, angrily denouncing the very premise of studying Brad Pitt. Their arguments were less principled than visceral, seething, and practically primal. Long-winded and angry, most of them spoke with a sense of self-righteous outrage. Somehow we had struck a chord in the profession, in individual scholars, and in the web intelligentsia that ran far deeper than we had ever expected. I was not surprised that an individual or two might roll their eyes bemusedly, but I had never imagined that a professional publication of record, legions of bloggers, and irate academics would even notice our work, let alone openly assault it. One disgruntled academic was so infuriated that he telephoned both my department chair and my dean demanding that my university should fire me for pursuing such frivolous studies. With people calling for my head, I started to feel more like a losing Big Ten football coach than a middling English professor. One thing, however, was certain: there was a line in the academic sand, and we had crossed it.

Our detractors' point was clear and unequivocal: do NOT talk about Brad Pitt. So we put the project on the back burner for a while until Chris picked it up again. One thing led to another until we ended up with this anthology of academic essays on the actor and celebrity Brad Pitt. Titled _Deconstructing Brad Pitt_, this anthology aims neither to simply praise Pitt nor to brutally bury him, but more modestly it seeks to seriously and critically analyze his career from a wide range of scholarly perspectives or, as the title of this anthology puts it, to deconstruct him.

Notes

1 Here is our original call for papers:

CFP: *The Cultural Logic of Brad Pitt*
For the 2005 Western Literature Association Conference in Los Angeles, we plan to organize a panel on the film icon, Brad Pitt. Why Brad Pitt? As one of this generation's most popular actors, Pitt has explored many of the cultural tensions of our emerging postmodern era. Depicting masculine American whiteness in various states of crisis, his characters generally enact complex postmodern agencies; they are never wholly coherent, they are often self-destructive, and they generally rely on a certain amount of play—between stability and instability, between life and death, between autonomy and alter-dependency, between control and abandon. Simultaneously reifying and challenging hegemonic codes of race, class, gender, and regional or national identity, his characters explore the complex and changing postmodern cultural landscape. Tracing his performances through a variety of films and theoretical texts we hope to explain Brad Pitt's multi-dimensional postmodernity by exploring: 1) the cultural logic of his performances, showing how they dramatize postmodern cultural tensions, and 2) the kind of cultural or political work that his performances accomplish, or the difference that they make and the impact that they have on the audiences who watch them. Some of the kinds of issues that we hope to explore include:

- Brad Pitt's West: From *A River Runs Through It* and *Legends of the Fall* to *Thelma and Louise* and *Kalifornia*, many of Pitt's performances explore the physical and cultural landscapes of the American West. How do Pitt's performances both reenact and revise more traditional western narratives and identities?
- Brad Pitt's postmodern subjectivity: How do Pitt's performances, especially in films such as *Fight Club* and *12 Monkeys*, explore new postmodern constructions of race, class, gender, and national identity? What makes these characters compelling or illuminating for contemporary audiences, and what do they tell us about how American culture is changing in response to new postmodern economic and historical contexts?
- Marketing Brad Pitt: While Brad Pitt has clearly emerged as a mainstream Hollywood star and box-office favorite, his characters frequently bristle with an undeniably rebellious and countercultural energy. But do his characters really explore radical or marginal locations outside the boundaries of the dominant culture, or are they only pseudo-revolutionaries-posing as rebels, but ultimately conforming to privileged, white, male, heterosexual, and American cultural norms? What do his performances teach us about the complex relationship between the culture and the countercultures of the postmodern, especially in the popular media? How is his revolutionary persona used as a marketing device to sell movies and/or postmodern culture?
- Please send a 1-page proposal and 1-page CV to Robert Bennett by Friday June 10, 2005.
- Proposals may be sent either by email (preferable): bennett@english.montana.edu [since changed, though I still accept hate e-mail] or by regular mail: Robert Bennett / 2-270 Wilson Hall / English Department / Montana State University / Bozeman, MT 59717
- More info about the conference is available online: www.usu.edu/westlit/conference2005.html.

2 James Brian Wagaman, "Postmodern Brad," *The Chronicle of Higher Education* online, https://chronicle.com/article/Postmodern-Brad/24659 [Accessed November 19, 2013].

3 Roger Kimball, "The Hermeneutics of Brad Pitt." http://www.
newcriterion.com/posts.cfm/hermeneutics-of-brad-pitt-3962
[Accessed November 19, 2013]; Rufus, "Proof that Academics
Read the *National Inquirer*." http://gradstudentmadness.
blogspot.com/2005/06/proof-that-academics-read-national.html
[Accessed November 19, 2013].

4 "La Logica Culturale di Brad Pitt." http://bottone.blogspot.com/
2005/09/paperi-call-for-crazy-papers.html [Accessed November
19, 2013].

5 "The Cultural Logic of Brad Pitt, or Does Tyler Durden Reify or
Challenge Hegemonic Codes of Race, Class, Gender, or Regional
and National Identities?" http://acephalous.typepad.com/
acephalous/2005/05/the_cultural_lo.html [Accessed December 3,
2013].

PREFACE

Christopher Schaberg

For many years the book you are holding in your hands existed as something of a joke: who would seriously write a serious book about Brad Pitt?[1]

In 2003, as a first-year PhD student at the University of California, Davis, I wrote an essay about how several of Brad Pitt's roles revealed contradictory ideals of the American West, and I presented this paper at the annual Western American Literature conference that year. Robert Bennett had been my mentor at Montana State University-Bozeman, where I had previously earned a Master's Degree in English, and he shared my obsessions with Pitt. At one point we hatched a plan for a whole book on Brad Pitt, and we attempted to put together a panel on this topic at another WAL conference. That panel never materialized, but our proposal for it produced strong reactions, as Robert delineates above in the Foreword. Luckily, I was obscure enough in my existence as a graduate student that I escaped the wrath of the responses to our call; but I do recall pulling off the road somewhere in Maine during a family trip in the spring of 2005, to entertain the skeptical and leading questions of a *Wall Street Journal* reporter who had picked up the story (nothing came of that interview—probably for the best).

So the idea that there might be a whole academic book organized around Brad Pitt was, for about a decade, simply a line that made people grin, cringe, or guffaw in disbelief. It was a good-humored joke about the capaciousness of cultural studies, about academics' ability to look at *anything* and "think critically" about it. (This technically falls under the long shadow of semiotics, or the study of signs.)

And yet, as Robert and I brainstormed this line of inquiry (let's call it Brad Pitt Studies), and we kept talking about this book idea with various scholars and students over the years, people inevitably insisted it could be done—even that it *should* be done. Brad Pitt represented certain hot button issues. For instance, his outspoken feelings about religion put rather bluntly what various philosophers have argued over the years, if in more elaborate language.[2] Then there are the ways that Brad Pitt and Angelina Jolie's relationship and parenting challenge the institutions of marriage and traditional family norms—these things running parallel to (if not outright precipitating) political shifts around who can marry who and how families are formed. Legalizing marijuana? Check. Sustainability? He's on it.

Still, there was always a lingering sentiment that scoffed at the very idea: Why think (much less *write*) about Brad Pitt at all? Isn't he just a pretty boy, a propped-up celebrity icon with passing interests in cool things like motorcycles, airplanes, exotic child adoptions, and postmodern architecture? Or even worse, if we *were* to take him seriously, might Pitt be little more than indicative of the most galling aspects of American white male privilege, the entertainment industry, and/or advanced global capitalism? In other words, don't we already know exactly what we will discover lurking in Brad Pitt, barely hidden under the surface?

Robert and I kept this book idea percolating for over a decade—half as a running joke, half as a real quandary. And in the meantime, celebrities became an increasingly respectable topic of inquiry: admirable books appeared on Johnny Depp, Lady Gaga, Clint Eastwood, and Tiger Woods (to name just a few). One potential contributor for this book (a poet and critic who writes very insightfully about popular culture) declined an invitation to write on Brad Pitt, but said he would have been glad to write about Daniel Day-Lewis. (Whether he was being sarcastic or not, I can't be sure; e-mail is tone-deaf.)

When I moved to New Orleans in 2009 for a tenure-track job at Loyola University New Orleans, my interests in Brad

Pitt flared up again. At one point I met Andrew Horton, a former film professor at Loyola, and he gave me a copy of a film he had written the screenplay for—Pitt's first feature-length role—*The Dark Side of the Sun*. This deferred, "lost" film blew me away: its curious blend of 1980's Americana mixed with European art cinema stirred something in me. And then of course, there was the emergent Pitt—everything there, yet disguised before his time.

Pitt is known around New Orleans for his post-Katrina work in the Lower Ninth Ward: his Make It Right project committed to building 150 green-designed affordable houses for residents who lost their homes when the levees broke. As of this writing, nearly 100 homes have been built under the auspices of Brad Pitt and Make It Right.

As Robert described above, our earliest ideas for this book were met with scorn and disbelief. Yet since moving to New Orleans, when I mention working on an academic study of Brad Pitt, people more often than not immediately respond, "What a great idea!" Around New Orleans, Pitt is generally taken seriously not only as an extension of the entertainment industry, but also as someone who has done something real for the city in the wake of a disaster. There's criticism mixed in with appreciation, for sure—but the point is that he is more than *just* a celebrity. (We have plenty of celebrities in New Orleans, thanks to the economic incentives for local film production; hang out at Whole Foods Uptown and count down from 60, and you're sure to spot at least one celebrity.)

To visit the Lower Ninth Ward in late 2013 is to see a space still ravaged by the flood after Hurricane Katrina, and yet that same space is also interspersed with brightly colored structures sprouting up amid empty lots and tombstone-like stoops and piers where old shotgun houses once stood. The "Brad Pitt houses" (as they are sometimes called) exhibit architectural audacity and verve; they also already show signs of wear, from the subsequent hurricanes and tropical storms since Katrina. Pitt's involvement in this effort has been instrumental and meaningful to many residents of the Lower Ninth Ward and to plenty of New Orleanians at large. I had known for a while that Pitt had a penchant for architecture—and that he had even completed an unofficial apprenticeship with Frank Gehry, one of the most influential architects of the last half century—and I felt an affinity with him when I learned that Pitt admired the work of Frank Lloyd Wright. My grandparents were proud owners of a Frank Lloyd Wright house that was designed and built for them in the 1950s, and many of my earliest memories involve that Usonian home.[3]

For me, then, this book involves personal attachments and my own narrative threads. Near and distant relations to architecture: my grandfather's love for Frank Lloyd Wright; my brilliant cousin architect Emily White, whose work I admire hugely; Brad Pitt, adjunct architect, who got involved in the rebuilding of New Orleans post-Katrina. Owning a 125-year-old shotgun house in New Orleans, I've become entranced by collisions and seepages between architecture, ecosystems, geography, and climate. Walking around the Lower Ninth Ward in October 2013 rendered me speechless. An incomplete project with its fair share of criticism, the Make It Right homes are nevertheless real acts of construction—even as they are enmeshed with politics, history, and questions of architectural style. Speaking of collisions, I've spent the last ten years writing seriously about airports and air travel, and one of the more frayed ends of this work wound up in these pages.

Then, of course, there is the scattered collection of movies with Brad Pitt in them, films I saw with no plan or system throughout college and graduate school. And these films were serendipitously framed by a surrounding wilderness of corresponding illuminations in books and essays, many of which happened in proximity to the name Jacques Derrida. Perhaps this book is evidence of how I dealt with the intensities of graduate school and the bleak academic job market of 2008 and 2009 (no less bleak in 2014, maybe even more so). This book has been an attempt to keep a sense of laughter and play in my academic work—or as a Loyola committee noted when they awarded me some funds to help with the completion of the book, "it's the lighter side of scholarship." (Though after reading Robert's Postscript, you might not be so sure.)

Relatedly, an upshot of this project has been the chance to surprise the students in my courses: "So anyway, I'm working on this book about Brad Pitt [. . .]"—you can imagine the looks on their faces, and the questions, exclamations, and conversations that follow. As an English professor it is nice to have ways to slip out of the preconceptions and clichés that come with the job—okay, even if nutty cultural studies topics *have become* one of those very clichés! The point of my digressions here is that this project has always been wrapped up with personal experiences, memories, and attachments. You'll see personal narratives weave in and out of the chapters of this book; another rule of Brad Pitt Studies seems to be that you can't escape *some* kind of attachment to him.

Notes

1 I don't mean a Hollywood biography (of which there are two) or a novel (of which there is one: Shannon Hammond's uproarious, offensive, abrasive, *Crying of Lot 49*-esque *Brad Pitt Won't Leave Me Alone*, published posthumously in 2011). I'm talking about a critical study, a study that takes seriously Brad Pitt as a complex icon, a "social text" replete with myriad meanings, understandings, assumptions . . . in short, a book that attempts to prove that Brad Pitt is something worth thinking about—not just something/someone to look at, to consume.

2 Compare, for instance, http://zerobs.net/media/brad-pitt-religion.jpg with the thinking of Friedrich Nietzsche.

3 http://en.wikipedia.org/wiki/Donald_Schaberg_House.

ACKNOWLEDGMENTS

This book would have been impossible to write and put together without the help of many kind, generous, and smart people. To start with, Brad Pitt inspired us in the first place and kept us interested and intrigued throughout the process, right up to the final assemblage of this book. Too many have contributed to this project, in ways both large and small, for us to list every individual by name. Moreover, while we sincerely thank the individuals named below for making significant contributions to our ideas and work, we also absolve them from any responsibility for endorsing what this book has to say. The following individuals have taught, assisted, and inspired us, but the Frankenstein's monster that we have made here—with its flaws, errors, absurdities, and strange attachments—is our own responsibility and ours alone. So please, don't blame anyone listed below.

We are indebted to our editors and their colleagues at Bloomsbury. Not only is Bloomsbury one of the smartest and hippest cultural studies presses going today, but it also has terrific editors (keeping Continuum alive in spirit if not in imprint). We thank Katie Gallof for acquiring the book and seeing it through its various stages, and for giving us a deadline extension when life and death intervened. Mary Al-Sayed provided thorough and savvy assistance in preparing the final manuscript. We also thank Haaris Naqvi for insight, ideas, and advice that helped shape the book early on. Four outside reviewers provided helpful feedback, advice, and insights, and we want to thank especially Roger Whitson for his enthusiasm for the project.

For their thoughtful suggestions, their accommodations and flexibility, and their careful attention to detail, we thank the following: Nancy Bernardo for the striking cover art and original collages; Erin Little, Loyola University Collaborative Scholarship Fellow, who arranged the bibliography as well as helped with dozens of minor tasks as the book came together; Stewart Sinclair, who read a good portion of the manuscript with shrewd eyes in the final hours; Emma Grimsley, research assistant through the Loyola Honors Program, for help researching an early chapter idea for the book; Richard O'Brien, for a burst of bright energy conveyed via Twitter in an otherwise dark moment; and Susan Clements, indexer, extraordinaire.

For their always insightful and stimulating conversation and ambient support, we especially thank Rob Wallace (the erstwhile Third Musketeer), Susan Kollin, Linda Karell, Kara Thompson, Mark Yakich, Tim Welsh, Hillary Eklund, John Biguenet, Tim Morton, Ian Bogost, Jeffrey Jerome Cohen, Neil Campbell, Steven Tatum, Alan O. Weltzien, Chris Schedler, and John Trombold—and the upstart intellectual provocateurs from the University of Utah and their friends. (You know who you are.) In addition, we wish to thank our colleagues and students in the English Departments at Loyola University New Orleans and at Montana State University-Bozeman. We also thank the Western Literature Association and Pacific Northwest American Studies Association—with their many thoughtful and engaging scholars—for providing venues where we could present early drafts of our work

For providing generous financial support throughout various stages of this project, we express our grateful appreciation to Loyola's Center for Faculty Innovation, Loyola's Marquette Summer Fellowship Program, the Loyola University New Orleans Honors Program (who knew undergraduate research assistants could be so helpful?), the Dean of Humanities and Natural Sciences at Loyola, the Loyola English Department, and the English Department at Montana State University-Bozeman.

Introduction

Christopher Schaberg and Robert Bennett

What is _Deconstructing Brad Pitt? It is a book about a famous actor, certainly. But it is also a book that exceeds the star, goes beyond him, and speculates about many topics that intersect or brush against the visages we recognize as Brad Pitt.

This is also a book that gets started ahead of itself, as indicated in the simple underscore before the title on the cover: _Deconstructing. As soon as you try to write anything about Brad Pitt, you realize that the writing has already begun. There's an audible, nearly palpable buzz around celebrities that preconditions every act of commentary or critique. It turns out that you cannot really write about Brad Pitt as a stable subject, but only about refracted images and wobbly meanings, hyperbolic performances and garish masks.

The underscore on the cover, then, says it all: even before you start *thinking* about Brad Pitt, deconstruction is happening. Brad Pitt isn't Brad Pitt. Or he isn't *just* Brad Pitt; he's _Brad Pitt, framed by some expectation, desire, notion—he's always something else, something more (or less). Some *thing* that we have to reckon with, coming from many angles and flashing across the various screens of our lives. On the one hand, maybe he is just another celebrity, another star to get excited about or at the mention of whose name you might roll your eyes. On the other hand, though, Brad Pitt is different: there's something about him specifically that needs to be thought about, teased out, agitated, articulated. At the same time, there is a veritable force field of opinions, attitudes, and shimmering surfaces that make him tricky to approach in a straightforward way. This is why the book in your hands offers you multiple ways to think about Brad Pitt—his roles, his various meanings in American culture, his subversive or mainstream qualities. This book was originally conceived for a series of books called "Guides for the Perplexed." The idea was that the book would pose a series of essays to satisfy readers who were perplexed about Brad Pitt. Is he really worth thinking about in a serious way? How precisely does he function as a sex symbol? Where does his acting end and his celebrity begin? Why does he never win an Oscar? Is he clearly a hyper-masculine figure, or might Pitt in fact challenge clear lines of gender and power?

The book still addresses these sorts of questions, but our editor thought that the book would do better on its own, outside an academic series dedicated to more recognizably scholarly topics. (After all, we weren't really imagining that professors would start designing classes around Brad Pitt Studies—though celebrity studies is a legitimate and thriving subfield of film/cultural studies.)

So who is this book for? We imagine several overlapping audiences. First off, this book is for readers who have been intellectually stimulated by one or more of Pitt's performances. Secondly, this book is for anyone who is turned off or even repelled by the utterance "Brad Pitt"—the chapters in this book show why Pitt is worth taking seriously, from a number of angles and for a variety of reasons. But the book is a far cry from mere biography, let alone hagiography. Instead our book takes an academic and critical approach to the actor and his many performances, offering a range of diverse perspectives both on his acting and his celebrity. However, we've tried to write this book in a way that is free of the kind of jargon that can make academic writing in the humanities turgid or abstruse.

Why, then, did we include a piece of academic jargon in the very title of the book? What does *deconstructing* mean? It does not mean a stripping away of Brad Pitt, or mere savage criticism. In fact, the term is *positive*. We admit right off to adopting the term "deconstructing" in a rather loose way; but to put it simply, deconstruction stands for three things for the purpose of this book: (1) Structure; (2) Signs; and (3) Play.

By *structure*, we mean the way Brad Pitt comes together, is made up, can be seen as a whole figure—even across the many roles that he plays, both on and off the screen. This is the common meaning of the word "deconstructing" as it has made its way into popular culture: you can order a "deconstructed sushi bowl" at a restaurant—which means all the parts of the traditional sushi roll are taken apart and made visible (and thus noticed differently) in the bowl. When we say we can *deconstruct* something, we might be claiming to see it for what it really is, to make apparent an otherwise hidden structure. This is how Woody Allen used the term to title his 1997 film, *Deconstructing Harry*, which peels back layers upon layers of the title character to show us certain psychological hang-ups, secret impulses, and concealed traits. *Structure* also suggests an architectural register, and indeed deconstruction has been applied to certain postmodern architectural styles and strategies; while this book does not touch directly on Pitt's interest in architecture, there is certainly potential for further inquiry on this topic.

By *signs*, we mean how Brad Pitt signifies things: from sexiness to strength, slacker stoner to stone-cold killer, white male privilege to progressive (even radical) politics, and so on. Deconstruction has been closely related to a widespread academic reading of signs in language and culture—and thus the term "deconstruction" and its attendant interpretive strategies have flourished in English departments across the

United States for several decades. (Not coincidentally, many of the contributors of this book are English professors.)

As for *play*, this is a key part of deconstruction: it means the way structures have *give*, or the way they flex and bend in order to stay intact. One of the tenets of deconstruction is that everything that seems fixed in fact requires room for slippage, or play. Where we might think Brad Pitt the actor (or celebrity) is a relative constant, a predictable persona or figure—we will discover him in fact to be anything but. He shifts around in ways that complicate and enrich the possible meanings we can associate with the name Brad Pitt. We will see how Pitt *plays* in different contexts—and even within the same context. In addition, and just as important, *play* suggests playfulness, or a certain basic pleasure in reading and interpretation.

Finally, and to return to the earliest point of this Introduction, consider one of Jacques Derrida's most adamant claims about deconstruction: it's not something you *do*, it's just something that *happens*. It is a necessary, ongoing condition for any structure, for any sign—for anything that *plays* (word-play, acting roles, a DVD, a YouTube clip...). Deconstructing Brad Pitt is actually not about *doing* anything special to the actor; it is about seeing how he acts, how he works, what he does—what *happens* around Brad Pitt. And it is already happening, whether you know it or not. The essays in this book are in turns playful and serious, personal and detached, biographical and theoretical. Together they comprise _Deconstructing Brad Pitt.

To begin again

This book takes Brad Pitt seriously as an actor—and not simply as an actor but also as a locus of larger cultural myths and narratives. Certainly, one can debate the quality of Pitt's acting or the value of his films, but his performances have inarguably shaped the last two decades of American and even global cinema: for better or for worse perhaps, but decisively nonetheless. Moreover, he has done so while playing a wide spectrum of popular, conventional, innovative, challenging, and even experimental roles: at one moment he plays an anarchist, terrorist, or insane person; the next he stars in a conventional Hollywood blockbuster, makes an art film about families (a kind of Ingmar Bergman meets *Lilo & Stitch*), or turns zombie hunter/savior of the post-apocalyptic world. For how ubiquitous and *seemingly* obvious a public figure Pitt has become—we think we already know him, we believe that we instinctively understand him, and we routinely reduce him to one simple cipher or another—his career as an actor, especially considered in its entirety, is both more complex and less self-evident than is commonly assumed. For all of the ink (not to mention glossy photographs) that have been spilled on the subject of Brad Pitt, surprisingly little of it—whether pro or con—actually takes Pitt seriously as an actor, explores his celebrity in interesting or nuanced ways, or attempts to explain his broader salience (or not)—as opposed to mere presence—in American culture at large. There are, to be sure, powerful counter-examples to this—critical cultural analyses of Pitt with genuine gravitas—but they remain little more than exceptions that prove the rule. If nothing else, this volume provides a counterweight to the salacious, unexamined Brad Pitt endlessly reproduced at supermarket checkout stands, offering in its place a portrait—however provisional and incomplete—of Pitt as an artist.

Approaching Pitt as an actor, however, first requires bracketing his celebrity—at least provisionally—to better foreground how his performances function as works of art. Even if only temporarily, the cultural critic must chart some path through the distorting fog of Pitt's often distracting celebrity persona. In short, the critic must seek to discover the hidden meaning, the essential form, or the inner structure of Pitt's acting as art. And yet, this critical gesture proves to be little more than a fool's errand, a sheer impossibility, because while the cultural logic of Brad Pitt does include his artistry, it always includes his celebrity and public persona as well.

Consequently, Pitt the actor and Pitt the celebrity are intimately interconnected in a Gordian knot, impossible to disentangle.

This presents the critic with an obvious dilemma—if not an outright paradox. On the one hand, Pitt's films have received both popular and critical acclaim, but his celebrity routinely eclipses, or alternatingly propels, his achievements as an actor, often inflecting—or at times even inflicting—his performances with a heavy atmosphere of cultural attitudes and predilections associated with Pitt as a public figure, icon, symbol, or even commodity. We can even talk about Pitt as a mere celebrity: a vessel (or, in occasional cases, a counterpoint) for myriad standards of physical beauty, sexual attractiveness, masculinity, and social norms (or not). In fact, Pitt's celebrity permeates his career so extensively that he may be better understood, first and foremost, as a celebrity rather than an actor, and even his best acting is frequently, if not absolutely, not dissociable from his highly visible celebrity and the cultural myths and narratives that surround it.

Consequently, this book also takes seriously Pitt's public life beyond the screen in the diverse roles, from tabloid icon to political activist, which have become associated with him. As the literary critic Jennifer Wicke has noted, "Celebrity is the whole ball of wax ... the interface or interstice where a celebrity pandemonium emerges . . . Celebrity is not a property or a substance or even, in a more supple sense, an exchange. It is a distinctive amalgam of production, consumption, and distribution."[1] Woody Allen's 2012 film *To Rome With Love* references Pitt himself to explain this logic of celebrity: at one point two characters (themselves caught up in an accidental celebrity swell) notice a thronging crowd in the streets of Rome, camera flashbulbs popping, and they say in passing that they think Brad Pitt might be in town. Here Brad Pitt serves as a metonymy for a vast population of celebrities, yet he is also more than an arbitrary figure.[2]

Cognizant of the tensions, at times even outright contradictions, between Pitt's acting and celebrity, this anthology explores the larger significance of Brad Pitt *both* as an actor *and* as a celebrity, taking each dimension of his career seriously and emphasizing the complex interrelationships between them. We proceed with the implicit understanding that Pitt's acting is always intertwined with his celebrity, and we openly embrace whatever conflicts, paradoxes, and incongruities this dual, de-centered, deconstructive perspective may present. In fact, in many instances Pitt's popularity (both critical and popular) often emerges largely out of the fertile ground where we must remain uncertain as to whether we are talking about him as an actor or as a celebrity, as an artist or as a person, as a cultural production or even as a reproduction. The media studies scholar Joy Fuqua has aptly described how "Pitt's image—an amalgam of on- and off-screen roles—offers what seems to be a conscious deconstruction of a conventional star identity that depends upon distance and inaccessibility of meaning."[3]

In Pitt's case then, the categories of actor and celebrity are far from incompatible—indeed, they overlap at almost every turn—though there is often tension and friction between them. Ultimately, we believe that deciphering the cultural logic of Brad Pitt requires a willingness to take seriously all of the complex, interconnected facets of his work, both as an actor—whose roles extend from critically acclaimed art films to Hollywood blockbusters and outright flops—and as a celebrity whose public image has not only filled grocery store checkouts with tabloid fodder but also contributed to the construction of low-cost, ecologically-minded housing in a sliver of New Orleans's devastated Lower Ninth Ward after Hurricane Katrina.

We acknowledge that with this book we as scholars have inevitably entangled ourselves with the brand of Brad Pitt. But this is no simple matter. The book is neither about Pitt himself, nor just his acting, nor his celebrity, nor his activism, nor the scholarly analysis of any of these things taken in isolation. Instead, we seek to explore a larger complex web that connects all of these things. Somewhere in the process— we ourselves aren't even quite sure where—this book itself began to get tangled up into that web as well. It is thoroughly deconstructive in this way. The book has been a confusing project at times, not least because it seems you cannot step twice into the same Pitt.

At this point we originally intended to include chapter summaries and a discussion of the conversations taking place between the chapters that follow. However, we have decided to forgo this standard academic strategy, and we invite you directly into the chapters themselves. Make connections, find your way, detect resonances and gaps; deconstructing Brad Pitt is an open-ended process, after all.

Notes

1   Jennifer Wicke, "Celebrity's Face Book." *PMLA* Vol. 126.4 (2011), 1134, 1137.

2   In fact, the line in *To Rome With Love* references not just Brad Pitt but Pitt *and* Angelina Jolie together. As Michele White demonstrates in her essay in this volume, "Brangelina Blend," the combined figure(s) of Brad and Angelina have only further extended their celebrity and its infiltration into everyday life and popular culture.

3   Joy Fuqua, "Brand Pitt: Celebrity Activism and the Make it Right Foundation in Post-Katrina New Orleans." *Celebrity Studies* Vol. 2.2 (2011), 192.

CHAPTER ONE

Making Montana

Ben Leubner

*I had a really good talk, good meeting with Redford,
but I think he's gonna find the guy. The guy
who just is that image—that Montana mountain boy,
fly-fisherman image.*

—RIVER PHOENIX, on auditioning for
A River Runs Through It

During my first semester as a university instructor in Bozeman, Montana, in 2002, I was surprised to hear a young student from the Flathead Lake region, a student with an avid interest in fly fishing, declare undying antipathy for both Brad Pitt and the film *A River Runs Through It*. I was of the opinion that both the film and the novella on which it is based were of a rather high quality and that they both did justice to their subjects, namely, Montana, fishing, and the often startling inability of human beings to help each other. "Ruined Montana," snarled the student, referring to both the film and its main star. I didn't want to ask him what he thought of *Legends of the Fall*.

Very frequently, when a book is being adapted for the screen, you will hear fans of the former lamenting in advance: "I hope they don't ruin the book with this film." Much less often will you hear people saying, "I hope they don't ruin the state with this film." Yet it remains a distinct possibility, for my student's logic is not hard to uncover and follow. Before Brad Pitt passed through Montana, first, in 1992, with Robert Redford, then again in 1994 with Edward Zwick, the state was relatively unknown and ignored, the homogeneous domain of its locals; the rivers weren't overcrowded with fishermen, and if tourism was indeed a part of Montana's economy, still, the closest most tourists came to the state was Yellowstone National Park. Post-Pitt, however, not even the Unabomber's eventual association with the state could keep the out-of-town, would-be fly fishermen from flocking to a paradise revealed, the "last best place." And along with the increase in tourism came an increase in relocation, which, in my student's view, meant people from California, particularly Hollywood, buying up land in Montana in order to escape the bustle of coastal city life. He now had to share Flathead Lake every summer with a small fleet of yachts whose owners were content to use the state as their own personal playground without taking a vital interest in its goings-on. Or, worse, they *would* take an interest in those goings-on, adopting patronizing and condescending attitudes and importing policies, values, and vocabularies inimical to the state's local (I won't say "native" yet) population. And so in the past twenty years the state has been transformed, even ruined, the surest sign of which is perhaps its population just recently having broken the magic number of one million, a statistic that might be explained by the fact that along with increased tourism and an influx of wealthy part-time residents, Brad Pitt also brought to Montana, in the wake of his passing, a number of new full-time residents inspired by the romantic image of the state conveyed in both the Redford and Zwick movies. I know that these people exist because I am one of them and know many others who have admitted it either willingly or reluctantly.

This perception of events, causes, and phenomena is of course at least as much imagined as it is factual, which is not to say, however, that there are not compelling facts to support it. A 2006 study conducted at the University of Montana showed that tourism in the state had "grown from 2 million visitors in 1988 to 10 million visitors in 2005."[1] Brad Pitt has something to do with this. The 13th of 41 facts about the 41st state at visitmt.com announces that several "movies have been filmed here. So if you're out on the Gallatin River catching cutthroat trout, look down at the rock you're standing on. Brad Pitt may have [stood there]" as well.[2] The montanafilm.com tourism brochure features the poster for *A River Runs Through It* (a silhouette of Pitt's character fishing from a boulder midstream) on its first page. And a 2005 study by *Montana Business Quarterly* estimated, according to a *Silver State Post* synopsis of it, "that four percent of all Montana tourists [come] here primarily to act out their fantasy of being Brad Pitt in *A River Runs Through It*."[3] Four percent might seem somewhat insignificant, but the number fails to take into account (1) those who come to the state for this reason but refuse to admit it either to others or even to themselves; (2) those who come to the state not to act out the fantasy of being Brad Pitt's character but instead the fantasy of meeting that character; (3) those who are similarly inspired not by *A River Runs Through It* but by *Legends of the Fall*; and (4) those who don't come to the state as tourists for these reasons but who instead simply move here and take up full-time residence as a result of reason (1), (2), or (3). I said to a friend of mine who has had experience of these phenomena as I myself have, "I'd think it was closer to 40 percent." "More like 400," she replied.

Still, a good deal of this perception concerning what might be called the Pitt Effect calls for tempering, and further statistical analysis indicates the extent to which it is chimerical, which is not to say insignificant, for chimeras are realities, too. My student's opinion in particular, though, is apparently not representative. The same 2006 University of Montana Study cited above found in its primary research that over 30 percent of Montana residents strongly feel that the benefits of tourism outweigh its drawbacks, that as tourism increases so will the quality of life in the state, and that the state is not becoming overcrowded due to tourism. Only 11 percent of residents strongly felt the opposite, with the rest occupying the middle ground.

In the final analysis, the yearly increase that Montana has seen in terms of nonresident visitors from 1993 to 2002 (save for 1996, when the number mildly decreased) cannot be laid *solely* at the feet of Brad Pitt in any strict sense. Even if one were to consider the national exposure which *A River Runs Through It* and *Legends of the Fall* gave the state (as one no doubt should), it seems that the two directors of the films, or even their producers, would be the ones to shoulder most of the responsibility and/or blame. This, however, is where the visibility of Brad Pitt comes into play, and it is this visibility, his star power, that makes it easy to eschew more complicated reasonings and instead simply render him a symbol of or easily intelligible stand-in for larger, more complex forces. From the standpoint of cultural studies, Brad Pitt is a highly combustible, densely concentrated cluster of symbols and significations, an identifiable and strongly magnetic part capable of representing more nebulous wholes.

And by late 1994, the one thing Pitt might have seemed a symbol of, perhaps before anything else save sex, and at least in the eyes of the movie-going public, was Montana. And no doubt a large part *of* his sex appeal had something to do with his association with Montana. Brad Pitt, we might say, made Montana sexy, but his own sex appeal derives in part from his having rubbed shoulders with Montana. *Legends of the Fall* came out in 1994 and *A River Runs Through It* two years earlier. In between came the Tom Cruise-driven blockbuster *Interview with the Vampire*. At the time these were the only lead roles Pitt had to his credit in films that had reached a wide audience (*Kalifornia* grossed only 2 million dollars). His only other big screen appearance that had garnered wide attention by this time was his supporting stint as a drifting, dreamy, small-scale robber in Ridley Scott's *Thelma and Louise*. Before the release of *Seven* and *12 Monkeys* it would have been hard to look at Brad Pitt without thinking, okay, first, of a pale, reluctant vampire, but then of either Paul Maclean, the fly fishing, gambling, alcoholic fatalist of *A River Runs Through It*, or Tristan Ludlow, the wild, roaming, bear-hunting bootlegger of *Legends of the Fall*. Both of these characters personify in their own way the rugged spirit of Montana, in sharp contrast to the characters who surround them: Norman (who leaves the state for academic pursuits) and Neal (who leaves it for a superficial existence in Hollywood) in *A River Runs Through It*; and Samuel (beneficiary of an East Coast education) and Albert (who for a time sinks himself in corrupt US politics) in *Legends of the Fall*. Paul, in the former, never leaves Montana, and Montana, it might be said, never leaves Tristan in the latter, despite his circumnavigations of the Earth. In both cases, according to the novelist Natalie Brown, "the beautiful, wild, natural, and untamed man is perfectly representative of the beautiful, wild, natural, and untamed state."[4] They reciprocate each other's sex appeal.

In *A River Runs Through It*, Paul (and therefore Pitt) even goes so far as to serve as a spokesman for Montana. When Neal, brother to Norman's love interest, shows up late for a fishing date, Paul tersely proclaims, "Neal, in Montana there are three things we're never late for: work, church, and fishing."[5] Earlier in the film when Norman declines a before-noon shot of whiskey, Paul informs his older brother that his several years spent at Dartmouth are "making [him] soft."[6] Paul is the punctiliousness of Presbyterianism crossed with the recklessness of the frontier gambler and drinker. In both judgments he draws a hard line to be on the other side of, which means to not be in Montana anymore, where Montana is not only a state but also a state of mind. Thus, when Norman insists at the end of the film that Paul come to Chicago with him to escape his gambling debts, Paul, standing wistfully on the bank of a river, says, "Brother, I'll never leave Montana."[7] And we understand that he can't; he is, at least in the film's depiction of him, Montana itself. Several of the film's fishing scenes are thus aptly shot in such a way as to indicate that the distinction between Paul and the rivers, trees, cliffs, and skies amidst which he stands is slight. In one scene in particular, Paul walks downriver from Norman, around some shrubbery, and disappears into water and light.

Pitt-as-Tristan is no less a representative of the land itself, than Pitt-as-Paul. From his advice to his overly Victorian brother Samuel regarding Samuel's sexual anxieties ("I recommend fucking") to the distance he keeps from his politically ambitious brother, Albert (the methods of politics and the wisdom of the land being diametrically opposed to each other), Tristan is all bluntness and honor.[8] If underneath Paul's decorousness there lurks an easy-to-provoke fearless fighter, then underneath Tristan's rugged exterior and flowing locks there exists a perfect gentleman more aristocratic than those at the state capitol. The ease with which Pitt exudes these dualities in both films is remarkable, even if he eventually came to regard his performance in *River* as among his weakest.[9] His characters oscillate between a strenuous exertion that somehow appears both graceful and languorous and a dead calmness that is in reality a fury. The delicate violence of fly fishing in *River* is recycled in Tristan's final, fateful waltz with the grizzly in *Legends*, and Tristan's smoldering actions of vengeance are carried out in the same stoic manner as Paul's dance with his Native American girlfriend amidst hostile, white eyes. In a remarkable case of circular transfusion, Pitt adopted this complex dynamic from the characters as they were written by Maclean and Harrison and then bestowed it back upon the state from which those characters were mined in the first place, in the process reinforcing the myth of Montana as a place full of enthralling contraries, a state where perfectly wild, perfectly debonair gentlemen might still be found practically spurting from the soil. And so the magnetism of Brad Pitt and the magnetism of the state of Montana became fused, and have remained so in some important way.

Even in Quentin Tarantino's 2009 film, *Inglourious Basterds*, Pitt's Lieutenant Aldo Raine—a sort of a cross between Tristan Ludlow and Tyler Durden (scalping Germans like the former, leading an ultra-violent renegade outfit like the latter)—claims to be descended from the mountain man Jim Bridger, who explored the west from the 1820s to the 1860s. When I saw the film in Bozeman, just under the shadow of the Bridger Mountains, the audience chuckled familiarly when Pitt's character revealed his ancestry, as if they were welcoming home a son who'd gone off to pursue other roles for fifteen years, or maybe it was a skeptical chuckle, a scoff that said, "He's pretending to be one of us again." It's a wonder that Pitt didn't get cast in 1998's *The Horse Whisperer*, though the fact that he didn't might explain that film's paling in comparison to the Montana films in which he was cast. It might have been a long and beautiful film, "not unlike driving through Montana," as a friend said to me, but it lacked the magnetism of Pitt, which apparently not even the combination of horses and an aging Robert Redford could make up for.

At the heart of this identification of Pitt with Montana, though, is a fairly relentless irony, given that before one can link him with the geographical entity of Montana by virtue of his roles as Paul and Tristan, one almost certainly must link him first and foremost with the geographical entity of Hollywood, a veritable hell on earth in the imaginations of most Montanans, a corrupt, plastic, concrete-covered seedbed of valuelessness. One needn't look far for confirmation of this opinion. In Maclean's novella itself, Paul, who epitomizes Montana, is asked by his brother, Norman, to take Norman's brother-in-law, Neal, fly-fishing (in the novella Norman and Jessie are already married). While Neal is originally from Montana, he has since abandoned it for Hollywood and has only returned for a brief visit. Paul does not like the prospect: "He'll be just as welcome as a dose of clap . . . I won't fish with him. He comes from the West Coast and he fishes with worms."[10] These words, had they been spoken verbatim by Pitt in the film, would have been wonderfully self-referential and ironic, perhaps too strongly so, for the movie tempers them: Pitt's Paul does lampoon the would-be Hollywood star Neal for being a bait fisherman and later wishes that he may "suffer from three doses of the clap and recover from all but the third," but he never identifies the source of Neal's villainy with his "[coming] from the West Coast."[11] One wonders just how many Montanans considered the invasion of their state by an entire West Coast film crew, spearheaded by Pitt, as "just as welcome as a dose of clap."[12] Certainly this was the way my student felt.

Redford sets the events of his film some ten to fifteen years earlier than the summer of 1937 during which most of Maclean's novella takes place. In this way a younger Norman can meet, court, and fall in love with Jessie, thus adding a romantic intrigue to a story that is primarily about two people (Norman and Jessie) being unable to help their brothers. In the scene when Norman professes his love to Jessie, he informs her that he has been accepted to graduate school at the University of Chicago but says he is not sure if he wants to leave, to which Jessie, initially failing to detect his drift, responds, "Montana, why? It'll always be here."[13] It is a line that appears nowhere in the novella, and it is supercharged with irony whatever Richard Friedenberg, writer of the screenplay, may have intended. The character Jessie, speaking the line in and from the 1920s, no doubt means what she says quite sincerely. And it may even be that the theater-going audience, viewing the film in the early 1990s, was meant to take it in no other way: Montana has always been here and will continue to always be here, a haven remote from the corruption and bustle of modern civilization, a romantic American River District, the lure of which is precisely its remoteness and emptiness. But the subsequent effect of the film, itself anchored by Pitt's charismatic performance, has been to jeopardize the very thing that Jessie regards as a certainty: the fact that Montana will always be here and that it will always be Montana, as opposed to, say, Montanafornia (a t-shirt currently being sold in Bozeman says Boze-Angeles in a script that calls to mind Los Angeles Dodgers' uniforms). One of the state's most famous nicknames is the "Last Best Place," a nickname that although uttered with pride by its residents would seem to ominously indicate that however remarkable it is that Montana has "been here" for as long as it has, it won't be here forever.

But if the Montana of the 1920s portrayed in both films has indeed already vanished in large part, it may be no substantial loss. For it may in fact have been a fiction all along, a fiction created in large part by the very films which have since drawn thousands to the state in search of it—though their coming would seem to necessarily preclude the very possibility of their encountering it. The fiction exists in novellas and on bumper stickers, it exists in tourist brochures and on celluloid, and it no doubt exists as an intractable reality in the minds of many people, both visitors and long-time residents alike. And it may indeed be the case that many of the latter blame the former for the state's ruination, but the truth of the matter is that those Pitt-inspired tourists and relocaters can give the overwhelming majority of the residents of Montana absolutely nothing to gripe and complain about, unless they themselves would willingly be shuttled from the state, as well.

For before there was the fiction of "Our" Montana, before there were local Montanans, there were indeed natives of the region (at least eleven distinct tribes) whom the soon-to-be locals themselves displaced, not infrequently ruining the land in the process (think strip mines as opposed to the more recent strip malls). Imagine if the Hollywood film crews rounded up all of the local Montanans, took possession of the places they and their ancestors had called home for generations, and relocated them to strategically placed reservations. This, of course, is precisely what happened to the state's native population at the hands of the US government, or to the small portion of that population that had managed to survive a veritable genocide, a fact brought home and emphasized in *Legends of the Fall*, both novella and film, in which Colonel Ludlow forsakes the US military in favor of a peaceful life in Choteau as a protest against the government's treatment of the region's native population. Tristan's own closeness to and spiritual identification with One Stab, his father's Cheyenne friend and confidante, echoes Paul's romantic relationship, in *A River Runs Through It*, with the half-Cheyenne woman whom Norman calls Mo-nah-se-tah. Part of what makes both Tristan and Paul such romantic, rebellious, outsiders then, is their intimacy with Native Americans, an intimacy that demands they brutally beat those who would question the humanity of their chosen companions.

The white savage Tristan (and to a lesser extent Paul) thus represents the interests of the very people whose way of life has been severely threatened by white encroachment, manifest destiny, and systematic murder. It is a complicated dynamic, one that by no means makes Pitt's characters hypocrites but instead places them on a precarious middle ground between two opposing cultures. It is not entirely dissimilar from the ground Pitt himself occupies as a member of the corrupt institution of Hollywood who, while he cannot completely divorce himself from it, can yet forsake it in large part in favor of the interests of various entities and organizations which struggle mightily against such institutions. In the case of the Treasure State, however, let no one be mistaken: its current identity crisis is one brought about by the competition of fiction with fiction. The reality was suppressed some time ago and for the most part continues to be today.

"I think this just might be my masterpiece," says Aldo Raine at the end of *Inglourious Basterds*, just before the credits roll and just after he has carved a swastika into the forehead of Hans Landa (Christoph Waltz) with a very large knife.[14] Compared to the many other swastikas Raine has carved into the foreheads of Nazis whom he has allowed to live that they might never successfully hide what they have been, this, he thinks, is his greatest work. The line, though, especially by virtue of its placement at film's end, can also be read as Quentin Tarantino's own acknowledgment of *Inglourious Basterds* as *his* masterpiece. In fact, such an alternative interpretation suggests itself immediately. But the line might additionally be read, I think, in a third way, as being spoken not by a character in the film or by the film's director, but by the actor who utters it. This is not only Raine's masterpiece and Tarantino's, but Pitt's as well, for his renegade lieutenant is in many ways a sort of apotheosis of so many of the other characters Pitt has played over the years. Raine, that is, is a sublimation of the rebel, outsider, drifter, alien, recluse, and conscientious madman that Pitt has played one variation of after another over the course of his career. From the violent boxers of *Fight Club* and *Snatch* to the southern outlaw Jesse James, Aldo Raine has something significant in common with several Pitt characters, including Paul Maclean and Tristan Ludlow. On the surface, he is a bootlegger like the latter and considers himself a kind of unconventional artist like the former. His and Tristan's predilection for scalping has already been noted. Perhaps most important, though, is Raine's being descended from Jim Bridger, all three of whose wives were Native American, which means that Raine has "a little injun in him," as he says.[15] Thus, as Raine scalps and carves his way across occupied France, both Paul and Tristan, through Pitt himself, are resurrected, and now able not only to empathize with but to fully play the Indian, and an Indian who, in Tarantino's counter-historical fantasy, emerges victorious with his Jewish comrade Utivich (nicknamed "The Little Man") against a force of unbridled evil.

Notes

1   Norma P. Nickerson, "Red or Blue? An Exploration of Political Party Affiliation and Resident Attitudes Toward Tourism in Montana." http://www.itrr.umt.edu/research06/2006TTRAParty affiliation.pdf [Accessed November 1, 2013].

2   "41 Facts from the 41st State." http://visitmt.com/experiences/montana_extras/montana_facts/ [Accessed October 18, 2013].

3   Patrick Duganz, "Warming Rivers May be the End of Trout Fishing." *Silverstate* Post online. http://ssp.stparchive.com/Archive/SSP/SSP08312011p02.php [Accessed November 8, 2013].

4   Natalie Brown, personal interview, December 20, 2011.

5   *A River Runs Through It*, directed by Robert Redford (Columbia Pictures, 1992).

6   *A River Runs Through It*, directed by Robert Redford (Columbia Pictures, 1992).

7   *A River Runs Through It*, directed by Robert Redford (Columbia Pictures, 1992).

8   *A River Runs Through It*, directed by Robert Redford (Columbia Pictures, 1992).

9   Gavin Edwards, *Last Night at the Viper Room* (New York: HarperCollins, 2013), 152.

10 Norman Maclean, *A River Runs Through It and Other Stories* (Chicago: University of Chicago Press, 1976), 9.

11 *A River Runs Through It*, directed by Robert Redford (Columbia Pictures, 1992).

12 *A River Runs Through It*, directed by Robert Redford (Columbia Pictures, 1992).

13 *A River Runs Through It*, directed by Robert Redford (Columbia Pictures, 1992).

14 *Inglourious Basterds*, directed by Quentin Tarantino (Universal Pictures, 2009).

15 *Inglourious Basterds*, directed by Quentin Tarantino (Universal Pictures, 2009).

CHAPTER TWO

Romantic Hero

Elizabeth Abele

Tragic Heroes are so much the highest point in their human landscape that they seem the inevitable conductors of the power about them, the greatest trees more likely to be struck by lightning than a clump of grass. Conductors may of course be instruments as well as victims of the divine lightning.

—NORTHROP FRYE, *Anatomy of Criticism*

When most people think of Brad Pitt as a "romantic" figure, they are most likely referring to Pitt as a man whose looks and charm have twice earned him *People Magazine*'s designation as "The Sexiest Man Alive" (in 1995 and 2000).[1] Pitt's personal life, as portrayed in the press, has likewise reflected the simpler definition of a romantic star, as he has moved serially between intense, monogamous relationships with beautiful actresses.

However, Pitt's stardom has been sustained not solely on his tabloid coverage but also on a persona sustained by two decades of film roles—a persona that fits more within the literary definition of the (often tragic) figure of the "Romantic Hero," also referred to as the "Byronic Hero." A rejection of the rationalism of the Enlightenment, the Romantic Hero makes an individual choice to triumph over the "restraints of theological and social conventions," a choice that often leads to personal melancholy and alienation—as well as the kind of destruction that Frye describes above.[2] American Romanticism, as embodied by figures like Benjamin Franklin and James Fenimore Cooper's Natty Bumppo, has been described as a deliberate journey away from rationality and civilization in favor of the freedom and purity found instead in nature and the imagination. In *Love and Death and the American Novel*, Leslie Fiedler describes how the American Romantic tradition developed this (often anti-sexual) figure:

> the typical male protagonist of our fiction has been a man on the run, harried into the forest and out to sea, down the river or into combat—anywhere to avoid "civilization," which is to say, the confrontation of a man and woman which leads to the fall to sex, marriage and responsibility.[3]

What makes Brad Pitt more than just a pretty face has been this development of an on-screen persona that reflects this classic definition of the Romantic Hero, a figure who—as Frye's Heroes above—often attracts tragedy to himself or to those with the misfortune to love him. The films of Brad Pitt directly address the allure of this American figure, as well as the dangers that accompany his physical and idealistic beauty.

Like other 1990s leading men—Tom Cruise, Keanu Reeves, and George Clooney—Brad Pitt embodied a leaner masculinity than the more muscular 1980s Heroes of Bruce Willis, Mel Gibson, and Kevin Costner. Cruise and Reeves came to stardom first, with their boyish, hot-dog ambition reflecting the drive of the Me-Generation. While Pitt's lithe physicality shares some similarities with Cruise and Reeves, his persona represents a more complicated, more personal code of masculinity. His early roles in films such as *A River Runs Through It* (1992) and *Legends of the Fall* (1994) established this passionate nature, as well as his charismatic beauty, directly portraying the dangerous allure of the Romantic Hero, an allure that is intensified by his inability to reciprocate. In mid-career films such as *Spy Game* (2001) and *The Mexican* (2001), his characters attempt to negotiate their passions with their professional obligations and personal intimacy. In his more mature films, these negotiations become more intense, involving direct action against the status quo: in *Mr. and Mrs. Smith* (2005) and *Moneyball* (2011), his protagonists directly take on the established order, where more genuine experience and personal relationships may be possible. Yet despite these films where Pitt's characters move toward personal intimacy, he continues to produce classic Romantic Heroes, like Rusty Ryan and Benjamin Button, who remain tantalizingly beyond anyone's reach.

Within the universe of his films, Pitt's characters even remain aloof from their male counterparts, unlike the homosocial bonds of typical Fiedlerian protagonists.[4] Even in his role as Danny Ocean's (George Clooney's) number two in the *Ocean's* series, Rusty Ryan purposefully remains at arm's length from Danny and the other crew members, keeping his personal secrets and desires separate from the caper at hand. Though aware of his professional obligations, Pitt's characters avoid losing themselves in the constructed personae of "soldier," "vampire," "cop," "outlaw," or "spy," declining to be bound by any preconceived notion of duty. His resistance to society's definition of his character's duty, in favor of his personal desires, alternately leads to tragedy and triumph. However, these negative consequences rarely deter the choices Pitt's characters make, as they largely choose personal integrity and emotions over unthinking conformity.

Pitt's filmography demonstrates the tension between the classic (and sexually desirable) Romantic Hero and an ideal romantic partner, as his characters are rarely satisfying husbands or lovers. Beginning with his brief role in *Thelma & Louise* (1991) through *The Curious Case of Benjamin Button*

(2008), his characters are more likely to abandon their lovers than characters played by his contemporaries; and as with Thelma, his pursuit of his own interest often leads indirectly to the deaths of his lovers. Likewise, Pitt's characters are more likely to die than those of other male stars, from *A River Runs Through It* to *Burn After Reading* (2008).

This chapter examines how the continuities in Brad Pitt's film roles model a version of masculinity that is distinct and decidedly Romantic, in the fullest sense of the word. In addition, it also notes the shifts within Pitt's personification of the Romantic Hero as he and his characters have matured.

Dangerous beauty

Literary critic Northrop Frye noted that the Romantic Hero is often "placed outside the structure of civilization and therefore represents the force of physical nature, amoral or ruthless, yet with a sense of power, and often leadership, that society has impoverished itself by rejecting."[5] Several of Brad Pitt's early film performances—such as *Kalifornia* (1992), *A River Runs Through It* (1992), *Legends of the Fall* (1994), and *Interview with the Vampire* (1994)—helped establish both Pitt's connections to physical nature, as well as his position outside of society's moral standards: Significantly, he is killed in three of these films, while his wife/lover is killed in two.[6] Unlike the masculinity of his *Interview* co-star Tom Cruise, his brand of hero is tied more to death than to triumph. These films present Pitt as an object of romantic desire, while portraying the ambivalence of his characters to romantic connections: the Romantic Hero as anti-(sexually) romantic.

This construction is most clear in *Legends of the Fall*, which established Pitt's ability to open a film, as well as his position as a pin-up for young women: the film's release and subsequent videotape sales were marketed with *Legends* posters featuring Pitt. These posters, like his appearance in *Interview with the Vampire*, solidified his position as a Byronic Hero, with his flowing hair and melancholic demeanor. Even his character's name, Tristan, evokes another tragic Romantic Hero. However, Tristan Ludlow's Romantic image is strongly linked to his dangerous nature. *Legends'* opening narration by One Stab (George Tootoosis) links Tristan to both American Indian culture and nature—including his long-standing feud with a grizzly bear, from which both wear scars. Though his brothers, Alfred (Aidan Quinn) and Samuel (Henry Thomas), are more refined, Susannah (Julia Ormond) is immediately drawn to Tristan, despite her engagement to Samuel.

Throughout the film's narrative, Tristan is a man led by his passions and instincts, often to the detriment of those who love him. Revenge and grief are particularly violent for him. When he is unable to protect his brother in World War I, Tristan goes on a literal rampage, scalping Germans. When he returns to the family ranch, in his grief he clings to Susannah before he abandons her, wandering the globe in search of intense experiences to numb his pain. The abandoned and deflowered Susannah finally accepts respectability and marriage to Alfred. When Tristan returns home the second time, he finds peace in marriage to Isabel Two (Karina Lombard), One Stab's granddaughter. However, in revenge against the government for the death of Samuel and actions against his father's ranch, he becomes a bootlegger ("screw the government"), flaunting both the law and organized crime.[7] His recklessness leads to Isabel Two's death—and another cycle of revenge—as well as Susannah's suicide.

Both Tristan's marriage to Isabel Two and her subsequent death solidify his character's connection to natural forces, as well as his unaware destructiveness. Caroline Brown compares the role of Isabel Two to Pitt's love-interest in *A River Runs Through It*. In both films, Pitt's character is the "troubled brother, the prodigal son"—and involved with a Native American woman, in defiance of his period's prejudices. As Brown argues, with respect to the Native American woman: "Although she serves to critique the corrupt, the wasteful, the discriminatory and hypocritical in white society, she herself is an oppositional force, idealized and abstracted."[8] While this relationship with Isabel Two marks Tristan's separation from societal restraints, Isabel Two and his family ultimately must pay the cost for his critique and freedom; as One Stab narrates: "It was those who loved him most who died young. He was a rock they broke themselves against, however much he tried protect them."[9] Even the traditional Alfred must sacrifice his values to save the life of the brother that, despite all, he still loves. After the trail of bodies, Tristan lives to be an old man, disappearing into the woods for his "good death"—a Romantic ending, living decades after the women who died for his love.

Together, Pitt's 1990s film roles established his screen presence as a natural force, existing outside of societal norms or morality, a force all the more exciting for its mortal danger.

Heroic melancholy

In the second decade of his career, Pitt's characters solidify their commitment to their Romantic ideals, while working to avoid the self-destructive pitfalls of more traditional masculine figures or their own demons. While maintaining Pitt's position as a Romantic Hero, his characters began to ask for more.

Linus (Matt Damon): You suicidal?
Rusty (Brad Pitt): Only in the morning.[10]

In 2001, Brad Pitt played three men who had passed their golden youth, but resisted entering the cynical resignation of their mentors: Rusty Ryan in *Ocean's Eleven*, Jerry Welbach in *The Mexican*, and Tom Bishop in *Spy Game*. Though Rusty has the charisma to charm television stars and to hold the 11 together, Rusty is aimless, waiting for something worth waking up for each day. He is able to play the long con with such calm ease specifically because he has nothing to lose. Though director Stephen Soderbergh remarked in the DVD commentary that Rusty's constant eating was originally conceived as the habit of a thief who eats when he can, audience members have read it as emblematic of the hole that Rusty cannot fill.

In *The Mexican* and *Spy Game*, Pitt's characters find someone they care about, a love for a woman that is connected to their ideals, rather than in conflict. But this quest for romance is as dangerous as the quests of Pitt's other Romantic Heroes. *The Mexican* is one of Pitt's few romantic comedies, though generically the film is more complicated than a traditional boy-meets-girl narrative. Jerry is torn between two commitments: his live-in girlfriend Sam (Julia Roberts) and his indenture to a crime boss Margolese (Gene Hackman).[11] Any other man would walk away from one or both: Sam is hysterical and unforgiving, and Margolese has bullied him into working for him. Throughout the narrative, however, Jerry puts himself last—even though everyone around him is self-serving and dishonorable—doing his best to honor his commitments to both Sam and Margolese. In addition, Jerry's own incompetence and bad luck make doing the "right" thing a major challenge, as he juggles recovering an antique gun (the "Mexican") with recovering Sam who has been kidnapped as insurance for the gun.

Jerry's integrity is unusual within the universe of this film. Since the rest of Margolese's gang has tried to steal the gun from him, Margolese assumes Jerry is likewise trying to extort him, asking Jerry what it would take for him to hand over the gun. Jerry is offended: "I don't know what it takes—I'm new in the fuck-you business!"[12] Jerry's sense of honor is as anachronistically romantic as the tale of the Mexican pistol that is retold throughout the film. Likewise, while Sam has given up on Jerry, vindictively throwing his clothes over the balcony, Jerry consistently refuses to give up on her. When Sam asks him the question, "If two people love each other, but they just can't seem to get it together, when do you get to that point of enough is enough?" Jerry is quick and definite with his response: "Never." While the gangster Margolese and Sam expect Jerry to welsh, Jerry sincerely does his best to be true to his word to both. Jerry refuses to allow therapy-speak or double-dealers to make him give up on his ideals, to join the "fuck-you business."

Spy Game presents an interesting contrast in the masculine ideals of two different generations, as CIA handler, Nathan Muir (Robert Redford) narrates the career of Tom Bishop (Brad Pitt) who faces execution by the Chinese government for a botched rogue mission.[13] While Muir enjoys the cynical detachment of the spy "game," Tom is presented from the beginning as a man who cares more about his principles than the exercise. In Scheherazade-fashion, Muir spins the tale of Tom Bishop to the CIA administration, as he tries to buy time and save his protégé's life.

From their first meeting, Muir notes both Bishop's talent as an operative and his Romantic integrity. Muir sees Bishop's ideals as having an ambivalent relationship to his potential as an operative: "Came across as one of those idealistic types, you know, a little bit of an attitude. Starts out trying to see what he is made of and ends up not liking the view."[14] Muir is amused that Bishop learned to shoot from the Boy Scouts: "Boy Scout" sticks as Tom's code-name, as it matches the personal integrity that he manages to hold on to, despite the ethical challenges embedded in each mission. Muir tries to counsel Bishop to be detached and self-preserving: "Don't spend your money for anyone, don't risk your life for an asset. If it is you or them, send flowers."[15] For a while, Bishop thrives as an operative, living by Muir's code. But after a physician who Bishop recruited is killed in a mission where Muir interfered, Tom asserts his break from Muir's mentorship: "I'm done with your reasons, Nathan. I'm done with you. I'm not ending up like you."[16] As proof of his break with Muir, Tom is captured trying to rescue his asset-lover from a Chinese prison. (And Muir is the person who handed her over to the Chinese to "protect" Tom.)

As Tom's capture and threatened execution coincide with Nathan Muir's last day before retirement, Muir's narration of Tom's story forces Muir to examine his own life choices. While

Tom has risked everything for love, Muir's four "marriages" were covers with agent "wives"—and so easily discarded. To save Tom, he breaks his own rules, spending his life savings to fund a rogue rescue mission. The last close-up shot of Tom is his realization that it was Muir who engineered his rescue—a shot that dissolves into Muir's eyes. Tom's Romantic ideals have finally infected the hardened pro.

In *The Mexican* and *Spy Game*, Pitt's characters operate in a masculine world where his characters choose an ethical and emotional path distinctly at odds with his mentors and colleagues—while still maintaining his commitment to the work at hand. Pitt's characters reject the traditional masculine mode of separation between business and personal (with the personal generally subjugated or even eliminated for business). Part of the Romantic nature of Pitt's characters is his awareness that it should always be personal.

The romance of losing

In the last decade, Pitt has embraced roles where his characters deliberately move away from traditional markers of masculine success. Like Rusty Ryan, Pitt's John Smith in *Mr. & Mrs. Smith* appears to be a man to be envied, living two "perfect" lives, as a suburban husband with a brilliant and beautiful wife Jane (Angelina Jolie) and as an accomplished spy/assassin.[17] However, as with Rusty, the film establishes his dissatisfaction early on: in a marriage therapist's office, it is clear that John is disconnected from his wife, based on body language, his pragmatic description of their relationship, and their reported lack of a sex life.

Though John in the opening scenes is willing to soldier on with their half-marriage, when their true identities and natures are revealed to each other, it is John who embraces the opportunity to have an honest relationship. He takes the personal and physical risks to tell Jane his true feelings, describing his thoughts when he first met her: "I thought you looked like Christmas morning. I don't know how else to say it . . . So there it is. I thought you should know."[18] Instead of revealing her feelings, she merely replies that he was the most beautiful mark she ever saw. After their fierce battle ends with guns pointed at each other's temples, it is again John who surrenders: "I can't do it . . . You want it? It's yours."[19] Though she urges him to take the shot, Jane finally collapses into his embrace. She is defeated not by his strength, but by his honest vulnerability. At the end of the film, John has lost his career and his house, but he is proud to report to their therapist that his marriage and his sex life are now more than satisfying. By sacrificing the trappings of success, John and Jane Smith win through *his* willingness to lose it all. Unlike the action-oriented hero who seeks the public acclaim of victory, the Romantic Hero often finds the personal rewards of "losing" more satisfying.

Pitt received his third Oscar nomination for Billy Beane in *Moneyball*—a less showy performance than his previously nominated roles, requiring less make-up and histrionics.[20] But this role epitomizes Pitt's brand of heroic masculinity that is more defined by ideals than by winning. Billy Beane is a former baseball player, who is currently managing the Oakland A's. The film opens as the A's lose the 2001 playoffs to the Yankees—a defeat followed by the loss of their three best players to free agency. The A's loser status is solidified as Billy unsuccessfully begs the manager for a larger budget (the lowest in professional baseball). Billy's position as a loser moves into his personal life, as his daughter is being raised by his ex-wife and her rich new husband; in addition, flashbacks reveal that his baseball career (for which he sacrificed a Stanford scholarship) never lived up to his golden-boy promise. As he says of himself, he is a "middle-aged man with a high-school diploma"—who has little personally, professionally, or financially to show for his life.

The advantage of being a man who has nothing is that he is open to new ideas. Facing the year ahead, he sees that he is doomed to fail again:

> The problem we're trying to solve is that there are rich teams and there are poor teams. Then there's fifty feet of crap, and then there's us. It's an unfair game. And now we've been gutted [. . .] We've got to think differently. We are the last dog at the bowl. You see what happens to the runt of the litter? He dies.[21]

In his quest against the Goliaths, Billy stakes his entire season (and career) on an unpopular theory, creating a team of "misfit toys" that his budget can handle. Instead of seeking to confirm his masculinity through the approval of other accomplished men, Billy can see the value in dweeby Yale economics grad, Peter Brand (Jonah Hill), who espouses the theory of Bill James—as well as baseball players who have been undervalued and discarded, as Billy was. Even as his new team loses game after game, Billy sticks by Peter and their shared vision.

However, unlike most baseball movies, when "victory" comes, it is mixed. The Oakland A's come back to set a record 20-game winning streak, finishing first in the American League West—only to lose in the playoffs *again*. Beane missed his personal goal of winning "the last game of the season"—"if we win, on our budget, with this team, we will change the game and that's what I want. I want it to mean something."[22] Instead of creating a way for poor teams to compete, Billy merely proved a theory that allowed rich teams to be more effective. As testament to this, the Red Soxs offer Beane $12.5 million to be their general manager, a record salary—which he refuses. Having chosen a major league contract over Stanford, he swore he'd never make a decision based on money again—and he doesn't.

Billy ends the film in almost the same position in which he started, having to build a team with an inadequate budget. As he ponders his choices, he listens to a CD that his daughter recorded for him. Before she begins singing Lenka's "The Show," she says: "Let me know if you change your mind and stay in California; if not, you *were* a really good Dad" (emphasis mine).[23] As she sings, Billy drives:

I'm just a little girl lost in the moment.
I'm so scared but I don't show it.[24]

As this song plays, titles reveal that Beane turned down the validation of the Red Sox contract to stay with the Oakland A's (and his daughter). The final title reveals that Billy is still tilting at windmills: "Billy is still trying to win the last game of the season."[25] As the audience reads this, they hear the words that his daughter has added to the final chorus, "You're such a loser, Dad. You're such a loser, Dad. Just enjoy the show."[26] Like Don Quixote, Billy has made losing a badge of honor, but he has also learned to enjoy the show, to enjoy being a father and making the best of his under-funded ballclub. As much as baseball is scored by wins and losses, and managed as mega-corporations, it is teams like the Oakland A's that maintain the human element of the game. As Billy asks: "How can you not be *romantic* about baseball?" (italics mine).[27] *Moneyball* directly characterizes Billy Beane as a Romantic Hero, equating him with the ultimate Romantic Hero, Don Quixote, and using the word "romantic" in its non-sexual sense, with baseball providing the only romantic moments of the film. Billy Beane may be Pitt's ultimate hopeless romantic, a man who cannot be resigned to losing yet for whom "winning" is not everything.

As varied as Brad Pitt's film roles may appear on the surface, the connective agent that binds the majority of his characters is a combination of passion with personal ethics—a masculine code that is both more flexible and more dangerous than the more traditional masculinity performed by his Hollywood peers. The quest of the Romantic Hero is not defined by traditional measures of success, and in fact often ends in failure or death: it is the integrity of the quest that matters. However, while the Romantic Hero might have tragic results for the individual protagonist and the characters who love him, in terms of Brad Pitt's career, this strategy in his film roles has succeeded in creating a long and respected career for him personally.

Pitt's persona as a Romantic Hero has built on and deepened Pitt's physical attractiveness, making his sex appeal more than genetic good fortune, giving his characters an ambiguity that is not easily resolved. As this examination of his key roles has attempted to demonstrate, his characters' journeys consistently challenge the universe of his films as well as his audience's expectations. The popularity of Brad Pitt over the past decades demonstrates the appeal of a more complex masculinity that includes self-awareness, personal integrity, and non-conformity. Together, the films of Brad Pitt offer a subtle yet sustained critique of any fixed notion of masculinity, relationships, or society. Instead, his Romantic Heroes argue for a more individual—a more romantic—approach to manhood as Hollywood has moved from the twentieth to the twenty-first century.

Notes

1   *People Magazine*, January 30, 1995, cover; *People Magazine*, November 13, 2000, cover.

2   James D. Wilson, "Tirso, Hat, and Byron: The Emergence of Don Juan as Romantic Hero." *The South Central Bulletin* 32(4) (1972), 247.

3   Leslie Fiedler, *Love and Death in the American Novel* (New York: Stein, 1966), 26.

4   Leslie Fiedler specifically notes the close bonds of Natty Bumppo and Chingachgook, Ishmael and Queequeg, and Huck and Jim, as establishing this American heroic model.

5   Northrup Frye, *A Study of English Romanticism* (New York: Random House, 1968), 41.

6   In this film, as in *Meet Joe Black* (1998), Brad Pitt's character trades a mortal life for death and an immortal existence. In *Interview*, Louis is overcome with grief over the death of his wife and child. In *Meet Joe Black*, his Young Man is so distracted by love-at-first sight, he is hit by a truck—Death takes over his body.

7 *Legends of the Fall*, directed by Edward Zwick (TriStar, 1994).

8 Caroline Brown, "The Representation of the Indigenous Other in *Daughters of the Dust* and *The Piano*." *NWSA Journal* 15(1) (Spring 2003): 17.

9 *Legends of the Fall*, directed by Edward Zwick (TriStar, 1994).

10 *Ocean's Eleven*, directed by Steven Soderbergh (Warner Bros, 2001).

11 Jerry's employment contract with Margolese demonstrates both his goofy clumsiness and his honor: he rear-ends Margolese in a car accident, leading to Margolese's imprisonment (there was a person in the trunk). As Margolese is sentenced to prison, Margolese "sentences" Jerry to work for his crew, an obligation that Jerry accepts without resentment.

12 *The Mexican*, directed by Gore Verbinski (DreamWorks, 2001).

13 The pairing of these stars has several extra-textual references. First, Robert Redford directed and narrated Brad Pitt in *A River Runs Through It*. Second, Pitt's golden-boy good looks naturally remind critics and movie-goers of the young Redford of *The Way We Were* (1973) or *The Great Gatsby* (1974). Their external similarities make the contrasts in their characters in *Spy Game* more striking.

14 *Spy Game*, directed by Tony Scott (Universal, 2001).

15 *Spy Game*, directed by Tony Scott (Universal, 2001).

16 *Spy Game*, directed by Tony Scott (Universal, 2001).

17 As an assassin, John's style is decidedly more romantic than Jane. While she is ever planned, precise, and detached, John is more creative and instinctual in his hits, creating a work environment that is warmer and more personal.

18 *Mr. & Mrs. Smith*, directed by Doug Liman (20th Century Fox, 2005).

19 *Mr. & Mrs. Smith*, directed by Doug Liman (20th Century Fox, 2005).

20 In 1996, Pitt was nominated for playing a mental patient/Philadelphia scion/eco-terrorist with bad hair and eyes in *Twelve Monkeys*. In 2009, he played the eponymous Benjamin Buttons, who aged backwards.

21 *Moneyball*, directed by Bennett Miller (Columbia, 2011).

22 *Moneyball*, directed by Bennett Miller (Columbia, 2011).

23 *Moneyball*, directed by Bennett Miller (Columbia, 2011).

24 Lenka, "The Show" (Epic, 2008).

25 *Moneyball*, directed by Bennett Miller (Columbia, 2011).

26 *Moneyball*, directed by Bennett Miller (Columbia, 2011).

27 *Moneyball*, directed by Bennett Miller (Columbia, 2011).

CHAPTER THREE

On Crashing

Christopher Schaberg

Heinrich came running down the hall, burst into the room. "Come on, hurry up, plane crash footage." Then he was out the door, the girls were off the bed, all three of them running along the hall to the TV set.

—DON DELILLO, *White Noise*

This is a really big honor for me, considering I'm a guy who had never ridden in an airplane until I was 25.

—BRAD PITT, ON ACCEPTING AN AWARD FOR BEST ACTOR BY THE NEW YORK CRITICS CIRCLE, JANUARY 2012

This is it: ground zero.

—TYLER DURDEN (BRAD PITT) in *Fight Club*

In his well-known novel *Crash*, J.G. Ballard combines the mysterious sensation of celebrity worship with the grinding realities of modern mobilities: "Driven on a collision course towards the limousine of the film actress, his car jumped the rails of the London Airport flyover and plunged through the roof of a bus filled with airline passengers" (p. 7). It is no accident that Ballard conjoins air travel, car culture, and star status in a single horrific image. The crash with which we are confronted in this passage has a lot in common with the usual figure of crashes that reigns in the domain of popular media: naïve or oblivious acts of tourism, the dramatic architecture of travel, and the specter of a rogue agent.

Think of the Asiana crash landing at SFO in July 2013—how experienced was the captain? Who tweeted the crash first? Did you see the smoke billowing across the tarmac? Think of the countless runway skids caused by failed landing gear, pilot error, wind gusts. Think of Sully and US Airways Flight 1549, the threat of non-migrating Canada Geese. Think of Air France Airbus A330 that plummeted into the middle of the Atlantic Ocean in the middle of the night in June 2009. Think of the Shoe Bomber. Think of 9/11. What fears, hopes, and dreams do we stake on crashing?

On crashing

Let us risk a detour. If, today, the term "crashing" is of any theoretical use, we must be able to analyze it in everyday figures. Figures like Brad Pitt—who, while we may not know him, we know *of* him. The way that in late 2012 we saw Pitt's face across airports, in malls, and on commercials advertising Chanel #5; and then the way that Dwight Shrutte in *The Office* stated glibly that people will buy anything sold by celebrities—snarkily citing Brad Pitt as an example. To risk what may seem a secondary tangent, let us turn to Tom DiCillo's 1991 film *Johnny Suede* to begin to draw connections between Brad Pitt and crashing.

Johnny Suede is a peculiar film displaying a sort of hybrid aesthetic, a mixture of Jarmuschian detached cool and Lynchian weird horror, weird yet recognizable consumer signs and charged yet inscrutable objects. We're clearly in the period of late American capitalism with, as David Foster Wallace once described a similar topos, "images and ironies all over the place."[1] Brad Pitt plays the proto-hipster and eponymous Johnny, who lives in a dingy apartment in Brooklyn where he can barely pay the rent. He is an aspiring musician, though *aspiring* may be too strong a word. He loafs about, styling his oversized pompadour and sulking in the corner of a nightclub. A pair of suede shoes fall from the sky, shattering a nearby telephone booth; Johnny is their happenstance beneficiary.

The first time we see Johnny play his guitar, he stumbles and stutters over lyrics that he appears to be making up as he goes. He pawns his guitar to pay the rent, and frustrated that he has had to resort to such an artistic compromise, briefly considers robbing a barbershop to get the money to get his guitar back— all he really wants to do is to get his band together. (The one time we actually hear them, they sound pretty good—Samuel L. Jackson is on bass.)

On the periphery of Pitt's performance, Nick Cave plays an apparently successful musician named Freak Storm. Cave's flamboyant rock star persona acts as a foil to Pitt's more timid Suede, but Freak Storm also becomes a bizarre mentor of sorts. Strangely, no one seems to recognize that Freak Storm is true to his name, a downward spiraling strung-out freak who looks pretty slick at first but by the middle of the movie is slouching in a derelict swivel chair and eating fried chicken found in a dumpster earlier that day. And then there is Pitt, mumbling "Thanks, Freak . . ." for his empty promises and hollow well wishes. Is this—a Freak Show—who Johnny Suede wants to become? Is this really what it means to "make it" as an alternative, free-spirited musician in the 1990s? (In a way, these scenes almost anticipate the way Edward Norton's quiet, anonymous character in *Fight Club* looks up to and in a way becomes the wild and sublime Pitt qua Tyler Durden.)

DeCillo's entire "ontology" throughout this movie is based upon the discordance or contrast between Cave, observed from a safe distance, and the absolute proximity of Pitt. DeCillo's elementary procedure consists in moving around

Pitt's grimy apartment with a disturbing proximity which renders visible the disgusting details of existence, the decaying walls and fraying of the grungy interior—in short, the habitat of a loner.

What do I mean by a loner? Suffice it to recall the opening sequence of *Johnny Suede*. After the shots that epitomize the nether regions of a nightclub—disgusting, graffiti laced bathroom walls—the camera settles on Johnny Suede combing his hair and mugging at himself in the mirror, while he sings softly the lyrics of Ricky Nelson's 1962 hit "Teen Age Idol":

> Some people call me a teenage idol
> Some people say they envy me
> I guess they got no way of knowing
> How lonesome I can be . . .[2]

These frames establish the loneliness and estrangement of Johnny Suede, a character who can only but dwell in an abject dive such as the studio apartment we see him skulking about in the following morning, wearing nothing but his magical suede shoes and some ripped and dirty undies, down which he plunges his hand. The tiny clattering refrigerator has nothing but a decomposing carrot and a cloudy jar of mayonnaise. But it is not merely the crash pad (a metonymic figure which will turn out to reappear here) that links Pitt to crashing. No, it hides in the lyrics that Pitt sings throughout the film with an eerie tone of reverence.

Johnny Suede hinges on a paradox of stylistic borrowing and the anxieties of influence that haunt such borrowing. On the one hand, the tortured artist is utterly alone in the world; on the other hand, the artist is strongly affected by previous artists as figures of devotion. As such, Pitt's Suede is a hyperbolic, self-aware, and tormented copy of 1950s rockers such as Ricky Nelson—and he is equally enamored with the contemporaneous figure of Freak Storm. As we have noted, as the film progresses, Freak Storm appears to be on a crash course of his own making—a kind of rock star flameout with which we are all too familiar, and which Johnny Suede seems all too ready to gravitate toward himself.

The musician Ricky Nelson, on the other hand, experienced a different kind of end: Nelson died five years before the filming of *Johnny Suede*—of all things, in a fiery plane crash. The band traveled around in a 1944 Douglas DC-3 said to have been "plagued with mechanical problems"—problems which apparently culminated in a fire in the cabin heater, causing the plane to crash and kill nine of the eleven on board.[3] This crash—indeed, the entire mythology around plane crashes and rock stars—might explain Johnny Suede's deep and ineffable sadness throughout the film: his hero not only died, but in a way that resists easy imitation.[4] Johnny Suede can pantomime Ricky Nelson's look and lyrics, but Nelson's crashing will always exist beyond him, inaccessible to the budding rock star. As for Johnny, his crash course ends with a philosophical quandary about free will versus determinism: can Johnny change his course, or will he always feel as if pushed around by a "big invisible hand"?[5] If he *can* change his course, does he have to hit bottom in order to do so?

Hitting bottom

In curious ways, Pitt's later role in David Fincher's 1999 cult film *Fight Club* revisits and ramps up the dilemmas of crashing. The house on Paper Street stands as the ur-crash pad, a dilapidated mansion where Brad Pitt resides as the countercultural yet wildly productive enigma, Tyler Durden. The nameless hero of *Fight Club*, played by Edward Norton, ends up living with Pitt in this abode. At one point, Norton quips in a voiceover, "Most of the week we were Ozzie and Harriet"—a weird echo of crashing, as it was Ricky Nelson himself who starred in this 1950s and 1960s TV program.

Backing up, though, we do not meet Pitt's character in the crash pad on Paper Street. We see Pitt clearly for the first time precisely after a crash fantasy—in Norton's words, "every time the plane banked too sharply on takeoff or landing, I prayed for a crash, or a midair collision."[6] Norton fantasizes that his plane has experienced a midair collision and passengers are getting sucked out, while Norton stares on in bland amusement. He wakes up to Pitt's Tyler Durden reading the emergency briefing instructions and lampooning the calm-looking passengers on the emergency briefing cards:

> "If you are seated in emergency row . . ."—*yup*—"and feel you would be unable or unwilling to perform the duties listed on the safety card, please ask your flight attendant to reseat you."
> An exit door procedure at thirty-thousand feet . . . Mm, hm. The illusion of safety.[7]

These lines revolve around the image of the "safety card," a text that is lampooned later by ironic parodies placed in seatback pockets by the Project Mayhem minions (Figures 3.1 and 3.2).

Fight Club hinges on this "ground zero" mentality. Pitt's Tyler Durden persona exuberantly embodies and celebrates the ways to "hitting bottom"—a condition that includes everything from car crashes to harmless pranks, self-mutilation

FIGURE 3.1 *Actual safety card in* Fight Club, © *20th Century Fox.*

FIGURE 3.2 *Project Mayhem safety card in* Fight Club, © *20th Century Fox.*

to wearing garish thrift store clothes. But what I want to linger on here in the above lines is the brash irreverence with respect to human air travel: Tyler Durden sees the whole project of flight as an "illusion of safety" that masks the airborne state of tenuousness, fragility, and absolute proximity to "hitting bottom." In other words, it is significant that Pitt is introduced in the airplane, as his character's purpose is to undermine the superstructures of progress—and air travel functions as a symbolic (if not exactly technological) lynchpin of contemporary culture.

And this is no fluke, this dance with crashing: we see it again and again, in different lights and at different angles. For instance, in a scene midway through the 2011 film *Moneyball*, Brad Pitt's character once again riffs on the nature of crashing, this time good-naturedly—but no less darkly and significantly for our purposes here.

In this scene, Pitt's baseball team general manager Billy Beane is trying to reassure his daughter Casey (played brilliantly by Kerris Dorsey) that he's not in trouble. Beane's job is definitely on the line at this point in the film. They are in the Oakland airport, with Casey getting ready to board a plane; she's an "unaccompanied minor," so the father is allowed to accompany her to the boarding gate. Here's the dialogue:

Billy Beane: "Do I look worried?"
Casey: "Yeah."
Billy: ". . . 'cause you're getting on an airplane; those things crash all the time."[8]

This is a classic example of what the journalist Dennis Lim has accurately described as Brad Pitt's "wild card" quality. It is part of the mythology of Pitt: his ability (often in single roles) to oscillate incredibly between cool, collected reason and erratic, emotionally charged physicality—to shift from the serious to the sly in a blink of the eye. In a word, Pitt is able to channel something wild—that is, *natural*—and in so doing, to throw into disequilibrium all the balanced measures of truth, law, and reason that structure society.

In *Moneyball* Pitt represents an adoring father and calculating manager. His professional recklessness is meant to be entirely compartmentalized: Billy Beane is trying to change the game of baseball, and regularly overturns desks and throws chairs, bats, and plastic water coolers into walls at the stadium. For the most part, the bonding scenes of Pitt and Dorsey seem to suggest that he leaves his rogue attitudes at the office—except for one scene at home in which he makes Casey a ridiculously huge ice cream sundae, to her delight—but we'll let that one slide. The point is that *Moneyball* shows us, for the most part, a balanced Pitt, a domesticated and professionalized Pitt.

Yet in the airport scene quoted above, a little glimpse of Tyler Durden bursts into view. In this brief utterance—"those things crash all the time"—Pitt sends up commercial air travel and mocks it as a dubious project, prone to crashing. The sterile white background of the scene—the generic concourse ambiance, the drone of automated things—underscores the sentiment here, as the exclusive privilege of flight is shown to be something drab, dull, non-distinct. And Pitt's characteristic sarcasm and dark humor punctuate the scene with something else: a specter of horrible violence (not just a plane crash, but with one's own child aboard) lurking just beyond the frame, but well within the realms of possibility. In the West Coast glow of speculative finance and sports fortunes, Pitt shows us once again that hitting bottom is always closer than we might think.

As in *Fight Club*, the crash in the mob film *Killing Them Softly* arrives in the figure of another actor: this time, James Gandolfini as the hit man Mickey who is brought in from out of town to do a special job—but because times are tight (it's late 2008), command is given from above to Brad Pitt's organizational character to "fly him in on coach." The economic crash is hereby signaled by the fact that even a high-end assassin can't fly First Class (or even Business) any more, and this fact is then echoed in the following scenes which show Gandolfini trudging up the jet bridge with all the other coach passengers, and then pulling a comically petite roller bag behind him through an ordinary, tattered baggage claim area. In this film about the hierarchies and bureaucracies of gambling, theft, and professional murder, Pitt's character stands as an awkward point of balance and perspective: a somewhat neutral observer of crashes on many levels.

Later in the film, when Pitt and Gandolfini square off in a hotel room—Mickey stupid drunk and bleary-eyed, Pitt crystal clear and sharp—we might recall an earlier scene with these two actors, roles reversed in yet another crash pad: In Tony Scott's 1993 *True Romance* the archetypal stoner Floyd (Pitt) smokes marijuana out of a plastic honey bear and unknowingly survives a run-in with a killer—played by none other than the cool, collected James Gandolfini. (This was the becoming-domestic of Pitt, not yet professionalized, but still at home on the couch.)

Killing Them Softly was filmed in New Orleans, where Brad Pitt has worked in real life since Hurricane Katrina to show that America is *not* "just a business," and is in fact a community where ecological design and human kindness can prevail.[9] It's also a city whose airport property is named after a plane crash: Louis Armstrong International is also known by its call sign KMSY, or MSY on your baggage tag—for Moisant Stock Yards, after John Moisant, the stunt pilot who crashed his plane and was killed in the stockyards that would become the travel hub of New Orleans. Crashing comes through *Killing Them Softly*, then, not just metaphorically in Mickey's downward spiraling character, but also in the very real architecture of the setting, Louis Armstrong Airport, a place with a history of plane crashes.

Significantly, *Killing Them Softly* was shot before Louis Armstrong was renovated for the 2013 Super Bowl, making it an exceptionally miserable baggage claim area. This familiar and loathsome realm stands as a metonymy for the economy at large: it is a repository for stuff, but it's shown to be empty, a junk space. As the critic Mark Fisher might have described this impersonal zone in the film, it is "all that is left to the consumer-spectator, trudging through the ruins and the relics."[10]

We can go further still into this eccentric connection. Terrence Malick's 2011 *The Tree of Life*, as the literary critic Nathan Brown has insightfully observed, "is one example of an effort to reframe existential questions concerning the relation of life and death as ontological questions concerning the being or non-being of life per se."[11] If, as Brown claims, the film "circulates around a central, singular event," it is worth noting that this event (the death of a son) is communicated to Brad Pitt's character (the father) over the phone in the cacophonous space of an airport, with a droning aircraft in the background drowning out the call. The existential crash of this film, which merges with a much broader ontological inquiry, is staged on a precarious field of flight. The airplane here functions as a muffled yet over-determined vehicle, a strictly teleological technology that is rife with the realities of the historical moment of the film. As Brown goes on to argue, "the problem, then, is not only that of the relation between matter, life, thought and spirit, but how this relation is mediated by technics and by capital." Pitt's struggling-to-hear at the airport is a point of immanent critique. If airports often stand for human progress, Pitt's defeated character struggling to communicate at the airfield is one of the most pointed and powerfully suggested critiques of human hubris in *The Tree of Life*. The idling aircraft engine mocks and remarks the "restlessness" (Brown) of Pitt's character, and underscores his propensity for crashing. Malick seems to imply a question through his impressionistic drama, the answer to which Pitt then embodies: What does crashing feel like? It feels like the universe, and it's exploding.

Nature lessons

Here at the edge of life and non-life, trembling in the presence of ground zero, we arrive at *World War Z*: Earth as the land of the humanoid undead. About thirty minutes into the film we find Brad Pitt's Gerry Lane on a military cargo aircraft with Elyes Gabel's Dr. Fassbach, a "virologist from Harvard" who has been tasked with figuring out the cause of (as well as a cure for) the wildly contagious zombie disease spreading over the planet. They are flying to South Korea, on a rumor that the zombie outbreak began there. En route, Fassbach pontificates about the subtlety and craftiness of Nature, musing on how "she loves to play tricks," and "she's a bitch." He even compares Nature to a serial killer. Toward the end of this airborne, spontaneous lecture, Dr. Fassbach gets a maniacal expression on his face, and Brad Pitt looks pensive if also a little disturbed.

Is it really a problem, though, if indeed the zombie outbreak is an extension of Nature? The thing about zombies is that they have supposedly broken *from* the natural order: they are the un-dead, they (non)exist beyond an allegedly "natural" human timeline of life and death. The zombies in this film click their teeth and sniff the air as if they are hungry, but they really just want to bite people—and only then to turn them into similar creatures. It's not about eating; it's about community, and a kind of asexual and finite reproduction.

Furthermore, they seem to have achieved a state of weird biological equilibrium, the sine qua non of certain ideas of ecology: this humanoid sub-species doesn't need to extract resources, exterminate other species, or build things—they just like to hang out. For when there are no more healthy non-zombie people to bite, the zombies go dormant, simply standing around and jerking occasionally (as we see later in the film). They don't have to work or struggle, they can just chill. Given contemporary culture's everyday wish images of vacation, retirement, off time, and vegging out—does zombie life really look so bad?

Nature is a strange problem that lurks throughout this movie. Nature plays a double role, both the background and the foreground, the riddle to solve and the inescapable condition. It is what *causes* the zombies in the first place (as a virus of some sort); yet it also, according to Dr. Fassbach, holds the keys and clues to the mystery. Nature in *World War Z* is something to "catch" in a double sense: as a virus and as a culprit who causes the virus. The reason they've sent a virologist on the mission is to figure out the disease and come up with a solution, a cure. Nature is figured as dynamic, adaptive, generative of new viruses and forms of life; some of this is threatening to human life, and thus humans push back, to keep the species from changing too much (or too quickly) or becoming extinct (at least not in our lifetime). At the same time, Nature is something to be held in check, perceived and controlled as an external entity.

Yet if Nature is something that at times needs to be recuperated or set in balance (*à la* those "Take Back America" bumper stickers), then it is precisely the *humans* who are ill-directed here: they should join the zombies, for the zombies have achieved a stable state *within a dynamic system*, a state that would seem to be able to exist in perfect harmony with the rest of Nature even within a broader state of flux. Humanoids as an entirely stable population of sloths: it's progress at its apex, satisfaction pretty much guaranteed.

Except that this is the foil of "Nature" as a concept. As the philosopher Friedrich Nietzsche describes it in *Beyond Good and Evil*, the desire to live according to Nature is incoherent, or at best tautological, as it sets up an opposition that always immediately collapses. It's like saying you want to live according to life. Well, how could it be otherwise?[12] Such too this mad mission of a species (humans, i.e., Nature) to rid Nature of something it generated, the zombies (again, Nature). The setting of Dr. Fassbach's Nature lesson is hardly coincidental. *World War Z* is in part, in fact, a startling and savage critique of modern air travel.

Earlier in the film, Gerry Lane's former boss Thierry Umutoni, U.N. Deputy Secretary-General (played by Fana Mokoena), briefs Lane on the situation and mentions offhand, concerning the virus, that "*the airlines were the perfect delivery system . . .*".

Later in the film, Gerry Lane barely escapes an overrun Jerusalem, enplaning onto a Belarus Airways wide-body jetliner at the last second before it takes off. Lane makes it out in the nick of time: from the airplane window on ascent, we see the teeming masses of zombies and the devastation below. Never mind: everything seems fine on the flight—a little relief, at last. That is, until the plane is making its descent into Cardiff, Wales, and Lane hears/feels some thumping toward the back of the plane. He cautiously strolls down the aisle to check it out. What I want to seize on here is the total banality of this scene: it is the pinnacle of modern progress, summed up in the interior space of the commercial airliner. But when Lane peeks through the divide that separates Business from Economy Class, he sees an awful sight: there was a zombie stowaway on the plane that finally broke loose from the nether regions of the aircraft, and is wreaking havoc and thus multiplying.

On the one hand, this is a terrifying scenario. On the other hand, though, it does not really look all that different from a normal scene of boarding, wherein people jockey for seats, armrests, and carry-on stowage. Incidentally, this whole episode was all the fault of a particular flight attendant: to wit, the crouching beige-clad woman in the mid-foreground, who unknowingly freed the secret sharer from a storage elevator in the rear galley. When she raises her head in preparation to attack Lane, we are presented with one of the exciting face-to-face moments in the film: the flight attendant is portrayed here with wild eyes, blood running down her chin, about to pounce.

Now having worked at an airport for a few years earlier in my life, I am fairly sympathetic to the grueling labor of air travel, and I do not wish to make fun of airline workers. But this sequence seems to me to be a clear jab: is this look so distinct from how we encounter (or at least hyperbolically imagine) irate, snippy flight attendants in so many mundane disciplinary contexts onboard commercial airliners? "*Sir, turn that phone off immediately!*"

At this point Lane's only recourse is to hurl a hand-grenade back toward the Economy section of the cabin, and duck. This rather takes care of the immediate zombie problem, but it doesn't bode well for the plane: a gaping rent in the fuselage, and the zombies (and most everyone else besides Lane and his sidekick) are sucked out of the plane as it depressurizes. In a moment of horrific hyper-verisimilitude, we even glimpse the aforementioned flight attendant qua zombie sucked into a turbine fan, her head actually denting the leading edge of the cowling as she is presumably churned into oblivion.

Mere seconds later, here we are back at Nature, which arrives in pristine form around a stunningly spectacular plane crash: the Airbus glides with gaping hole and engine on fire over a mountain ridgeline, and the pilots prepare to crash land the plane in an evergreen forest. The plane at first seems poised to land somewhat gently in the resplendent foliage, but soon erupts in a fireball and disintegrates, its nose breaking off and crumpling as it tumbles toward the audience.

This is an example of what I call the "environmentality" of plane crashes.[13] The environmental scholar Arun Agrawal uses the term "environmentality" to describe how people become political subjects through the creation and dissemination of environmental policies and ecological knowledge.[14] Agrawal demonstrates that as land and resources become objects of statistics, ordered consumption, and conservation, environmentality emerges through people becoming certain kinds of subjects: environmental subjects. This is not necessarily a specific way of inhabiting or treating an environment, but rather accounts for how people gradually become implicated in and subject to specific cultural and political designations about what an environment *is* in the first place. Here, I am adapting Agrawal's term to think about how air travel disasters are represented and mediated in contemporary U.S. culture.

Risking yet one more detour, we can circle back around to the theme of safety briefing cards in *Fight Club* to see environmentality at work. Such cards, as provided in the seatback pockets of commercial airliners, cultivate certain ideas of Nature.

On this Alaska Airlines briefing card, an idyllic alpine scene is depicted outside of the crash-landed aircraft. Let us suspend disbelief for a moment concerning the implausibly intact landing gear or the slim chances of such a graceful emergency landing in rugged terrain. Let us focus, instead, on the outside environment that appears in this info-graphic. Upon first glance, the scene simply suggests an open space that one can dash into after an emergency landing. And yet, as we consider further the informational incongruities located in these processual frames, the contrasting images become more

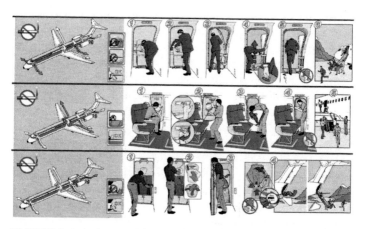

FIGURE 3.3 *Safety card from an Alaska Airlines MD80, circa 2003.*

curious. The technical diagrams detail various contingency escapes from the aircraft, including materially specific directions about how to deploy the tail slide, for instance. These diagrams are somewhat offset by boldly rendered landscape features, such as fecund foothills and sublime mountains jutting up on the horizon. What is the function of this highly aestheticized *outside*? My theory, as evinced in this example and reappearing in the crash scene from *World War Z*, is that there is a critical relationship between ideas of environment and the procedural aesthetics of plane crashes.

Lingering on this emergency briefing card, we can see how the potentially harrowing event is tied to an environmental-aesthetic register: the sky is intensely blue, and the dramatic snow-peaked mountains give way to verdant forests—it is an encompassing ecosystem rendered in miniature. The beauty and eco-logic of a world beyond thus somehow buttress the violence of the plane crash. Outside the wrecked airplane and its tight seating configurations, one finds oneself in an ecological *tabula rasa*, a space open to inhabitation and free mobility. The shattered dream of the passenger traveling by air ends up on the ground, and the violence of the crash becomes a portal into a pristine, beautiful wilderness. The air travel disaster becomes a zero point for a survivalist fantasy, a reset button that places the human subject back in a pure state of nature, like Robinson Crusoe on his island. In other words, the techno-culture of modern air travel is subtended by a mindset of naturalism and by an idea of beautiful wilderness as an always-available foundation point where human progress can begin afresh.

Back in *World War Z*, the plane crash serves as if to say, "*You want Nature? You got it!*" It's all around: in the mountains, the white barked aspens, the firs and pines, the heavy clouds—it's a ridiculously scenic vista, re-marked as it were as a "scene" where Nature really resides. Human flight always comes crashing back to the ground. The wild landscape frames this disaster, and clears away something of a blank slate for the human subject qua survivor, in the singular form of Brad Pitt.

A tree trunk in the foreground of this shot reminds us that here, amid the redundant wire tangles and calamitous wreckage, we're in the realm of Nature. This is where we can start fresh, back at ground zero. It is no wonder that the crash scene is precipitated by a sequence that wonderfully and uncannily calls to mind Edward Norton's own mid-air collision fantasy in *Fight Club*.

These are fantasies of getting back to Nature, to real experience—in Henry David Thoreau's words, "*Contact! Contact!*"[15] Yet if we really wanted this immediacy in the context of *World War Z*, we would need only allow ourselves to be bitten. The zombies aren't struggling against—or to get closer to—Nature. They are it. As are we.

And here again lies a harsh critique of air travel, instantiated by various roles and acts of Brad Pitt: just when we thought we were farthest from Nature, nestled in our elaborate techno-cultural tubes of flight, we were in fact closer than ever to it. We can fly, but we cannot hide. This is Nature—ground zero—reached by plane and yet always already there, in us as well as beneath us, the condition and the possibility, the baseline and the endlessly receding horizon.

Expiry

In Martin Brest's 1998 film, *Meet Joe Black*, Brad Pitt's character as Death comes to life paradoxically after Pitt's former fictional self is killed, spectacularly struck and flung by multiple cars as he is crossing the street. The scene of the crash is immortalized in a GIF that shows Pitt flying through the air again and again, a 3-second eternal return of the same death.[16]

There are more than enough indications here to suggest we might perceive Brad Pitt and crashing as sharing a charged space in our cultural imagination. Here there is a sort of fantasy, call it oblique, which we can only glimpse through scenes and metaphors of collisions, effects of gravity, and subjective breakdowns. I employ these words, I admit, with full knowledge that this is a strange and uncertain connection—but also with the conviction that there is something about crashing that taps into an as yet unnamable feeling or condition, something we can only inadequately call *Nature*. It is something we identify with, but that we also turn our eyes away from, some "terrifying form of monstrosity" that proclaims itself uniquely in the guise of Brad Pitt when we see him crash on screen.[17]

Notes

1   David Foster Wallace, "E Unibus Pluram," in *A Supposedly Fun Thing I'll Never Do Again* (New York: Back Bay, 1998), 36.

2   Ricky Nelson, "Teen Age Idol." (Imperial 5864, 1962).

3   See http://en.wikipedia.org/wiki/Ricky_Nelson#Death.

4   Another link between nostalgia for a real American style of rock music and plane crashes can likewise be seen at work in "The Day the Music Died." http://en.wikipedia.org/wiki/The_Day_the_Music_Died.

5   *Johnny Suede*, directed by Tom DiCillo (Lions Gate, 1991).

6   *Fight Club*, directed by David Fincher (20th Century Fox, 1999).

7   *Fight Club*, directed by David Fincher (20th Century Fox, 1999) (DVD 22:47).

8   *Moneyball*, directed by Bennett Miller (Columbia, 2011).

9   *Killing Them Softly*, directed by Andrew Dominik (Weinstein, 2012).

10 Mark Fisher, *Capitalist Realism* (Winchester: Zero Books, 2009).

11 Nathan Brown, "Origin and Extinction, Mourning and Melancholia." *MUTE*, September 9, 2012. http://www.metamute.org/editorial/articles/origin-and-extinction-mourning-and-melancholia [Accessed December 17, 2013].

12 Friedrich Nietzsche, *Beyond Good and Evil*, trans. Walter Kaufmann (New York: Vintage, 1989), 15.

13 Some of this discussion is drawn from my essay, "Environmentality and Air Travel Disasters: Representing the

Violence of Plane Crashes," in *Beauty, Violence, Representation*, ed. Lisa Dickson and Maryna Romanets (New York: Routledge, 2013).

14 Arun Agrawal, *Environmentality: Technologies of Government and the Making of Subjects* (Durham, NC: Duke University Press, 2005).

15 Henry David Thoreau, *The Maine Woods* (New York: Viking Penguin, 1988), 96.

16 See http://stream1.gifsoup.com/view2/1756535/brad-pitt-gets-hit-by-two-cars-o.gif.

17 Jacques Derrida, "Structure, Sign, and Play in the Discourse of the Human Sciences," in *Writing and Difference*, trans. Alan Bass (London: Routledge, 2001), 370.

CHAPTER FOUR

Suburban Rage

Robert Bennett

Well, I would say that I'm just drifting.
Here in the pool.
—BENJAMIN BRADDOCK (DUSTIN HOFFMAN), in *The Graduate*

I am willing to die, but not of boredom.
—MARK (MARK FRECHETTE), in *Zabriskie Point*

Mike Nichols's 1967 film, *The Graduate*, opens with an extraordinary image: a deliberately off-center close-up of Benjamin Braddock (Dustin Hoffman) staring vacantly into the distance. Weighed down (in advance) by the monotony, banality, and superficiality of suburban life, Benjamin's absolutely blank expression conveys, as forcefully as any image in American cinema, an acute sense of suburban alienation. He is deeply disturbed, and yet he seems unable to muster anything more than the most passive response. We later learn that he wants something "different," but—more resigned than resistant and largely incapable of articulating any viable alternative of his own—he does little more than "just drift" in his family's pool.[1] Disaffected, disoriented, and directionless, Benjamin feels trapped by post-WWII Southern California's emerging suburban landscape of sprawling tract homes, manicured lawns, and swimming pools; its facile culture of conspicuous consumption, social conformity, and intellectual incuriosity; and its ersatz lifestyle of fast food, fast music, and fast cars.

It is Benjamin's expressionless expression, however, that best captures the psycho-social geography of this brave new "plastic" world.[2] On the one hand, his passivity reflects the 1950s quietist "square" cultural consensus, described by William Manchester as "withdrawn, cautious, unimaginative, indifferent, unadventurous, and silent."[3] At the same time, however, his troubled face also expresses his own generation's growing discontent. Trapped like a deer in the headlights, Benjamin is caught precariously between suburbia's Golden Age in 1950s Southern California and its explosive aftermath, even blowback, a decade later. Henry David Thoreau aptly described Benjamin's predicament, *avant la lettre*, as a life of "quiet desperation," and *The Graduate* essentially provides a case study in this particular emotional quandary: confused to the point of bewilderment, distraught almost to panic, and silenced practically to muteness, Benjamin is silently but desperately trapped by suburbia.[4] Like Sartre, he can find no exit.

Or can he? Despite its recurring images of entrapment, *The Graduate* still holds out a ray of hope, suggesting that other counter-suburban worlds might be possible. Even in his first conversation with his father, Benjamin attempts to express, though falteringly, that he wants to be "different," and he struggles, albeit largely unsuccessfully, to break free from the suburban world that constrains him.[5] Like T. S. Eliot's Prufrock, he is "pinned" but still "wriggling," and ultimately he does take action, overdue as it may be.[6] Subversively redeploying the same car that he initially spurned as a symbol of suburban consumerism, conformity, and parental ineptitude, Benjamin races to the church where Elaine

Robinson (Katharine Ross), the daughter of his ex-lover, Mrs. Robinson (Anne Bancroft), is about to marry another man. Belatedly finding his voice—though only in the form of an inarticulate scream—he interrupts the ceremony, steals the surprised bride (already wed) at the altar, and escapes with the bride-to-have-been in a passing school bus. Initially laughing happily, the couple seems to represent some hopeful counter-suburban alternative though the film ultimately concludes with the couple's laughter turning into more tentative and apprehensive expressions. The newly unweds may have finally escaped their past suburban lives, at least for a day, but their ambiguous expressions suggest that they are hardly in the clear. At best, they have achieved a partial, uncertain victory. At worst, their defiance may prove little more than one more turn of the suburban screw; their escape route but another dead-end suburban cul de sac. Nevertheless, uncertain as their future may be, Benjamin's anguished cry and the couple's gutsy insubordination provide a powerful reminder: suburbia's quicksand may not be escaped easily, but one need not simply roll over and play dead either, at least not without first putting up a fight.

Released only three, albeit a significant three, years after *The Graduate*, Michelangelo Antonioni's *Zabriskie Point* (1970) advances a radically different anti-suburban critique. Like Benjamin, Antonioni's characters are painfully disillusioned, and *Zabriskie Point* explicitly connects their disillusionment to the rapidly suburbanizing American Southwest, which he depicts as a site of conspicuous consumption, insipid superficial lifestyles, rigid gender roles, the exploitation of minority workers, irresponsible real estate speculation, and environmental destruction. Antonioni's film, however, depicts this suburban alienation as spreading to larger groups of disaffected youth, if not an entire generation, who seek to transform their precursors' passivity into active resistance, open rebellion, and even full-blown revolution. In fact, the film opens with a room full of student radicals and civil rights activists planning acts of civil disobedience, debating racial politics, and advocating the use of violence to achieve their ends. Impatient even with this heightened level of political agitation, Antonioni's protagonist, Mark (Mark Frechette), walks out on the proceedings mid-deliberation, boldly declaring his resolve to die—"though not of boredom"—for the cause.[7] He then buys a gun, seriously contemplates shooting a police officer, and steals a plane, first risking and then later losing his life as a result. Meanwhile, even his resolutely apolitical, peacefully-inclined hippie girlfriend, Daria (Daria Halperin), vividly contemplates, if not quite actually commits, an audacious act of anti-suburban terrorism. In what is arguably the most powerful anti-suburban visual montage ever filmed, Daria evocatively imagines exploding a luxurious suburban home on the fringes of the Phoenix desert—together with the furnishings, clothes, and food inside it—over and over again in a series of breathtaking slow-motion images taken from diverse angles and perspectives—all accompanied by a Pink Floyd soundtrack. If *The Graduate* critiques suburbia, *Zabriskie Point* outright damns it, openly advocating its utter destruction, transforming Benjamin's quiet desperation into an anti-suburban rage that extends well past lawlessness to the brink of terrorist violence.

This may seem an odd introduction for an essay on Brad Pitt, but I contend that this history of anti-suburban critique plays a crucial role in two of his most significant performances: his role as John Smith in one of his highest grossing films, Doug Liman's *Mr. & Mrs. Smith* (2005, henceforth *MMS*); and his tour de force performance of Tyler Durden in David Fincher's *Fight Club* (1999, henceforth *FC*), arguably the best and most critically acclaimed performance of his career. Consequently, anti-suburban rage provides a crucial reference point for understanding the popular appeal, artistic scope, and larger social and political significance of Pitt's career. One might even say that underneath Pitt's boyish good looks and ripped body runs what *FC* refers to as "Jack's raging bile"—an acute, piercing political sensibility that Pitt has drawn upon judiciously, but forcefully, to articulate a formidable sense of anti-suburban rage.[8]

While this political undercurrent to Pitt's career generally follows the post-WWII American counterculture's broad critique of suburbia, it also extends *The Graduate*'s sociological satire toward Antonioni's more radical political analysis of alternative sites of resistance, lines of flight, and revolutionary possibilities. After all, if suburbia is simply an ersatz world constructed out of plywood, plastic, and ticky-tacky, then its defenses cannot possibly be impregnable. Its flimsy spatial, social, and ideological façades must have structural weaknesses that can be exploited, whether by eloping lovers (*The Graduate*), would-be terrorists (*Zabriskie Point*), pirate radio DJs (*Pump Up the Volume*), drug-dealing widows (*Weeds*), cyborg freaks (*Edward Scissorhands*), professional assassins (*Grosse Pointe Blank*), demented rabbit hallucinations and kiddy porn dens (*Donnie Darko*), toxicity (*Safe*), or various animated cartoon superheroes (*The Incredibles*), animals (*Over the Hedge*), and brats on skateboards (*The Simpsons*). Pitt's films, therefore, occupy a turbulent crossroads where post-WWII American cinema's critique of suburbia's endless rows of "little boxes" crosses paths with more violent representations of anti-suburban rage which envision other counter-suburban possibilities, new social and political structures of feeling, and alternative emergent spatial and cultural landscapes.[9] More specifically, I argue that Pitt's performances have played a crucial, possibly unsurpassed, role in articulating this revolutionary anti-suburban critique for his generation. In something like a cinematic avatar of Jane Jacobs's *The Death and Life of Great American Cities* or a celluloid version of Mike Davis's *City of Quartz*, Pitt's performances in *MMS* and *FC*, in particular, criticize the suburban spatial, social, cultural, and political restructuring of American cities—and by extension of American society and culture at large—with the urgency, audacity, and fury of "raging bile."[10]

Sex in the suburbs

"There's this huge space between us, and it just keeps filling up with everything that we don't say to each other. What's that called?"

"Marriage."

> —JANE SMITH (ANGELINA JOLIE) AND HER MARRIAGE
> COUNSELOR, DR. WEXLER (WILLIAM FICHTNER), in
> *Mr. & Mrs. Smith*

"Ask the sex question again . . . Ten."

> —JOHN SMITH (BRAD PITT) in *Mr. & Mrs. Smith*

In most respects, *MMS* simply retells a rather unexceptional, practically formulaic, variation on the standard anti-suburban narrative that has become a bread-and-butter staple, if not the past use-date sour milk, of post-WWII American cinema and television—something between, say, *Edward Scissorhands* and *Desperate Housewives*. Like *The Graduate*, *MMS* establishes its anti-suburban critique with its first image: a shot of the eponymous Mr. John and Mrs. Jane Smith (Brad Pitt and Angelina Jolie) sitting uncomfortably in a therapist's office discussing the "huge space" that has developed between them.[11] Like the eloping Benjamin and Elaine, their initial laughter quickly devolves into a series of awkward glances—fake smiles, tensely pursed lips, barely audible sighs, incredulously raised eyebrows, and impatiently rolled eyes—as they fidget nervously while answering, when not simply evading, their marriage counselor's questions. Between John's transparent denial—"we don't really need to be here"—and the couple's inability to even "understand," let alone answer, their therapist's questions about their sexual satisfaction—both familiar tropes in anti-suburban narratives—the film immediately suggests that the couple's marital issues may somehow be related to their suburban lifestyle.[12]

This suspicion is quickly confirmed as the film soon moves on to depict a series of iconic suburban images: a school bus and paper boy on a stereotypical wide tree-lined suburban street, John and his neighbor simultaneously retrieving their morning papers, the highly affected manners displayed at a neighborhood party, and the Smiths' banal discussions of home repairs, passive aggressive mini-feuds over new drapes, unromantic bedroom routines, and dinner conversations about passing the salt. The film does occasionally reinterpret these worn-out tropes in new ways, and when it does reduce them to cliché it usually does so with an ironic wink. Its recurring suburban imagery, together with that imagery's implicit critique of the dull blandness of suburban life, however, unmistakably draws on long-established cinematic conventions that blame marital dissatisfaction in general—and sexual dissatisfaction in particular—on the cold emotional calculus of suburban life with its dutiful role-playing, shallow materialism, conformist tendencies, faux intimacies, and desperate attempts to shore up façades of happiness. When Jane asks their therapist whether "zero" should "technically" be considered as a possible answer to his question about their sex life, *MMS* may use a different narrative device than *The Graduate*, but it essentially advances the same anti-suburban critique represented by Benjamin and Mrs. Robinson's affair, drawing such a strong connection between suburbia and loveless, perfunctory marriages that it essentially blames suburbia—in very broad brushstrokes—for marital failure at large.[13]

Sitting awkwardly in their therapist's office—much like Benjamin and Elaine at the back of the school bus—the Smiths soberly, but uncynically, reflect upon what they have gotten themselves into. Again like the renegade lovers, the Smiths are exploring alternatives, looking for solutions, and struggling to break free from suburbia's psycho-social-sexual straitjackets—imperfect as their attempts may be—and nowhere is their struggle represented more clearly than in the repartee and banter, especially the nonverbal facial expressions and body language, that they exchange in their therapist's office. Consequently, these scenes are where much of the film's larger conceptual work takes place: where its themes are most clearly articulated, where its central conflict is most explicitly negotiated, and where much of its best acting and most clever dialogue occur. Ultimately, it is also where the Smiths finally defeat, or at least where they announce that they have defeated, the suburban marital doldrums with John's concluding line: "Ask the sex question again ... Ten."[14] Simultaneously resolving both the film's romantic comedy and its anti-suburban critique, the Smiths not only have fallen in love again, but they have also psychologically escaped suburbia.

And yet, *MMS* is far from a mere morality tale about psycho-therapy's relative advantages over infidelity, let alone some simplistic declaration that love can conquer all things suburban, turning domestic unbliss into hot sex steamily ever after. The Smiths do resolve their marital problems, and their therapist's office is where John scores their triumph a perfect ten, but the analyst's couch is not itself where they most directly confront and resolve their differences. If anything, their therapy sessions function merely as a barometer that measures the emotional progress they make elsewhere. Consequently, a more accurate description of the Smiths' situation might be found in something like Gilles Deleuze and Félix Guattari's anti-Freudian adage that a "schizophrenic out for a walk is a better model than a neurotic lying on the analyst's couch."[15] Only when the Smiths take their neuroses out for a walk, they pack serious heat and work out their marital issues through a series of high-power firefights and bare-knuckle death matches. Pat Benatar called love a "battlefield," but for the Smiths it is much closer to a warzone, a warzone where the Smiths do their own kind of therapy—between periodic exchanges of gunfire and knives, of course.[16]

Ultimately, *MMS* is neither a salacious tell-all about sex in the suburbs (or the lack thereof), nor some moralizing sermon on the benefits of marriage counseling, but rather a Homeric song of arms and man (and woman) whose central narrative logic revolves largely around issues of violence, especially the violence that seethes just behind suburbia's placid façades: the couple's vast arsenals of weaponry concealed in their suburban home—John's cache of guns hidden under the backyard shed and Jane's clandestine knife collection stashed behind the kitchen stove—their secret identities as professional assassins, and the ensuing violence and mayhem they ultimately produce both against each other and against the larger world around them. That this violence results in the complete and utter destruction of their suburban home, the demolition of an iconic suburban box store (a thinly-veiled version of a Home Depot located adjacent to a Costco knock-off), and a lethal high-speed chase in an explicitly suburban minivan further suggests that *MMS* uses this violence specifically to critique suburbia. In the end, however, the Smiths neither adapt to nor escape suburbia, but instead they outright destroy it, blowing up their suburban lives one house, one minivan, and one big box retail store at a time. Not since *Zabriskie Point* have filmgoers seen suburbia blown up with such exquisitely violent imagery, and it is precisely this violence—together with its implied critique of suburbia—that saves their marriage. It is not until they find themselves overlooking what Joyce described as the "ruin of all space, shattered glass and toppling masonry," standing knee-deep in the smoldering ruins of their self-demolished suburban home, that their love begins to rise anew, phoenix-like from suburbia's ashes.[17] In many ways, however, this violent turn is simply a return to their pre-suburban roots. After all, the Smiths first christened their budding romance, after escaping soldiers while on assignments in Bogotá, with the toast: "To dodging bullets."[18]

Domestic violence

"That's the second time you've tried to kill me today."

"Oh, come on, it was just a little bomb."

—JOHN AND JANE SMITH (BRAD PITT AND
ANGELINA JOLIE) in *Mr. & Mrs. Smith*

"There were times I just wanted to kill her."

"Likewise."

"But I just couldn't take the shot.". . .

"That's marriage?"

"You take your best shot and . . ."

>   —JOHN AND JANE SMITH (BRAD PITT AND
>   ANGELINA JOLIE) in *Mr. & Mrs. Smith*

In the simplest sense, *MMS* uses the genre of a domestic suburban romantic comedy, together with its trope of marital and sexual dysfunction, to critique suburban life, but its larger analysis of suburbia extends much further, mixing the conventions of both romantic comedies and spy action thrillers to produce a new hybrid genre. Much of the film's creative energy—including its unique approach to the problems of marriage, sexuality, and suburbia—derives largely from the tension and friction that it develops by crisscrossing these two genres. In this sense, *MMS* finds its truest counterparts not in *The Graduate, Desperate Housewives*, or other films that use images of sexual dissatisfaction to critique suburbia, but in films such as *Zabriskie Point*, Joel and Ethan Coen's *Raising Arizona* (1987), George Armitage's *Grosse Pointe Blank* (1997), Pixar's *The Incredibles* (2004), and Shawn Levy's *Date Night* (2010). In different ways, each of these films depicts characters who draw upon the adventure, excitement, and even violence found in lives of espionage, crime, or crime-fighting to help alleviate suburban boredom, ennui, and alienation.

In fact, *MMS* finds its most direct precursor neither in John Huston's *Prizzi's Honor* (1985)—which also depicts married assassins with assignments to kill each other—nor in Alfred Hitchcock's 1941 *Mr. & Mrs. Smith*—from which Liman's film borrows only its title and a vague sense of resolving marital difficulties through heated argument. Instead, *MMS* draws its essential plot and larger themes most directly from James Cameron's *True Lies* (1994). Like *MMS, True Lies* describes a deteriorating marriage between a bored suburban housewife,

Helen Tasker (Jamie Lee Curtis), and her boring salesman husband, Harry (Arnold Schwarzenegger). Their marriage is revitalized, however, when Helen discovers that Harry is really a secret agent and then gets drawn into one of his action-packed covert operations. Like the Smiths, the Taskers escape suburban monotony, reinvigorate their uninteresting lives and marriage, and ultimately fall in love again through daring acts of espionage and mortal combat as they join forces to defeat a group of heavily-armed terrorists. Moreover, *True Lies* explicitly presents the couple's thrilling adventures as an antidote to their suburban malaise. After Helen is seduced into a fake espionage plot by Simon (Bill Paxton)—a used car salesman who preys upon "bored housewives" who are "stuck in a rut" and need the "promise of adventure" or "danger" to free them from their "daily suburban grind"—she confesses that Simon's plot ensnared her because she wanted to do "something outrageous" that would make her feel "reckless" and "wild" in order to escape her uneventful suburban life.[19] Like *MMS*, *True Lies* also depicts the lethal attraction of violent covert operations as ultimately having a therapeutic effect that helps ease, or even cure, the pains of suburban discontentment. (This sentiment is echoed in "Mr. & Mrs. Simpson," *The Simpsons'* parody of *Mr. & Mrs. Smith*, when Homer declares, "so killing people together has really spiced things up in the bedroom."[20])

The most direct connection, but also the most significant difference, between the two films, however, lies in their respective tango scenes. Both beginning and ending with a tango scene, *True Lies* uses its dance scenes as a narrative framing device—much like the therapy sessions in *MMS*. Its opening tango, however, is thoroughly conventional and virtually indistinguishable from similar scenes in many James Bond-style action films: Harry uses an elaborate ruse and various technological gadgets to infiltrate a party in an elegant ballroom; then after stealing various computer files he begins flirting—and eventually tangoing—with a sexy art dealer, Juno Skinner (Tia Carrere), who unsurprisingly turns out to be an undercover agent herself; and when Harry is finally detected, again unsurprisingly, he proceeds to blow up half of the estate while escaping a phalanx of armed pursuers. The scene's centerpiece, however, is Harry and Juno's passionate tango which pointedly contrasts Harry's exotic—and erotic—life as a secret agent with his—and his wife's—dull domestic suburban lives back home. Consequently, the tango scene helps measure, by contrast, the initial state of the Taskers' lackluster marriage, just as the couple's concluding tango, in turn, measures the successful rekindling of their romance. Dancing together flirtatiously with the intimacy and erotic passion that their relationship initially lacked, the Taskers upstage even Harry's earlier tango with Juno, while Helen, now a newly appointed agent in her own right, humiliates Simon—whose predatory ruse once symbolized her vulnerability as a bored suburban housewife—by making him pee his pants at the point of her lipstick case (mistaken by Simon for a gun). Much like John's self-scored ten, the Taskers' final tango signals the simultaneous resolution of the film's two principal plotlines: the Taskers' relationship is renewed and their boring suburban lives are re-energized with the thrill and excitement of violence, rather than sex per se, providing the primary catalyst driving both transformations.

While the tango scene in *MMS* unmistakably references its counterpart in *True Lies*, the two scenes ultimately function inversely. Instead of revitalizing their marriage, the Smiths' tango actually marks the beginning of its dissolution. John asks Jane pointblank for a divorce (in the same restaurant where he once proposed), she curtly refuses his request to sit with her, he impudently sits anyway, and they both pull guns on each other under the table while John explains their "unusual" situation: "You obviously want me dead, and I'm less and less concerned for your well-being."[21] Even the couple's dance is marked by conflict and violence: they exchange witty insults, sharp accusations, and barbed replies; their dance moves, ranging from twisted arms to slammed heads, frequently double as acts of violence; and they repeatedly frisk each other for weapons with double-entendred dance moves that fuse eroticism with violence, occasionally even employing gestures—such as Jane's crouched frisking of John's leg—that make explicit, parodic reference to *True Lies*. Consequently, instead of celebrating the couple's happy reconciliation the Smiths' tango reveals the unraveling of their entire relationship with Jane rejecting happy endings as stories that have not yet finished while John advances his "newly formed" theory about why their marriage failed.[22] With the Smiths simultaneously attempting to blow each other up on their way out the door, the scene further underscores how underneath the passionate surface of the Smiths' tango, like their suburban lives and marriage, lurks a seething cauldron of violence boiling over with repressed anger, deep-seated resentment, secret death wishes, hidden weapons, and cloak-and-dagger identities. Ultimately, the film ends up redefining its own earlier definition of marriage as the "huge space" that develops between spouses over time, amending it to a couple's shared secret desire to "kill" each other—with the primary difference being simply that spouses, unlike assassins, just cannot bring themselves to "take the shot."[23] Aligning itself closer to *Zabriskie Point* than *The Graduate*, MMS seemingly shares Antonioni's sense that liberating ourselves from suburban banality requires, in some sense, engaging in acts of real or imaginary anti-suburban counter-violence.

Consequently, MMS is anything but some kind of *True Lies II*. Like the Taskers, the Smiths may resolve their marital differences, but they do so only within a very different, more or less diametrically opposed, narrative and ideological framework. Immediately before its final tango scene, *True Lies* depicts the Taskers laughing together in their suburban home as an iconic all-American, white, middle-class suburban family before effortlessly transitioning to the couple's final covert assignment and passionate tango. By unmistakably implying that the Taskers' double lives as suburban spouses and government agents can be seamlessly reconciled, the film largely re-inscribes, if not reinforces, post-WWII America's dominant cultural values and hegemonic political ideologies, ranging from traditional gender roles and the illusion of suburbia as a haven of domestic tranquility to exceptionalist cold war metanarratives (represented both by Harry's bombastic personification of America's inflated sense of its military power and through racist stereotypes of Arab terrorists).

In stark contrast, whatever resolution the Smiths may find, they do not find it within the protective confines of either suburbia or the paranoid cold war nation-state. Instead, the Smiths' happiness, even survival, as a couple requires that they outright destroy both their suburban home (à la Antonioni) and a suburban big box store (an icon of global capitalism at its most suburban). Moreover, by the end of the film it is not only the Smiths' home and local strip mall that lie in ruins, but the entire ideology of suburbia with its rigid gender roles, façades of domestic harmony, emotional sobriety, architecture of middle-class respectability, and insatiable consumerist fantasies. And if the film does allegorize post-WWII America's larger political economy, it depicts it as mere crass materialism (the fetishized conspicuous consumption of home improvements and interior decorating) or even merciless gangster capitalism (corporations that literally kill for profit) rather than as some kind of benevolent military state whose secret agents protect its citizens from foreign threats while the suburbs shelter them from domestic harm. Defanged for post-9/11 audiences, MMS may present a simpler, more entertaining, and less strident narrative than Zabriskie Point or even FC, but their central political critiques are much closer than they might seem at first glance. After all, all three films essentially end with spectacular explosions—of suburban homes, big box retail stores, and corporate skyscrapers—that most emphatically do not represent conventional action thrillers' mere violence-for-violence's-sake destruction, let alone paranoid cold war wet dreams, but instead advance genuine political critiques, essentially revolutionary manifestos, that openly advocate what Chuck Palahniuk's novel, Fight Club (1996), describes as "break[ing] up civilization so we can make something better out of the world."[24]

Suburban spleen

Martha Stewart is polishing the brass on the *Titanic*.

—TYLER DURDEN (BRAD PITT) in *Fight Club*

Deliver me from Swedish furniture.

—CHUCK PALAHNIUK, *Fight Club*

FC's larger political ideology is, of course, more obvious, better known, and largely derived from Palahniuk's novel, so I need not restate its essential anarcho-terrorist tenets or rehash the largely petty—partisan and sermonizing—critical debates that surround them. Without question, *FC* is much more aggressively political than *MMS*, or even *Zabriskie Point*, but all three films share a similar core political critique: that modernity has gone off its rails, devolving into a toxic mixture of fetishized techno-rationality, insatiable consumerism, and irresponsible hyperdevelopment that is both destroying the environment and hollowing out the human spirit. These films concur that suburbanization has played a leading role in creating this mess and that only radical, and quite possibly violent, opposition to suburbia can correct these problems. Consequently, *FC* differs from *MMS* and *Zabriskie Point* more in degree than in kind.

More superficially, however, *FC* also differs because it is clearly an urban, not a suburban, film. Its tough, gritty ethos draws on specifically urban settings, situations, characters, and imagery. The film's narrator and Tyler live in a "dilapidated house" in a "toxic waste part of town," their fight clubs are housed in abandoned industrial spaces underneath seedy bars, and Project Mayhem's anarcho-terrorists rampage from rooftop to rooftop across the urban skyline—that is until they blow it up altogether.[25] However, this gritty urban setting is precisely what Tyler's space monkeys are fighting to defend, while the world that they assault is strikingly suburban*ized* even if not suburban per se. What Palahniuk's novel, and by extension Fincher's film, criticize is a postmodern landscape where everything—urban *as well as* suburban—has been deracinated, standardized, miniaturized, atomized, commodified, domesticated, emasculated, and corporatized. In short, suburban*ized*, or what *FC* might even call suburban-*sized*—a world where suburbia's "little boxes made of ticky-tacky / little boxes all the same" have both proliferated and shrunk.[26] As Palahniuk puts it, postmodern subjects now live not little but "tiny" lives full of "tiny soap, tiny shampoos, single-serving butter, tiny mouthwash," and even "single-serving friends."[27] If *MMS* and *Zabriskie Point* critique suburbia's little box homes and big box commercial stores, then *FC* criticizes even the corporate city itself as little more than an extension of suburbia's cultural and political logic writ large across the entire urban landscape. Project Mayhem does target urban institutions—condos, museums, and skyscrapers—but not for being urban. On the contrary, it attacks a highly gentrified postmodern corporate city that lost its Whitmanian urban soul long ago, and nowhere is this more evident than when the narrator, seeking "deliver[ance] . . . from Swedish furniture," blows up his "pornograph[ically]" commodified condo full of "clever Njurunda coffee tables in the shape of a lime green yin and an orange yang," "Rislampa/Har paper lamps made from wire and environmentally friendly unbleached paper," "Mommala quilt-cover set[s]. Design by Tomas Harila and available in the following: Orchid. Fuschia. Cobalt. Ebony. Jet. Eggshell or Heather," and refrigerator full of "fourteen different flavors of fat-free salad dressing" and "seven kinds of capers"—the stuff it takes a "whole life to buy."[28] The world that Tyler rages against—the one that has become a "slave to the IKEA nesting instinct," where dining sets can "define [you] as a person," where "everything is a copy of a copy of a copy," and where the "things you own end up owning you"—may not be so different from, or even less suburban than, Benjamin's, Daria's, and the Smiths' worlds after all.[29]

Recontextualizing *MMS* and *FC* within this tradition of anti-suburban critique, however, raises several crucial questions about Brad Pitt as an actor: what is the essential relationship between Pitt the actor and this anti-suburban critique, how does his *performance* of these roles articulate anti-suburban rage so compellingly, and why have *his* performances resonated so powerfully with the American public? Without question, Palahniuk's novel provided exceptional material already well-suited for the cinema, and Fincher's adaptation is in many respects as daring and inventive as the novel itself. I argue, however, that Pitt's performance—and more specifically his performance of madness—provided a, if not *the*, key ingredient or sine qua non that transformed *FC* into the voice of a new lost generation. Absent Pitt's signature style—his delivery, his wit, his body language, his intensity, and his idiosyncratic devil-may-care nonchalance—*FC* could have easily become *Rebel Without a Cause* without James Dean. The ideas, the political message, the character, the narrative, and the lines themselves were all there for the taking—already embedded in Palahniuk's novel, then reinscribed onto Uhls's screenplay—but it was Pitt the actor who delivered those lines in a manner that communicated them powerfully and viscerally to the American public. In short, Pitt's performance played a catalytic role in electrifying the film, supplying the performative spark that helped bring Palahniuk's monster of a novel to life for a much broader—not to mention more sympathetic—audience than it might have otherwise reached.

Let me briefly discuss three crucial scenes that demonstrate different ways that Pitt's acting transformed the film. First, Tyler's conversation with the narrator during their initial encounter on the airliner illustrates Pitt's extraordinary ability to deliver a complex, Hamlet-esque dialogue full of nuanced and ambiguous meanings, seemingly illogical non-sequiturs, and a string of cryptically charged messages—all with a studied nonchalance. With almost every line, Pitt's timing and inflections add additional layers of meaning: he segues seamlessly from a monotone recitation of airplane safety rules to wild-eyed conspiracy theories, his paranoid glances breathe life into his conspiratorial murmurings, his pauses add urgency to his ramblings, his rhetorical questioning probes the narrator (and audience) to consider his cryptic messages more deeply, he offhandedly denounces civilization or proposes revolutions in mere asides, he switches deftly between committed anarchism and deadpan apathy, and his smirks add impish glee to his already devilish philosophies. Moreover, Pitt delivers these lines while sporting an outrageously flamboyant outfit. The clothes may make the man, and Pitt's garish fashion statement seems to offer the very model of such man-making clothes. In this case, however, the reverse seems equally plausible: it is Pitt the actor—with his timing, facial expressions, gestures, and mannerisms—who makes his costumes, impeccably designed as they may be. While one could claim that the film's brilliant costume design provides its actors with a sartorial crutch, already performing half of their act for them, this would only be halfway true because ingenious costuming also raises the stakes for actors' performances by requiring their acting to properly fit, match, and pull off such extraordinary clothes. Pitt admirably fills the shoes not only of his costume but also of Palahniuk's and Uhls's lines, and he draws on a broad array of well-honed acting skills to accomplish this.

In addition to simply performing his lines well, Pitt demonstrates a unique ability to balance impassioned rants with stark emotional detachment. While this adroit emotional gear-shifting recurs throughout the entire film, it is particularly evident in Tyler's second significant conversation with the narrator just before Tyler introduces the idea of the fight club by asking the narrator to hit him "as hard as you can."[30] At one moment, Pitt is eating while talking on the phone, casually asking what is up, staring around the room with palpably distracted boredom, obviously fake commiserating with the narrator for his lost possessions, and striking up seemingly tangential conversations about what duvets are. The next minute, however, he has already launched into a diatribe against the evils of rampant runaway consumerism and pervasive media saturation which culminates in telling Martha Stewart to "fuck off" and calling for the end of consumer culture as we know it—only to stop on a dime and reverse directions again, self-deprecatingly dismissing his own tirade as mere bluster: "but that's me. I could be wrong. Maybe it's a terrible tragedy."[31] With one final rhetorical summersault he again prophetically warns—"the things you own end up owning you"—only to retreat once more behind a mask of indifference—"but do what you like, man"—as he dismissively turns away from the conversation altogether.[32] If James Dean mastered the persona of the rebel without a cause, Pitt extends this persona one step further, transforming it into the anarchist without a cause—or even a care. Ultimately, Pitt channels his diverse acting skills to create an apathetic anarchism that matches its revolutionary manifestos with passive shrugs and declarations of faith with a devout agnosticism, and this enables the film to raise radical political issues without falling into the ideological pit of mere agitprop. As Pitt delivers the lines, the film questions, interrogates, and challenges what seem to be political and economic certainties, but it does so without advocating any new totalizing or totalitarian alternatives.

In fact, the political vision that slowly emerges in the film as it passes from a self-inflicted *mano a mano* brawl in a parking lot to fight club's bloody communal melees and Project Mayhem's anarcho-terrorist acts of violence does not reflect some kind of political manifesto. Rather, the film, like the book, offers its anarchist vision only as the symbolic, imaginary, fictional, illusionary and delusionary, hallucinations of a madman. If Tyler Durden knows which way the wind blows, it is because he resembles the melancholy, brooding Hamlet or the moody, scatologica, demi-revolutionary impulses of Bob Dylan's "Subterranean Homesick Blues" or "Ballad of a Thin Man"—not because he literally advocates some latter-day restoration of Weather Underground-style terrorism. And this is where Pitt's performance reaches its most impressive complexity as he ratchets up his already Hamlet-esque cryptically-encoded confusion, with its bipolar swings between revolution and resignation, into a full-blown portrayal of madness. Ultimately,

Tyler Durden is neither a Malcolm X nor a Ted Kaczynski but rather a contemporary variation on the haunted Hamlet who, seeing intimations of things gone terribly wrong, becomes a spectral gadfly spurred on by ghostly hallucinations in his "mind's eye"—but without the certainty or direction that might ossify these visions of madness into some kind of new direction or vision. Like *Hamlet, Fight Club* explores unanswerable questions more than it proposes final solutions, and Pitt's performance brings this kind of unhinged probing madness to life—or at least to the screen. In the film's last couple scenes which begin to reveal Tyler as a projected phantasm of the narrator's disintegrating mind, Pitt adds to his performance a heightened emotional intensity, increasingly urgent pleadings, angry ranting, maniacal laughter, wild-eyed stares, and the occasional all-out freak out. And, of course, once again there are the clothes—as unmistakably mad as the deranged hallucination wearing them. But here the viewer also has another moment of realization: Pitt has been playing Tyler as mad from the get-go, only with a stealthy understated subtlety. He has dropped hints everywhere throughout his performance that in retrospect only make sense as scattered pieces of Tyler's madness, but Pitt drops these hints carefully without playing his hand outright. Then, just at the moment when Tyler finally openly states that the seemingly normal, albeit eccentric as hell, character of Tyler is actually insane, Pitt again reverses direction to depict this lunatic, with his madness in full open view, as absolutely normal: "people do it every day. They talk to themselves. They see themselves as they'd like to be."[33] Instead of urging caution as the narrator approaches the brink of insanity, Tyler encourages him forward into the abyss, praising his ability to "just run with it."[34] Counterintuitively, Pitt's logic and delivery even straighten out as this epiphany of insanity is revealed. Tyler's paranoia dissipates, his bipolarity flattens out, and his non-sequiturs turn into lucid logical syllogisms. As Tyler and the narrator negotiate the semi-permeable membrane that divides their split-personality, Pitt's performance continually shifts between deadpan normalcy and unhinged madness. In the end, Palahniuk's character, Tyler Durden, is not a political revolutionary with a manifesto in hand but rather the melancholic ghost of a philosopher and poet gone mad who, like Hamlet, probes the boundary between madness and the stark, raving sane almost to the point of its erasure, making normalcy seem bizarre and madness appear perfectly natural. Renaissance humanists might have called such well-studied and willful nonchalance *sprezzatura*, and Pitt performs Tyler's raging madness with a deliberate carelessness that at times almost resembles the casual manners of Renaissance courtiers. Even at its most nonchalant, however, Pitt's *sprezzatura* is a *sprezzatura* that you don't want to fuck with.

Notes

1   *The Graduate*, directed by Mike Nichols (MGM, 1967).

2   *The Graduate*, directed by Mike Nichols (MGM, 1967).

3   "The Silent Generation." Wikipedia: The Free Encyclopedia, http://en.wikipedia.org/wiki/Silent_Generation [Accessed September 27, 2012].

4   Henry David Thoreau, *Walden and "Civil Disobedience."* (New York: Signet, 1999), 5.

5   *The Graduate*, directed by Mike Nichols (MGM, 1967).

6   T.S. Eliot, *The Waste Land and Other Poems* (New York: Signet, 1998), 8.

7   *Zabriskie Point*, directed by Michelangelo Antonioni (Warner Brothers, 1970).

8   *Fight Club*, directed by David Fincher (20th Century Fox, 1999).

9   Malvina Reynolds, "Little Boxes," *Ear to the Ground.* (Folkways, 2000).

10 *Mr. & Mrs. Smith*, directed by Doug Liman (20th Century Fox, 2005).

11 *Mr. & Mrs. Smith*, directed by Doug Liman (20th Century Fox, 2005).

12 *Mr. & Mrs. Smith*, directed by Doug Liman (20th Century Fox, 2005).

13 *Mr. & Mrs. Smith*, directed by Doug Liman (20th Century Fox, 2005).

14 *Mr. & Mrs. Smith*, directed by Doug Liman (20th Century Fox, 2005).

15 Gilles Deleuze and Félix Guattari, *Anti-Oedipus: Capitalism and Schizophrenia* (Minneapolis, MN: University of Minnesota, 1983), 2.

16 Pat Benetar, "Love is a Battlefield," *Live From Earth*. (Chrysalis, 1983).

17 James Joyce, *Ulysses* (New York: Vintage, 1986), 475.

18 *Mr. & Mrs. Smith*, directed by Doug Liman (20th Century Fox, 2005).

19 *True Lies*, directed by James Cameron (20th Century Fox, 1994).

20 "Mr. & Mrs. Simpson," *The Simpsons*, season 19, episode 5 (1997).

21 *Mr. & Mrs. Smith*, directed by Doug Liman (20th Century Fox, 2005).

22 *Mr. & Mrs. Smith*, directed by Doug Liman (20th Century Fox, 2005).

23 *Mr. & Mrs. Smith*, directed by Doug Liman (20th Century Fox, 2005).

24 Chuck Palahniuk, *Fight Club* (New York: Henry Holt, 1996), 208.

25 *Fight Club*, directed by David Fincher (20th Century Fox, 1999).

26 Malvina Reynolds, "Little Boxes," *Ear to the Ground*. (Folkways, 2000).

27 Chuck Palahniuk, *Fight Club* (New York: Henry Holt, 1996), 28.

28 Chuck Palahniuk, *Fight Club* (New York: Henry Holt, 1996), 43–5.

29 *Fight Club*, directed by David Fincher (20th Century Fox, 1999).

30 *Fight Club*, directed by David Fincher (20th Century Fox, 1999).

31 *Fight Club*, directed by David Fincher (20th Century Fox, 1999).

32 *Fight Club*, directed by David Fincher (20th Century Fox, 1999).

33 *Fight Club*, directed by David Fincher (20th Century Fox, 1999).

34 *Fight Club*, directed by David Fincher (20th Century Fox, 1999).

CHAPTER FIVE

Abyss of Simulation

Randy Laist

In both the book and the film adaptation of *Fight Club*, Tyler Durden sums up Gen-X angst by explaining that "the middle children of history" have been "raised by television to believe that someday we'll be millionaires and movie stars ["movie gods" in the film]. . . but we won't, and we're just learning this fact."[1] Tyler offers this insight as a diagnosis for the wellspring of resentment and disillusionment that motivates the acts of violence perpetrated in Fight Club and its spinoff, Project Mayhem. According to Tyler's sociological formulation, the rage that fuels Fight Club is a result of a clash between the transcendental expectations of a media-saturated childhood that every American child is destined for the transfiguration of mass-media celebritydom and the crushing realities of an anonymous adulthood.

This dialectic of an illusory unreality coming into conflict with a brutal baseline reality informs the entire structure of the *Fight Club* narrative. It underscores the opposition between the Narrator (real) and Tyler (illusory), as well as that between the subversive community of Fight Club (real) and the inauthenticity of the surrounding culture (illusory). The consistency of this dynamic underscores the standard reading of *Fight Club* as a Nietzschean celebration of authentic Dionysian energies pitted against the self-deception of rationalism and order.

In the film version, however, Tyler's diagnosis of *fin-de-millénaire* malaise is complicated by the fact that Tyler's words are coming out of the mouth of Brad Pitt, an actor who emerged from obscurity to become a millionaire and movie star, the epitome of the fulfillment of television's allegedly false promise. The mixed message embedded in this contrast between the indictment of the American dream expressed by Tyler and the achievement of the American dream personified by Pitt is an example of a tension that runs throughout the film itself, which articulates a radically anti-corporate jeremiad in the guise of a big-budget, mass-marketed corporate product. The director and writers of *Fight Club* demonstrate a keen self-awareness concerning the contradictory nature of their undertaking, and the casting of Brad Pitt in the role of the narrator's schizophrenic alter ego is a semantic gesture alluding to the structural schizophrenia in the corporate/anti-corporate ethos of the movie itself.

The adaptation of a transgressive novel into a commercial film is always attended by the anxiety that the movie will appear to be a watered-down, sanitized, or even censored forgery of the original text. This risk must have seemed particularly acute for the adaptors of *Fight Club*, which levels such a violent critique not only at mass-produced corporate products, but more specifically at the propagandistic effects of mass media. It was arguably in an effort to preempt such criticism that, rather than softening the message of *Fight Club*, the film adaptation pushes the extreme anarchism of the book into a bottomless nihilism, extending the book's cynicism to a terminal degree.

The novel *Fight Club* shares the utopian politics of the neo-Situationist collective the Cacophony Society, with which its author, Chuck Palahniuk, was affiliated while he was writing the book. Project Mayhem engages in acts of what the Situationists called *détournement*, the subversive defacement of capitalist imagery, and what Adbusters calls "meme warfare." "Liberating" billboards, posting "subvertisements," and disrupting the daily patterns of consumer behavior are incursions intended to take people "outside market-structured consciousness long enough to get a taste of real living."[2] It would be easy to imagine either Palahniuk's or Fincher's Tyler saying the same thing. Tyler consistently appeals to the authenticity of visceral experiences. The acts of violence he oversees are experiments in "real living." In both the book and the movie, the Narrator states: "You aren't alive anywhere like you're alive in fight club."[3]

The nihilistic turn in the film itself, however, is to nullify this opposition between real and unreal by implying that Tyler Durden, self-proclaimed docent of the real world, is himself a trickster with a distinctly cinematic ontology. The casting of Brad Pitt in the role of Tyler is the quintessential gesture through which the movie announces its intention to one-up the transgressive mood of its source novel. Whereas Guy Debord denounced the "Society of Spectacle," Fincher's *Fight Club* nihilistically suggests that the denunciation of the spectacular society is itself merely an extension of the spectacle.

In this development, Fincher's *Fight Club* follows the trajectory described by Jean Baudrillard, who has remarked on his own Situationist roots. Baudrillard's writings share the Situationists' formulations of the influence of mass media and the coded nature of the spectacular environment. Steven Best explains, however, that "Baudrillard soon rejected the Situationist analysis as itself bound to an obsolete modernist framework based on notions like history, reality, and interpretation, and he jumped into a postmodern orbit that declared the death of all modern values and referents under conditions of simulation, implosion, and hyperreality."[4] In the same gesture, Baudrillard rejected the Marxian utopianism that undergirds the Situationist critique, concluding that "the universe is not dialectical: it moves toward the extremes and not towards equilibrium; it is devoted to radical antagonism, and not to reconciliation or synthesis."[5] In Baudrillardian terms, the Situationist concern that "actual reality has been eroded by the overdeveloped commodity economy" is stunted at the second phase of the image, that in which "the image masks and denatures a profound reality."[6] Palahniuk's novel carries forward its Situationist inheritance, but it also invests it with an appetite for destruction that reverses the 1960s-era idealism characteristic of that inheritance.

Fight Club the novel is a vast statement of negation. Not only do Tyler and the Narrator negate the values of capitalist society, but they negate the values of life itself, embracing pain, death, despair, and negationism as vehicles towards "hitting bottom."[7] In the book, however, this mood of negationism does not amount to nihilism; the absurd terrorist acts of Project Mayhem, like the self-destructive compulsion of the main character(s), signify a desperate attempt to resurrect the profound reality that is so conspicuously absent in the world of Palahniuk's novel. "It's Project Mayhem," the Narrator explains, "that's going to save the world. A cultural ice age. A prematurely induced dark age. Project Mayhem will force humanity to go dormant or into remission long enough for the Earth to recover."[8] The Narrator expresses a strategy of leaping into the black hole of absence and negation as a way of recovering an original Eden of profound reality.

Significantly, this line does not appear in the movie, which never articulates any political aspiration as lofty as saving the world, even ironically. Rather than articulate a conventional critique of consumer culture, *Fight Club* the movie adopts the fatal strategy of pursuing the logic of Baudrillard's fourth phase of the image in which "it has no relation to any reality whatever. It is its own pure simulacrum."[9]

For his role in *Fight Club*, Pitt was able to attract one of the largest salaries in Hollywood in 1999 despite his uneven history as a lead actor. None of his movies had been a great box office success; his most recent film up to that date, *Meet Joe Black*, had been an outright flop, with Pitt's performance as a personification of death receiving a share of the blame, and, indeed, his top-billing in *Fight Club* did not prove enticing enough to the mass-audience to make that movie a box office success.

Pitt has always enjoyed the kind of celebrity that is not tied to his appearances in any particular film. Pitt's screen persona blends together Robert Redford's boyish grin, Paul Newman's charm, James Dean's obligatory squint, and early Brando's famous pout. But Pitt's resume lacks anything like what *Butch Cassidy and the Sundance Kid*, *Cat on a Hot Tin Roof*, *Rebel without a Cause*, or *A Streetcar Named Desire* were for those actors. Rather, Pitt rose to fame as a result of a bit part in *Thelma and Louise*, in which he played the avatar of a female fantasy of anonymous male attractiveness. His success in this role was a reflection of his ability to channel an archetypal image that both men and women recognized before they ever laid eyes on Pitt himself.

By 1998, "Brad Pitt" was a household name indicating a certain ideal of masculine sexual attractiveness, as demonstrated by the prominent use of his name in that capacity in *Billboard*'s number three song of that year, Shania Twain's "That Don't Impress Me Much" ("So you're Brad Pitt? That don't impress me much").[10]

Unlike his predecessors Brando, Dean, and Newman, whose origins in the Actors Studio encouraged them to practice acting as a study in depth psychology, Pitt is more of a celebrity than an actor, and a celebrity's ontological status is rooted not in the profundity of the unconscious, but in the stark superficiality of proliferating surfaces. Moreover, the collective recognition of Pitt as an ideal of masculine attractiveness works to elevate him beyond the tabloid variety of celebrity to equate him with a Platonic principle. As Roland Barthes said of Greta Garbo, Brad Pitt's "singularity [is] of the order of the Concept;" he is a literal "movie god," a visible apparition representing the manner in which the iconography of consciousness itself is populated with preexisting two-dimensional images.[11]

The casting of this idealized entity in the role of Tyler Durden is a key component of how Palahniuk's social critique is reimagined in Fincher's film. The master-conceit of the novel, that Tyler and the Narrator are actually one character using "the same body, but at different times," is sustainable due to the nature of the medium of prose.[12] Because novelists rarely provide a thorough physical description of their characters, a reader is accustomed to having an imprecise mental impression of what a novel's characters look like and, as a result, Palahniuk's mirror-trick is relatively easy to pull off. Palahniuk's Narrator even reports that "Tyler and I were looking more and more like identical twins," which makes sense in retrospect because they were always the same person.[13]

Obviously, the first hurdle the screen adaptors faced was the fact that a movie does not have the porous visual quality of prose. A movie takes place in a surface world of absolute visibility, where nothing can exist that cannot be seen. Tyler cannot be faceless and, moreover, he cannot have the same face as the Narrator because that arrangement would give the game away to the audience as well as to the Narrator. The screenwriters' dilemma results from the fact that the film medium is limited, strangely, by its inability to withhold information—its inability to *not see*.

The writers seized on this paradox, so appropriate to the anti-Enlightenment mood of the source text, as the inspiration for their decision to cast Pitt. If we have to make Tyler Durden visible, they might have said, we will give him the hyper-visibility of Pitt's archetypal celebritydom. The movie replaces the novel's ambiguous blending of Tyler and the Narrator with a visual opposition. In an interview, Edward Norton recalls, "We decided early on that I would start to starve myself as the film went on, while he would lift and go to tanning beds; he would become more and more idealized as I wasted away."[14]

The movie's Tyler explains to the Narrator (and the audience) why Tyler looks like Pitt: "All the ways you wish you could be? That's me. I look like you wanna look, I fuck like you wanna fuck."[15] As an expression of the Narrator's deepest aspirations for himself, Pitt's Tyler contributes an ironic twist to Palahniuk's Tyler. It turns out that Tyler represents not only the Narrator's dreams of freeing himself from mental enslavement to consumerist society, but also, paradoxically, his dreams of having baby-blue eyes and washboard abs, of looking like someone who spends a lot of time lifting weights and going to tanning beds—who looks, in short, like Brad Pitt.

Linking Tyler Durden to Pitt's celebrity image of fashion-model photogenic-ness completely contradicts everything that Tyler Durden supposedly stands for, yet, in the spirit of nihilist anarchy, there is a distinctly Durdenesque quality to the film's subversive casting choice, which is actually a kind of perverse subversion of Palahniuk's subversive novel, a kind of reverse *détournement*. The voice denouncing mass media culture is coming out of the very idealized face of that culture. This irony, however, also articulates a devastating critique of naïve models of countercultural resistance, suggesting the depth to which even our fantasies of resistance are always already colonized by mass-cultural influences.

As if to explicitly communicate to the audience that the filmmakers are intentionally drawing on Pitt's celebrity status to make an ironic point, the background of one shot includes a marquee advertising *Seven Years in Tibet*, a Pitt vehicle from 1997. The suggestion is that Brad Pitt exists as a celebrity within the diegetic world of *Fight Club*, and may even literally be the model for the Narrator's idealized self-projection. In the DVD commentary, Edward Norton explains that the filmmakers had planted another marquee advertising Norton's film, *The People vs. Larry Flint*, in the same scene, but it had been blocked by a bus and did not make it into the film. This is perfectly appropriate because the Narrator's character exists in a permanent state of occlusion throughout the story, subordinated in every way to the cinematic charisma of his alter ego.

Norton himself, although he appears in every single scene in the entire movie, took in one-seventh of Pitt's salary and received second billing. Similarly, Norton's Narrator character gets all the dregs of the life he shares with Tyler. Tyler gets all the sex, power, swagger, and understanding, while the Narrator doesn't even get a name. In lieu of a name, the Narrator identifies himself by a series of pseudonyms, all drawn from movies: Cornelius, Rupert, and Travis. Cornelius, the simian scientist from *The Planet of the Apes*, is an obvious choice, since he is a kind of prototypical "space monkey," Tyler's term for pioneers of the posthuman.[16] Cornelius is a movie-creature who represents the transcendent possibility of fast-forwarding evolution to reveal new possibilities for human being. The allusions to Rupert Pupkin and Travis Bickle, Robert De Niro's characters in Martin Scorsese's films, *The King of Comedy* and *Taxi Driver*, respectively refer to two other space monkeys, movie-people who have sought (and arguably found) transcendental, posthuman possibilities in the merging of their own personalities with the circuits of the mass media. In this context, the Narrator's other proxy-name, Tyler Durden, is an extension of his pattern of compensating for his anonymity by identifying himself with images of people from the silver screen, and so it is fitting that the Narrator should hallucinate a Tyler who looks like the famous movie star Brad Pitt.

The movie officially introduces Tyler in a sequence that begins immediately after Tyler's memorable request to the Narrator to "hit me as hard as you can."[17] The image freezes on a close-up of Pitt, accompanied by the Narrator's proposal to tell us a little about Tyler Durden. The freeze-frame captures Pitt with an expression of bright-eyed mischievous intensity. With his butterfly collar and with accent lighting framing his jawline and highlighting his facial structure, his hair tousled to perfection, the image is the ideal Brad Pitt glamor shot, a perfect visual representation of Brad Pitt as a celebrity face.

After lingering over this image, the scene cuts to a shot of the lens of a movie projector. By cleverly adjusting the depth of field, Fincher's camera carries us into the lens of the movie projector to see the image on the actual strip of film being projected. The movie interrupts our study of the lineaments of Pitt's cheekbones to plunge us into the rabbit hole of the apparatus that generates this image, deconstructing it by exposing the technological intervention responsible for weaving the moving illusion of the filmic image. When Fincher's camera cuts from Pitt's image to the image of the camera lens, we discover that the image being projected through that lens is a frame from a pornographic movie depicting a semi-erect penis. In this way, this sequence invites us to recognize Pitt's face as a sublimated variation of what Baudrillard calls "the phallic instrumentalization of the body."[18] The sequence as a whole suggests that Pitt's face is, fundamentally, a fetishistic representation of the male body as an expression of a "phantasmic cut" that separates a body part from any existential continuity—the body enframed as an absolute commodity.[19]

When we cut away from the penis image, we are in the editing room with Tyler. His editing of the strip of film is itself represented in a slickly edited sequence—a second of the guillotine snipping the celluloid strip on the editing block, a second of the scotch tape being tugged out of the dispenser, a second of Tyler depressing the splicer—which draws our attention to the fact that this deconstruction of the image is in fact highly artificial and has itself been deftly manipulated by the very trickster who is supposedly being deconstructed. In détourning the cinematic experience of its own audience, Fight Club abducts its viewers into an acknowledgment of their own participation in the oscillation of images between movie screen and lived experience.

Retroactively from this editing room scene, the Fight Club audience may realize that they have already been victims of Tyler's cinematic trickery. Repeat viewers of Fight Club usually come to consciously perceive the two appearances of "subliminal Pitt" that precede Tyler's physical introduction into the diegetic narrative. In a symbolic atmosphere in which castration is such a predominant threat—Bob has had his testicles surgically removed, while the police commissioner and then the Narrator are both directly threatened with the same form of dismemberment—Tyler enjoys the ontological status of being invulnerable to this danger because he exists in the form of a cut phallus. His subliminally spliced-in image is the equivalent of the penis that Tyler cuts and splices into movies with "celebrity voices" (Brad Pitt, Edward Norton, Meat Loaf).

By drawing this equivalence between the dismembered penis and the image of Brad Pitt, the film implies that the reason Tyler Durden is so free of castration anxiety is that he is himself a "phallic effigy," always already castrated, "a fetishistic object to be contemplated and manipulated, deprived of all its menace."[20] The movie's spokesmodel for agency and authenticity is a passive object, a celebrity image, which nonetheless asserts a viral kind of potency, editing itself into consciousness in a manner that is both aggressive and coy. Another variation on the subliminal Pitt is the one that appears in a crowd of waiters on a television in the Narrator's hotel room. When a physical Pitt appears in a crowd scene traveling in the opposite direction from the Narrator on an airport moving walkway, it is as if these subliminal cinematic images are starting to punch through into the Narrator's reality. Of course, the reverse turns out to be true—the Narrator's phantasmal celebrity-projection is leaking out of his brain and into his perceptual environment—an inversion which is itself subordinated to a more implosional sense in which Tyler's ability to edit himself into the Narrator's (or our) consciousness discloses the cinematic quality of the Narrator's consciousness itself (as well as of our own).

The manner in which Brad Pitt's image is manipulated as celebrity icon throughout *Fight Club* has the effect of problematizing a simple reading of Tyler's character as an advocate for a profound reality. One of the movie's parallels to the subliminal Pitts is the image of a nude male Gucci model whose black and white photograph is backlit (like a film image) on a bus stop shelter that Tyler and the Narrator walk past. Of course, we are accustomed to seeing such images in the subliminal background of our contemporary media-scape, but the presence of this advertising image of the male body as enframed instrumentalized phallus suggests a manner in which our daily lives have been *détourned* by invisible Tylers, splicing pornographic images into the margins of quotidian awareness.

When Tyler and the Narrator board a city bus several seconds later, they encounter the same Gucci advertisement, again cinematically backlit. Paralleling Tyler's movement over the course of the film from a subliminal presence to an object of consciousness, the Gucci model becomes a subject of explicit commentary in both the Narrator's voiceover monologue and his conversation with Tyler. As the camera cuts to the advertisement, the Narrator reflects, "I felt sorry for guys packed into gyms, trying to look like how Calvin Klein or Tommy Hilfiger says they should."[21] As if to validate this sentiment, the Narrator confers with Tyler, asking him, "Is that what a man looks like?"[22] Tyler scoffs, naturally, cryptically equating "self-improvement" with "masturbation."[23]

Tyler's aphorism, however, backhandedly affirms an anterior assumption that the project of looking like a Gucci underwear model is a viable path to "self-improvement," a mixed message that is underscored even more deliberately by the fact that Tyler himself, thanks to Brad Pitt, has a fashion model's body, a fact which is increasingly accentuated throughout the film.[24] The very next cut after the conversation about the Gucci model is to a fight scene in which a bare-chested Brad Pitt flexes his glistening muscles under a light that is expressly positioned to highlight the contours of his arms, chest and abdomen as he subdues an opponent. When he stands up after the fight, the light plays across his clearly gymnasiumed physique, his pants ride low on his hips, and his shoulders are thrown back, as he strikes the same contrapposto pose as the model in the Gucci ad. The irony of the Narrator asking his imaginary friend what a real man looks like is amplified by the fact that his imaginary friend is himself modeled after the same hyperreal standards as the media images that he defines himself in opposition against.

Baudrillard critiqued a world in which everyone had fallen "under the sign of behavior models inscribed everywhere in the media or in the layout of the city. Everyone falls into line in their delirious identification with leading models, orchestrated models of simulation."[25] The Narrator's attempt to resist the models of simulation represented by a fashion model takes the form of a parallel "delirious identification" with his fashion-model alter-ego, an ironic inversion that demonstrates the deep complexity and ambivalence of the relationship between the urban consumer-citizen and his ambient media-scape.

The aestheticized destruction of the urban skyline in the final scene of *Fight Club* recalls Baudrillard's assertion that "terrorism itself is only a gigantic special effect."[26] In Fincher's film, Brad Pitt's Tyler Durden personifies the conflation of politics and entertainment, of terrorism and the media, and of activism and spectacle that Baudrillard identifies as characteristic of the late twentieth century. The casting of Brad Pitt in the role and, more importantly, the manner in which the film weaves Pitt's status as a celebrity icon into *Fight Club*'s semantic texture, reorganizes the psychological and political implications of Palahniuk's original narrative. Psychologically, the movie collapses the distinction between the real Narrator and his unreal alter ego, replacing this duality with an all-consuming sense of hyperreality in which the Narrator has been abducted into a cosmos ruled absolutely by a celebrity "movie god."[27]

Politically, Fincher's film reflects the observation of the Critical Art Ensemble that knowing "what to subvert assumes that the forces of oppression are stable and can be identified and separated—an assumption that is just too fantastic in an age of dialectics in ruins."[28] With celebrity-Tyler genetically implicated in the entire fabric of reality, and with the psychology of the Narrator populated by images from the corporate mass media, there is no possibility of staging any traditional kind of dialectical political struggle.

In mirroring this abyss of simulation, Fincher's film suggests a more challenging political paradigm than the conventional oppositional model that brought Marxist-Situationist activists onto the streets of Seattle in 1999 to protest the World Trade Organization. In adopting Baudrillard's nihilistic variation on Situationism, the movie extends Tyler's philosophy of "hitting bottom" to political agency itself, replacing the utopian aspirations of Marxism with the fatal strategy that "there is no liberation but this one: in the deepening of negative conditions."[29] This is indeed a bleak conclusion, but in the same way that Baudrillard's playfulness as a writer imbues his nihilistic prose with a mischievous sense of fun, Brad Pitt's glowing hyperreality as a celebrity endows his performance as Tyler with an ironic glee.

A month after the release of *Fight Club*, Pitt appeared in a cameo role as himself in *Being John Malkovich*, another film that uses cinematic celebritydom as a metaphor for the strange kind of fun that can be had with the subversion of ontological categories. Early in the twenty-first century, as the *fin-de-siècle* spirit of hyperreality gave way to a new decade of war and terror, Pitt still appeared in roles that emphasize his celebrity identity—*Ocean's Eleven, Ocean's Twelve,* and *Mr. & Mrs. Smith*, in particular—but these films are entirely lacking in ironic content; rather, these are movies devoted to the worship of Pitt as a movie god, as opposed to movies like *Fight Club* or *Being John Malkovich* which use celebrity actors to stage surprising confrontations with celebrity deification. In more recent years, Pitt has turned away from roles that allude to his own celebrity status in order to develop his talents as a "serious" actor in movies like *Babel, The Curious Case of Benjamin Button, Tree of Life, Moneyball,* and *World War Z.*

More fundamentally than his movie roles, however, Pitt's celebrity consists of the manner in which "subliminal Pitts" have been edited into the lifeworld of contemporary American consumers. The fact that he occasionally appears in movies is incidental to his more pervasive cultural presence as a tabloid fixture. Boosted into the tabloid pantheon by a love triangle (Brad–Jennifer–Angelina) that promised to be a second coming of the legendary Eddie–Debbie–Liz sensation of scandal sheet lore, the subsequent stability of Pitt's relationship with Angelina Jolie has solidified his status as a perennial fixture in the supermarket aisle firmament. His activities as a philanthropist, green activist, producer, and head of a large and photogenic family all follow this trend toward viralization which has always been immanent in Pitt's particular mode of celebrity.

Despite its underwhelming box office performance, *Fight Club* remains the movie for which Pitt is most well known, at least according to the Internet (*Fight Club* appears as the first movie result in a Google search for "Brad Pitt Movies," for example; Tyler Durden was named *Empire Magazine*'s number-one greatest movie character, etc.). The cult response to Fincher's movie and Pitt's performance, still noticeable almost fifteen years after the movie came out, suggests that *Fight Club*'s critique of image-culture—and its critique of that critique—remain relevant. The enduring hyper-celebritydom of Pitt himself continues to reinforce the manner in which his most popular role deploys the actor's fame as an element of its bleak representation of a society lost in a mirror-world of simulation.

Notes

1   Chuck Palahniuk, *Fight Club* (New York: Henry Holt, 1996), 157.

2   Kalle Lasn, *Culture Jam* (New York: HarperCollins, 1999), 106.

3   Chuck Palahniuk, *Fight Club* (New York: Henry Holt, 1996), 42.

4   Stephen Best, "The Commodification of Reality and the Reality of Commodification," in *Baudrillard: A Critical Reader* (Oxford: Blackwell, 1994), 42.

5   Jean Baudrillard, *Jean Baudrillard: Selected Writings* (Stanford, CA: Stanford University Press, 2002), 185.

6   Guy Debord, *Society of the Spectacle* (London: Rebel Press. 1977), 24; Jean Baudrillard, *Simulacra and Simulation* (Ann Arbor, MI: University of Michigan Press, 1994), 6.

7   Chuck Palahniuk, *Fight Club* (New York: Henry Holt, 1996), 69.

8   Chuck Palahniuk, *Fight Club* (New York: Henry Holt, 1996), 116.

9   Jean Baudrillard, *Simulacra and Simulation* (Ann Arbor, MI: University of Michigan Press, 1994), 6.

10   Shania Twain, "That Don't Impress Me Much," *Come on Over* (Mercury 1997).

11   Roland Barthes, "The Face of Garbo," in *Mythologies* (London: Vintage, 1993), 57.

12   Chuck Palahniuk, *Fight Club* (New York: Henry Holt, 1996), 155.

13   Chuck Palahniuk, *Fight Club* (New York: Henry Holt, 1996), 105.

14   Quotes in S. F. Said, "It's the Thought that Counts." *The Telegraph*, online, April 19, 2003, http://www.telegraph.co.uk/ culture/film/3592955/Its-the-thought-that-counts.html [Accessed November 9, 2011].

15   *Fight Club*, directed by David Fincher (20th Century Fox, 1999).

16   Critical theorists have used the term posthuman to refer to conceptualizations of human identity that depart from classical, Enlightenment-era formulations. If the icon of Renaissance humanism is Leonardo Da Vinci's sketch of Vitruvian Man, a perfectly formed individual sealed within geometric shapes, the space monkey—a creature part animal, part technological, and of indeterminate sex—would be the perfect representative of the posthuman.

17   *Fight Club*, directed by David Fincher (20th Century Fox, 1999).

18   Jean Baudrillard, *Symbolic Exchange and Death* (London: Sage, 1993), 109–10.

19   Jean Baudrillard, *Symbolic Exchange and Death* (London: Sage, 1993), 102.

20   Jean Baudrillard, *Symbolic Exchange and Death* (London: Sage, 1993), 102.

21   *Fight Club*, directed by David Fincher (20th Century Fox, 1999).

22   *Fight Club*, directed by David Fincher (20th Century Fox, 1999).

23 *Fight Club*, directed by David Fincher (20th Century Fox, 1999).

24 *Fight Club*, directed by David Fincher (20th Century Fox, 1999).

25 Jean Baudrillard, *Symbolic Exchange and Death* (London: Sage, 1993), 78.

26 Jean Baudrillard, *Fatal Strategies* (New York: Semiotext(e), 2008), 62.

27 *Fight Club*, directed by David Fincher (20th Century Fox, 1999). In critical theory, hyperreality refers to a condition in which the conventional distinction between real and unreal is rendered obsolete, as when the real life you appear to be living turns out to have been an elaborate fiction, or when your fictional friend who doesn't exist nevertheless produces measurable effects in the real world.

28 Critical Art Ensemble, *The Electronic Disturbance* (New York: Autonomedia, 1994), 12.

29 *Fight Club*, directed by David Fincher (20th Century Fox, 1999); Jean Baudrillard, *Fatal Strategies* (New York: Semiotext(e), 2008), 223.

CHAPTER SIX

Brangelina Blend

Michele White

A "Brangelina" wedding cake topper depicts Angelina Jolie's and Brad Pitt's heads fused onto a single tuxedo-clad body.[1] This blended or conjoined twin sports a fairly traditional tuxedo and two bowties. The cake topper also has breasts bulging from underneath the black tuxedo and a large pregnant belly, which spreads the tuxedo because of its mass and looks like the Earth. Dangling from the arms of this sculpture are two sets of conjoined baby triplets that represent Jolie and Pitt's biological and adopted children. One sculptural group of children is light-skinned and is supposed to resemble Jolie and Pitt while the other group is dark-skinned and intended to stand in for their adopted children. While these bodies are fused into a family, they do not all occupy the same position. The Jolie head looks out at viewers with open eyes and a smile on her full lips. However, Pitt is turned away, distracted, and staring off into space. Jolie and Pitt's affective positions are further mapped onto the infants. The pale infants are on Jolie's side and are craning their necks into space, expressing themselves with open mouths, and appear to be engaged with and looking at their surroundings. The brown babies are leaning away from Pitt and viewers, have their eyes closed, are frowning, and appear to be ill or asleep. The topper uses these features to make unfortunate distinctions based on people's skin color and indicates that Jolie, Pitt, and the children respond to their familial coupling in different ways.

The wedding cake topper of Jolie and Pitt's family encapsulates many of the cultural reactions to this group. It consolidates different people into the blended identity and term "Brangelina," associates the couple with excessive reproduction, makes racial distinctions, uses the figure of the conjoined and pregnant body (and combinations of different genders and races) to mark them as monstrous, references their global reach and politics, and suggests they collect people. The features of the wedding cake decoration and the use of Jolie and Pitt's blended names to label the topper and represent the couple make them into a stand-in for unions and couplings. While toppers represent togetherness and Jolie and Pitt sometimes seem inseparable, their figuration as an archetypal married couple is strange.[2] They announced their engagement in 2012 but have not married, and wedding cakes are usually consumed after the wedding.

The term "Brangelina" contributes to cultural conceptions of these individuals as deeply intermeshed. Such combinations suggest that the referenced people do not have coherent bodies (and are therefore fluid and monstrous), are overly attached to their partners and families, and are multiple rather than individual. Cultural conceptions of fluid, monstrous, emotionally excessive, and intermeshed bodies are associated with femininity and women and are thus less likely to challenge the ways Jolie is understood. Pitt's position is more liable to be destabilized by these feminine and female attributes. Pitt's less-normative choices are also culturally notable. His gym-produced hard body and claims to ideal white masculinity are undermined by the feminizing and monstrous connotations of the Brangelina blend. This may explain recent commentary about Pitt's aging and changing body and physiognomy. Pitt's consolidation into the Brangelina blend thus provides an important site from which to consider the construction of his identity and masculinity. This chapter addresses these issues by deploying such Internet representations as the Brangelina wedding cake topper; web-based posts about Jolie and Pitt's family; and critical literature on gender, race, and embodiment.

Thinking about Brangelina as blend, mesh, and portmanteau

The terms "blend," "mesh," and "portmanteau" describe combinations of names or word parts that create different meanings than the individual components. For instance, "brunch" is now used to describe a meal that combines the features of breakfast and lunch. The word "Brangelina" identifies Jolie and Pitt as well as their family. Such instances of blending are frequent cultural and linguistic processes through which new words, and potentially different ideas, are introduced into languages.[3] The resultant words are known as portmanteaus because these suitcases have two parts that are united when closed. Lewis Carroll, who is credited with developing this term, writes, "'SLITHY' means 'lithe and slimy' . . . You see it's like a portmanteau."[4] His description and word choices also associate portmanteaus with mutability and the grotesque.

People now combine proper names to create portmanteaus that describe intermeshed partnerships, especially when the individuals are well known and involved in heterosexual relationships. Commonly mentioned blends of people's names include Bennifer (Ben Affleck and Jennifer Lopez) and TomKat (Tom Cruise and Katie Holmes)—even though these couples are no longer romantically involved. While the popular media represents other celebrity couples with blends, Brangelina is the exemplary portmanteau couple. For instance, entertainment news site Zimbio argues that Brangelina is the "biggest, most-often used celebrity portmanteau," "it might be the only one that's seen steady use even after its novelty has long worn off," and it may be "the only reason you've ever heard the word 'portmanteau.'"[5] According to these and related texts,

Jolie, Pitt, and their combination into Brangelina constitute and continue the blend.

Portmanteaus render couples as two mirroring parts of a suitcase that make one form when together and touching. The popular media's tendency to figure male/female celebrity couples as ideal portmanteaus continues the societal privileging of heterosexuality. Heterosexual couples are also adopting portmanteaus as a means of articulating their own relationships. People's blending of names, according to linguistic anthropologist Benjamin Zimmer, "often indicates the inseparability of the two blendees" and therefore their physical and emotional coupling.[6] Reporter Denise Winterman argues that such blends could be a way of resisting the sexist tradition that encourages women to take men's names. However, she also notes that most blends list the man's name before that of the woman's. This includes the ways the Brangelina blend features Pitt's first name before Jolie's. Thus, portmanteaus of couples' names tend to constitute gender and sexual norms *and* dissolve stable identities.

Blends provide ways of representing people's shared lives and connections. They also tend to eradicate the agency of individuals. Jonathan Gabay, a marketing executive, argues that meshes give "people an essence of who they are within the same name."[7] With hyphenated names, the hyphen appears to be "pushing one name away from the other" and asserting each person's uniqueness. Meshing "says 'I am you and you are me,'" which according to Gabay, "is rather romantic."[8] It also works against second-wave feminist interests in women maintaining lives and identities that are distinct from their position within relationships. Blends challenge masculinity because the man is figured as attached to the woman rather than having a singular and coherent body. For instance, the Brangelina wedding cake topper depicts Jolie, Pitt, and their family as corporeally fused and dependent. Other media commentary similarly suggests that Pitt is being changed, controlled, and absorbed by Jolie. These beliefs conjure ongoing fears about the feminine.

Theorizing Brangelina and Pitt

The Brangelina wedding cake topper and the more general construction of Brangelina imply that Jolie and Pitt have one body and identity. Yet men and masculinity are ordinarily associated with very different bodily constructs than women and femininity. Feminists suggest how women and femininity are usually related to fluidity, hybridity, monstrosity, and reproduction.[9] Contemporary society, as feminist philosopher Elizabeth Grosz argues, negatively constructs the female body "as a leaking, uncontrollable, seeping liquid; as formless flow"; and as lacking "self-containment."[10] Females are thus conceptualized as repellent because they are too wet and open and blended with other things. For women who bear children, these ties include their intermeshed corporeality and mixed identities with fetuses and children. According to feminist scholar Rosemary Betterton, pregnant women disrupt cultural conceptions of individual subjectivity and sexed positions.[11] They are not one person or two subjects because they carry within their bodies a fetus whose sex is, at least for a time, unknown. The pregnant woman, as she argues, is "like the monster" and "destabilizes the concept of the singular self, threatening to spill over the boundaries of the unified subject."[12]

Years after giving birth, women can still be understood as multiple because "'non-self' cells" from fetuses, as sociologist Aryn Martin describes them, remain in women's bodies.[13] In other words, women who have been pregnant are modified at the cellular level by the processes of reproduction. This is particularly significant in Jolie's case because she has been consistently associated with maternal reproduction and more recently with the BRCA1 "mutation," which is a gene that produces a protein that can make people susceptible to breast and ovarian cancer. In addition to these narratives about excessive reproduction and out-of-control genes, conceptions of feminine mutability have historical and cultural precursors. Women in Western culture were, until the last few decades, expected to use their husband's last name and sometimes their husband's first name to represent them after marriage, whereas men have been less reconceptualized by relationships and marriages.

The ideal man is imagined to be coherent, impenetrable, and hard—and he is associated with rationality and the mind rather than the body. Sociologist Klaus Theweleit indicates how soldiers, and men more generally, want to be men of "steel" and "dam in" and conquer anything that threatens to change them "back into the horribly disorganized jumble of flesh, hair, skin, intestines, and feelings."[14] In a similar manner, film scholar Richard Dyer notes, a "hard, contoured body does not look like it runs the risk of being merged into other bodies."[15] This hard and toned male body has been promoted by contemporary celebrity culture. Stars like Pitt are thought of as ideal representations of masculinity and are expected to maintain fit and muscled bodies.

Pitt's role as a perfect man has been connected to cultural admiration of his physique. Like women, he is admired for being a body, but this form is also understood as hard and controlled. Celebrity coverage and blog posters offer Pitt's exercise regimens so that other men can attain his form and attract women. For instance, PYGOD argues that Pitt's hard body and its associated exercise program will "make all the chicks wet."[16] This continues and alters cultural conceptions of women's fluidity. PYGOD supports sexist conceptions that women are passive and uncontrollable bodies and that men do things to them. PYGOD does not recognize women as agentive subjects. Of course, men like Pitt labor over the male body in order to produce such effects. Articles suggest that Pitt's "body is still iconic today" because "he represents the modern ideal male body—muscular without being overly bulky and exceptionally lean."[17] He is consistently identified as having "one of Hollywood's best bods."[18] However, this ideal muscled form is not always aligned with his familial position. Starpulse argues, "When he isn't adopting kids with his life partner, Pitt makes a living having impossibly rock-hard abs and a chiseled face for a man of his years."[19] Starpulse thereby suggests that there is a gap or temporal lapse between Pitt's hard form and his familial role. Posters also provide a proviso by indicating that he has an admirable physique for a man of his age. In addition, Pitt is believed to have transformed from a "Hollywood heartthrob" to a "house husband" and "father of six" who "loves a bit of housework" and is "domesticated."[20] Pitt is thereby imagined to do work that is coded as feminine and to have been changed by these experiences. In other words, these texts dismissively suggest that Jolie has emasculated him.

Jolie and Pitt are also depicted with mutable gender and sex features in an illustration for a *GQ* article about men and pregnancy.[21] In the image, Jolie and Pitt celebrate their pregnancy. However, it is Pitt rather than Jolie who carries the fetus. Pitt's highlighted and below-the-shoulder hair, goatee, and mustache reference an amalgam of gender positions, including that of the girly girl, groomed metrosexual, and manly man. However, the contrast between his slender and almost concave chest, which deviates from the usual emphasis on Pitt's muscularly-defined torso, and his bulging pregnant belly splinter the male body and masculine norms. He is the body that is conceptually and cellularly changed by pregnancy. Pitt's traditional masculinity is further challenged by a small limp bow that hangs below his pregnant belly and secures his sweat pants. The tie acts as a corollary for his genitals and suggests his penis is also tiny and flaccid.

Pitt's position as an empowered white heterosexual man is troubled because the image references contemporary pregnancy photography but reverses the associated gender roles. In most pregnancy photographs, the man stands in back of the woman and holds her around the stomach. This allows him to best display her pregnant belly and the reproductive "success" of the couple. These photographs ordinarily position men as producers rather than reproducers of the family and as heads of households. Yet in this image, Jolie is in the male position. She holds Pitt's belly and has a body without being the swollen and reproductive body. Jolie is in the position of power. Other representations also indicate that Jolie controls Pitt. Posters note that "Angelina wears the trousers in the relationship and Brad is happy to go along with anything that will make her happy."[22] "He had freedom and masculinity with Jen [Aniston]," writes rebecca, "the way he never will with Angie."[23] These comments imagine that Jolie is too assertive and that such feminine behaviors compromise men's masculinity. Pitt is associated with an undesirably revised and feminine masculinity and seen as part of a fused and excessive family.

The figure of "Bat Boy Jolie" as critique

The popular press and Internet posters often mention Jolie and Pitt's commitment to creating a "rainbow family." Yet Jolie and Pitt's interest is often tied to monstrous, disproportionate, and avaricious accumulations rather than tolerance. Allie Pruitt performs such an interrogation in a *Weekly World News* article where she claims that Jolie and Pitt are trying to adopt Bat Boy—an apocryphal bat-human "mutant" whose adventures are pleasurably chronicled in the paper.[24] Pruitt writes that Jolie and Pitt's interest in adopting Bat Boy is the "perfect example" of their commitment to a rainbow family. In the story, Jolie declares that it is her "duty to be photographed while rescuing" Bat Boy and giving "him a better life in front of millions of people."[25] sunshine coast girl explores a similar theme and argues that Jolie "collects children like trophies and pays other people to look after them (except during photo shoots)."[26] Jolie and Pitt are thereby imagined to extend their visibility and personal interests by adopting children. In a related manner, critical literature indicates that high profile transnational adoptions work to erase the details of birth parents' lives and their relationships with children.[27] Jolie figures Bat Boy "all on his own" in the story, but adoptions by such celebrities as Madonna have been questioned because birth parents and extended families were still involved with the children. megsx responds to the possibility that Jolie and Pitt are going to adopt again by suggesting that the child "might still have friends and even a family still alive!"[28] Popular and academic authors indicate that not all biological parents or birth countries are willing participants in such adoptions.

Bat Boy's resistance to being incorporated into Jolie and Pitt's family and the Brangelina structure functions as a humorous critique of the family's behaviors. In an image that accompanies Pruitt's story, Jolie smiles invitingly at the camera and viewer while holding her adopted child Zahara so that they can both be seen. Jolie would be the beautiful and caring celebrity mother if Bat Boy was not running away from this relationship. He holds his arm up in a resistant fist, his mouth is open in a wide and toothy scream, and his eyes bulge. Pruitt writes, "Jolie used mosquitoes as bait to lure and trap him. With Brad Pitt's assistance, she dragged him kicking and screaming to the local courthouse to have the adoption finalized."[29] In a related manner, adoptmebrangelina imagines that when "Taiwanese village" women learn that "Brangelina might be passing through," they advise people in the community to "hide the orphans!"[30] Dirty Girl Gardening describes "Brangelina's obsession with kidnapping" children so that they can adopt them.[31] They figure Brangelina avariciously absorbing cultures and individuals.

Bat Boy is imagined to compromise Jolie and Pitt's position and relationship rather than providing positive media and familial images. Bat Boy "nipped Pitt on the cheek, who dropped him and began screaming, 'My face! My beautiful face!'" Pitt risks hurting the child and lets him escape because of his vanity. Jolie later learns that Bat Boy is at a local mall and tries to get Pitt to detain him. "Pitt vehemently refused, fearing such an action might endanger his precious face. They began a fight which lasted for two days and nearly dissolved their marriage."[32] Through these narratives, Pitt is rendered as self-involved and as a "beautiful face" and body, rather than being intellectually and ethically focused. His masculinity is also compromised because concerns about being beautiful are associated with femininity and women.

The couple's failed hopes of adopting Bat Boy, like the reports about them considering adoptions from many other countries, are always followed by indications that they are interested in another country and child. According to Pruitt, Jolie and Pitt are now "adopting a Tibetan yeti to supplement Jolie's new interest in Buddhism."[33] In transnational adoptions, children are sometimes understood as commodities and accessories. Raka Shome argues in her research on transnational adoptions that "collecting children becomes a way of engaging with different national cultures, and the children become a commodity through which race/culture can simply be bought, and engaged with, at will."[34] ashley writes that Jolie and Pitt "act like kids are collectibles" and they should "get a better hobby!"[35] "Hollywood is now collecting these kids like bottle caps," writes Screamname.[36] Pruitt's narrative is thus a knowing critique of Jolie, Pitt, and their media images. And yet, Pruitt also relies on some underlying intolerant conceptions of gender, race, and sexuality.

Race, monstrosity, and the "Brangelina brood"

Jolie "has made a bold choice," according to Pruitt, in trying to adopt Bat Boy and "further diversify her brood."[37] Other members of the popular press and Internet posters also use the term "brood" as a method of coding Jolie and Pitt's family. They emphasize the ethnicities, racial positions, and number of Jolie and Pitt's children. Bat Boy stands in for these conceptions of difference by not being fully human. Unfortunately, society still sometimes renders people of color as inhuman and links them to animals in a pejorative move. The discourse about the "Brangelina brood" continues these conceptions because non-white women are called "brood mares" in order to emphasize their purportedly excessive reproduction. According to John Lennard's research on speculative fiction, "brood now carries a very strong taint from horror movies of demonic lairs filled with progeny" and the term continues to be associated with excessive reproduction.[38] Thus, the term "brood" renders dismissive conceptions of race and related ideas about monstrous reproduction. Jolie and Pitt are imagined to have not only a large but also a monstrous family.

Jolie, Pitt, and their family are identified as a brood and as representative of larger reproductive and adoptive behaviors. Hope Carson describes Justin Bieber and Selena posing with a "Brangelina-like brood of babies and tots."[39] Elizabeth Hurley and Shane Warne's "collective brood looks set to rival that of Brad Pitt and Angelina Jolie."[40] Heidi Klum and Seal's mixed-race family is described as "not a Brangelina-sized brood, but it's pretty big."[41] Their reproduction is also rendered as monstrous and not fully human because of references to their "seal pups" and Heidi Klum's speaking and thereby grotesque vagina. In a similar manner, Jolie and Pitt are imagined to be outside of contemporary culture and its medical and empowering developments. According to Lauren Paxman, "Most couples now stop adding to their brood at three or four children"—after all, "that's kind of what contraception was invented for," but Jolie and Pitt "are not like most couples."[42] They and their children are associated with non-Western cultures and coded as being backwards and different.

Conclusion: Brangelina and Pitt as too much

The media is often fascinated by celebrities and provides narratives about their purported excesses, including stories about drug overdoses, serial relationships, public misbehavior, and arrests. Jolie and Pitt's additions to their family, while distinct from these types of spectacles, are also identified as excessive and too much. Lauren Franklin responds to an announcement that Jolie and Pitt are going to adopt and asks, "Is seven children too much?"[43] pinksugarxxx replies, "Dont they have enough?????"[44] "Just typing the names of all their kids exhausts," says The Celebrity Stork.[45] Thus, Jolie and Pitt's supposedly excessive behaviors are imagined to have an embodied influence on readers. This is because such perceived excesses are destabilizing.

The postfeminist author Naomi Wolf argues that Jolie and Pitt rework contemporary conventions. The "well-thought-out multiethnicity" of their family works against cultural beliefs about people's relationships and "what 'family' is expected to look like."[46] She identifies Jolie and Pitt's family as part of a political project that rethinks relationships and how families look and culturally function. However, the blended family is also identified as a problem. Anonymous notes that the "family would be a whole lot cuter if the adopted kids would be white and not adopted."[47] According to Adam, Jolie and Pitt are "trying to blend biological and adopted kids," but they have "bitten off more than they can chew."[48] People use the term "Brangelina" and the attributes of this group to figure Jolie, Pitt, and their family as a disturbing blend and to continue racist investments in purity and whiteness. Individuals exaggerate the number of Jolie and Pitt's children as a method of critique. For instance, Sunnye writes about "Brangelina" having "95 babies."[49] People propose that Jolie and Pitt's family is not normal and is less socially acceptable. They thereby model the kinds of families and relationships that communities should generate. Folks usually do not see the "entire Brad Pitt/Angelina clan," notes Mimi, "although that may well be because most normal camera lens aren't big enough."[50] These authors argue that the size and constitution of Jolie and Pitt's family are so much that it is incomprehensible and humanly and technologically unmanageable. This allows people to refuse integrating such families and relationships into their worldview.

When the individual's style is "too much," notes Jack Babuscio in his analysis of camp, "it results in incongruities:

the emphasis shifts from what a thing or a person *is* to what it *looks* like; from *what* is being done to *how* it is being done."[51] In addition, Babuscio suggests that "too much" is a critical strategy that can undo traditional forms of gender and other identity positions. Too much emphasizes that people are performing and constructing their identities rather than just *being*. Thus notions that Jolie and Pitt's family and public image are too much emphasize their roles as actors and producers of representations. Their choices and positions undermine cultural expectations that parenting is an authentic, unmediated, and private practice. Jolie and Pitt are still identified as embodying ideals because of their beauty and position as celebrities. However, their lives, as I suggest in this chapter, also conflict with cultural standards. For instance, Pitt is identified as an agentive hard male body *and* as emasculated. It is because of his position as an ideal male that Pitt's body and actions disrupt ideas about the functions and features of masculinity. His cultural status is also why society patrols his less-normative choices.

While many individuals find the excesses and behaviors of such celebrities to be deeply pleasurable, Jolie's and Pitt's *too much* and the non-normative actions of other public figures have political resonance. In being exemplary, their everyday actions point to inconsistencies in cultural standards and values. What requires further interrogation is how society has such individuals stand in for cultural norms while trying to ignore and resolve their transgressions. A group of popular authors has attempted to retain Pitt's coherent and iconic body by situating the family's excesses in relationship to Jolie and the hybrid body of Brangelina. These actions are troubling because they further denigrate women. They also tend to produce more versions of Jolie, Pitt, and Brangelina. When these varied forms of identity are highlighted, they illustrate the dissonances in these actors' positions and relationships rather than providing support for traditional structures.

Notes

1   Mike Leavitt, "Brangelina.jpg," Intuition Kitchen Productions,
     11 February 2013. http://www.intuitionkitchenproductions.
     com/actionfigures/caketoppers/Brangelina.jpg. In the citations
     in this chapter, detailed information about website references
     is included. The constant reconfiguration of Internet
     representations and changes in Internet service providers
     make it difficult to find previously quoted material and
     important to chronicle the kinds of depictions that happen in
     these settings. Many Internet texts include typographical
     errors and unconventional forms of spelling, uppercase and
     lowercase typefaces, punctuation, and spacing. I have retained
     these formatting features in quotations and Internet references
     without such qualifications as "intentionally so written" or
     "sic." The date listed before the URL is the "publication"
     date or the last time the site was viewed in the indicated
     format. When two dates are included, the first date points to
     when the current configuration of the site was initially
     available and the second date is the latest access date. Some
     versions of referenced sites can be viewed by using the
     Internet Archive's Wayback Machine. Internet Archive,
     "Internet Archive: Wayback Machine," December 6, 2013,
     http://www.archive.org/web/web.php.

2   Cele Otnes and Elizabeth Pleck, *Cinderella Dreams: The Allure
     of the Lavish Wedding* (Berkeley, CA: University of California
     Press, 2003).

3   Paul Cook and Suzanne Stevenson, "Automatically Identifying
     the Source Words of Lexical Blends in English," *Computational
     Linguistics* 36(1) (2010), 129–49.

4   Lewis Carroll, *Through the Looking-Glass* (Seattle, WA:
     Madison Park, 2010), 69.

5   Zimbio, "Brangelina and Other Famous Portmanteaus."
     24 February 2013, http://www.zimbio.com/Brangelina+and+Oth
     er+Famous+Portmanteaus/articles/EGHTgVLEAN6/Brangelina.
     [Accessed February 24, 2013].

6   Benjamin Zimmer, "A perilous portmanteau?" Language Log,
     November 2005. http://itre.cis.upenn.edu/~myl/languagelog/
     archives/2005_11.html. [Accessed December 27, 2012].

7   Jonathan Gabay, as quoted in Denise Winterman, "What a mesh," BBC News, August 3, 2006. http://news.bbc.co.uk/2/hi/uk_news/magazine/5239464.stm. [Accessed February 22, 2013].

8   Jonathan Gabay, as quoted in Denise Winterman, "What a mesh." BBC News, August 3, 2006. http://news.bbc.co.uk/2/hi/uk_news/magazine/5239464.stm. [Accessed February 22, 2013].

9   Rebecca Bell-Metereau, "Searching for Blobby Fissures: Slime, Sexuality, and the Grotesque," in *Infamy, Darkness, Evil, and Slime on Screen*, ed. Murray Pomerance (Albany, NY: State University of New York Press, 2004), 299.

10 Elizabeth Grosz, *Volatile Bodies: Toward a Corporeal Feminism* (Bloomington, IN: Indiana University Press, 1994), 203.

11 Rosemary Betterton, "Prima Gravida: Reconfiguring the Maternal Body in Visual Representation," *Feminist Theory* 3(3) (2002), 255–70.

12 Rosemary Betterton, "Promising Monsters: Pregnant Bodies, Artistic Subjectivity, and Maternal Imagination." *Hypatia* 21(1) (Winter 2006), 85.

13 Aryn Martin, "Microchimerism in the Mother(land): Blurring the Borders of Body and Nation," *Body & Society* 16(2) (2010), 23.

14 Klaus Theweleit, *Male Fantasies*, vol. 2 (Minneapolis: University of Minnesota Press, 1989), 160.

15 Richard Dyer, "The White Man's Muscles," in *The Masculinity Studies Reader*, eds. Rachel Adams and David Savran (Malden, MA: Blackwell, 2002b), 265.

16 PYGOD, "Brad Pitt in *Fight Club*," StrengthFighter.com, April 24, 2012. http://www.strengthfighter.com/2012/04/brad-pitt-in-fight-club.html. [Accessed April 24, 2013].

17 admin, "Brad Pitt Workout – The Fight Club Workout," Prove You're Alive, September 7, 2011. http://proveyourealive.com/brad_pitt_workout_fight_club_workout. [Accessed April 24, 2013].

18 Kevin McMillian, "Brad Pitt Troy Workout," *Squidoo*, 24 April 2013. http://www.squidoo.com/brad-pitt-troy-workout. [Accessed April 24, 2013].

19 *Starpulse*, "Top 10 Metrosexual Celebs," March 3, 2008. http://
    www.starpulse.com/news/index.php/2008/03/03/top_10_
    metrosexual_celebs. [Accessed February 15, 2013].

20 Rebecca Merriman, "'Mr Muscle' Brad Pitt Loves Getting His
    Hands Dirty," *Entertainmentwise*, September 17, 2012. http://
    www.entertainmentwise.com/news/88170/Mr-Muscle-Brad-Pitt-
    Loves-Getting-His-Hands-Dirty-. [Accessed April 24, 2013].

21 John Ueland, "Congratulations, You're Man-Pregnant," *GQ*,
    February 2013. http://www.gq.com/entertainment/humor/
    201303/man-pregnant. [Accessed December 19, 2013].

22 "INSIDE THE WORLD OF BRANGELINA'S BROOD,"
    Mirror, March 17, 2007. http://www.mirror.co.uk/3am/
    celebrity-news/inside-the-world-of-brangelinas-brood–459160.
    [Accessed April 6, 2013].

23 rebecca, "Brad and Angie vs. Brad and Jen!" *thinkfashion*,
    August 15, 2007. http://www.thinkfashion.com/blogs/stylosity_
    hollywood_hookup/archive/2007/08/15/brad-and-angie-vs-
    brad-and-jen.aspx. [Accessed April 7, 2013].

24 Allie Pruitt, "BAT BOY JOLIE?" *Weekly World News*,
    November 21, 2008, http://weeklyworldnews.com/
    mutants/4036/bat-boy-jolie/. [Accessed April 29, 2013].

25 Allie Pruitt, "BAT BOY JOLIE?" *Weekly World News*,
    November 21, 2008, http://weeklyworldnews.com/
    mutants/4036/bat-boy-jolie/. [Accessed April 29, 2013].

26 sunshine coast girl, "Angelina Jolie," *The Tyee*, 28 December
    2012, http://thetyee.ca/Views/2009/06/10/Jolie/. [Accessed
    December 28, 2012].

27 Jodi Kim, "An 'Orphan' with Two Mothers: Transnational and
    Transracial Adoption, the Cold War, and Contemporary Asian
    American Cultural Politics," *American Quarterly* 61(4) (2009),
    855–80; Robert A. Saunders, "Transnational Reproduction and
    its Discontents: The Politics of Intercountry Adoption in a
    Global Society," *Journal of Global Change and Governance*
    1(1) (2007), 1–23.

28 megsx, "Angelina 'planning to adopt Haitian child.'"
    Sugarscape, February 10, 2010. http://www.sugarscape.com/
    main-topics/celebrities/464465/angelina-planning-adopt-
    haitian-child?page=1. [Accessed December 31, 2012].

29 Allie Pruitt, "BAT BOY JOLIE?" *Weekly World News*,
    November 21, 2008. http://weeklyworldnews.com/
    mutants/4036/bat-boy-jolie/. [Accessed April 29, 2013].

30 adoptmebrangelina, "Brangelina," Urban Dictionary, August 28,
    2009. http://www.urbandictionary.com/define.php?term=
    brangelina. [Accessed December 27, 2012].

31 Dirty Girl Gardening, "DIRTY LOVE," February 2012.
    http://dirtygirlgarden.com/2010/02/valentines-day-propagation/.
    [Accessed December 29, 2012].

32 Reginald Cunningham III, "BRAD AND ANGELINA
    SPLIT," *Weekly World News*, January 26, 2010. http://
    weeklyworldnews.com/celebs/15324/brad-and-angelina-split/.
    [Accessed August 25, 2013].

33 Allie Pruitt, "BAT BOY JOLIE?" *Weekly World News*,
    November 21, 2008. http://weeklyworldnews.com/
    mutants/4036/bat-boy-jolie/. [Accessed April 29, 2013].

34 Raka Shome, "'Global Motherhood': The Transnational
    Intimacies of White Femininity," *Critical Studies in Media
    Communication* 28 (5) (2011), 388–406.

35 ashley, "Brangelina to Expand its Brood?" *Hollywood
    Gossip*, December 10, 2008. http://www.thehollywoodgossip.
    com/2008/12/brangelina-to-expand-its-brood/. [Accessed
    April 5, 2013].

36 Screamname, "Angelina set to adopt another baby," *Free
    Republic*, October 27, 2006. http://www.freerepublic.com/
    focus/f-chat/1726790/posts. [Accessed May 1, 2013].

37 Allie Pruitt, "BAT BOY JOLIE?" *Weekly World News*,
    November 21, 2008. http://weeklyworldnews.com/
    mutants/4036/bat-boy-jolie/. [Accessed April 29, 2013].

38 John Lennard, *Reading Octavia E Butler: Xenogenesis/Lilith's
    Brood* (Penrith, UK: Humanities-Ebooks, 2007), 86.

39 Hope Carson, "Why Justin Bieber-Selena Gomez's Love Will
    Last Forever," *Gather*, January 27, 2012. http://celebs.gather.
    com/viewArticle.action?articleId=281474981066030. [Accessed
    December 30, 2012].

40 Yahoo! Cricket News, "Will 'S-Hurleys' outnumber Brangelina
    brood?" Cricket ON, December 20, 2011. http://cricketon.com/

uncategorized/will-s-hurleys-outnumber-brangelina-brood/. [Accessed February 11, 2013].

41 Julie Gerstein, "Total Speculation: 9 Potential Reasons Heidi Klum & Seal Are Breaking Up," *The Frisky*, January 23, 2012. http://www.thefrisky.com/2012–01–23/total-speculation–9-potential-reasons-heidi-klum-seal-are-breaking-up/. [Accessed December 30, 2012].

42 Lauren Paxman, "Are Brangelina adding to their brood? The Jolie-Pitts were spotted visiting an orphanage," Alison Jackson Online, November 28, 2012. http://www.alisonjackson.com/ brangelina-adding-to-brood-brad-pitt-and-angelina-jolie-spotted-visiting-orphanage/. [Accessed February 17, 2013].

43 Lauren Franklin, "Angelina 'planning to adopt Haitian child,'" *Sugarscape*, February 10, 2010, http://www.sugarscape.com/ main-topics/celebrities/464465/angelina-planning-adopt-haitian-child. [Accessed December 31, 2012].

44 pinksugarxxx, "Angelina 'planning to adopt Haitian child,'" *Sugarscape*, February 10, 2010, http://www.sugarscape.com/ main-topics/celebrities/464465/angelina-planning-adopt-haitian-child. [Accessed December 31, 2012].

45 The Celebrity Stork, "The Brangelina Brood Hits New Orleans (PIC March 2011)," *Flickr*, March 20, 2011, http://www.flickr.com/photos/35965850@N04/5545100670/. [Accessed February 11, 2013].

46 Naomi Wolf, "The Power of Angelina," *Harpers Bazaar*, June 8, 2009. http://www.harpersbazaar.com/magazine/cover/angelina-jolie-essay–0709. [Accessed April 1, 2013].

47 Anonymous, "The Brangelina family in Hello!" *Celebitchy*, August 9, 2007. http://www.celebitchy.com/2397/the_brangelina_family_in_hello/. [Accessed February 11, 2013].

48 Adam, "Angelina Jolie and Brad Pitt's Kids Turn Nasty," *ShowbizSpy*, March 17, 2011. http://www.showbizspy.com/ article/228633/angelina-jolie-and-brad-pitts-kids-turn-nasty. html. [Accessed December 27, 2012].

49 Sunnye, "Namibia: Diamonds on the soles of my shoes, Part I," *nomadamorphose*, May 10, 2012. http:// nomadamorphose.blogspot.com/2012/05/namibia-diamonds-on-soles-of-my-shoes.html. [Accessed December 29, 2012].

50 Mimi, "SPOTTED: BRANGELINA'S BROOD," *Beauty and the Dirt*, March 21, 2011. http://www.beautyandthedirt. com/entertainment/gossip/spotted-brangelina-brood/. [Accessed February 11, 2013].

51 Jack Babuscio, "Camp and the Gay Sensibility," in *Camp Grounds: Style and Homosexuality*, ed. David Bergman (Amherst, MA: The University of Massachusetts Press, 1993), 24.

CHAPTER SEVEN

Art Muse

Sarah Juliet Lauro

Emily Dickinson once wrote, "If I feel physically as if the top of my head were taken off, I know that is poetry." And when I feel as if my sternum has been knocked out of my chest cavity, I know I'm looking at a matinee idol. (Why *is* beauty so violent? Never mind. It just is.) Yet, I never carried a torch for Brad Pitt the way many other women of my generation did. Our childhood bunk beds still bear the scar, written as it is in permanent marker, of my little sister's tortuous, decade-long crush: "Mujy loves Brad Pitt." "Loves" is signified with a drawing of a lopsided heart and a crooked "s." I was more of a Johnny Depp girl, myself. And River Phoenix. And Christian Slater. (It was the 1990s.) The only film, in fact, during which I felt afflicted with what my sister had been suffering from since *Thelma & Louise* (1991) was *Meet Joe Black* (1998).

In *Meet Joe Black*, Brad Pitt is cast as the human personification of Death. Pitt plays him as an alternatingly child-like and zombie-like imitation of life, performing the vessel for this version of *Death Takes a Holiday*, the 1934 film that inspired this update. In *Meet Joe Black*, the Grim Reaper comes to Earth to experience life, attaching himself to a very wealthy media mogul; this provides opportunity for a subtle defense of capitalism that masquerades as critique almost as prettily as Death masquerades as a beautiful man. Bill Parrish (Anthony Hopkins) has been granted a stay of execution in exchange for hosting Death's vacation, and, aside from his impending demise, the plot is driven by his need to defend his company from a merger that would, it is repeatedly stated, destroy his life's work. In articulating his decision to reject the sale of Parrish Communications, Hopkins's character soliloquizes at a board meeting:

> I knew I wasn't going to write the Great American Novel, but I also knew that there was more to life than buying something for a dollar and selling it for two. I hoped to create something . . . Sure I want to make a profit, you can't exist without it. But John Bonicue is all profit . . . Reporting the news is a privilege and a responsibility, and it is not exploitable. Parrish Communications has *earned* this privilege. John Bonicue wants to *buy* it.[1]

In this way, the film serves as a kind of time capsule for the halcyon days of the late 1990s, before the neoliberal bubble burst.[2]

This gorgeous Grim Reaper is introduced to Parrish's family as a mysterious stranger named Joe Black, and he promptly falls in love with the rich man's daughter, Susan, who mistakes him for a man she had met in a coffee shop earlier that day, whose body Death has borrowed for his tour among the living. In the end, Death realizes that Susan is not truly in love with *him*, but only with the young man he has been imitating. He fulfills his obligation as the great equalizer and ferries Parrish to his fate after a lavish 65th birthday bash; the party recalls what is considered by many to be *the* great American novel Parrish alludes to in the boardroom scene, F. Scott Fitzgerald's *The Great Gatsby*.

In his farewell address, Parrish says to the partygoers, "I'm going to break precedent and tell you my one candle wish: that you would have a life as lucky as mine, where you could wake

up one morning and say, 'I don't want anything more.' "[3]
Ensconced as the speaker is on the stately grounds of his out-
of-town mansion (the other half of the film takes place in an
Upper East Side palace complete with indoor pool), standing
on a dais lit with a "saffron-glow" meant to convey "tea-dance
twenties" (as the older, somewhat neglected, party-planning
daughter Allison describes it), this statement (and the film in
general) send mixed messages about the meaning of life.

The film has moments that, like its references to Fitzgerald's
cautionary tale about the pitfalls of the American Dream, seem
like oblique self-critique: At one point, Parrish hands Black
some cash and says to him, "You know about money, don't
you?" to which Death responds, "It can't buy happiness?"
"Yeah," Parrish says sardonically. But except for the fact that
Death has come to dinner, Parrish appears quite happy, as he
does in his Manhattan apartment's lavish library full of leather-
bound books, among which we are informed is an original
edition of Dickens's *Bleak House* and copy of Jefferson's
"Parliamentary Manual." The former, with its plot concerning
a will in legal dispute, is invoked to allude to the perils of those
who would try to protect their legacy beyond their earthly
demise; the latter cheekily foreshadows the other higher power
invoked repeatedly in the film: the law of the land. Bemused by
the phrase "Nothing's certain but Death and taxes," our not-
so-Grim Reaper later impersonates an IRS agent.

In a pivotal scene set in this library, Parrish regards the
beautiful stranger as he asks:

> Parrish: You're coming to take me? What is that? Now,
>   who the hell are you?
> [The stranger approaches and they regard each other.] You
>   are?
> Black: Yes . . . Who am I?
> Parrish: Death . . . You're . . . Death
> Black: Yes.
> Parrish: Death?
> Black: That's me.[4]

These few lines take one minute and twenty seconds of screen time to deliver, due to the actors' pauses between words and lines, many of which include several different shots. It is this scene that digital artist Jillian Mcdonald hijacks in her 2008 piece "Staring Contest with Brad Pitt."

In "Staring Contest" Mcdonald splices together shots from this scene to create a loop that goes on *ad infinitum*. In this minute-long video loop the artist acts as a surrogate for Parrish in the scene in which he first sees the man he will call Joe Black, whom he understands to be Death cloaked in human form. Here the artist steps into the role of Hopkins in order to stare down Death. Or it might seem this way. Yet, Mcdonald's piece is not called "Staring Contest with Death" but rather "Staring Contest with Brad Pitt," and the title stresses the immovability of the Hollywood image. Aren't we always, in some sense, aware that we're looking at Brad Pitt, no matter who he's playing? Cutting between takes of herself blue-screened into Pitt's over-the-shoulder angles, and shots of Pitt into which she has inserted herself into the frame in place of Hopkins, she depicts an unlikely pair embroiled in a staring match (Figures 7.1 and 7.2).

Mcdonald makes the kinds of goofy faces one might make in such an endeavor: trying not to blink, trying to make one's opponent blink, trying to concentrate and not to look away, opening and closing her mouth, adjusting her hair in an attempt at distraction, boldly swaying without breaking eye-contact, piquantly arching an eyebrow. Pitt's unflinching glare, crafted originally as the gaze of Death looking upon a mortal, takes on new and comic tones set in this context, embroiled in a staring contest with a woman who clearly doesn't belong in the frame. Though the digital match-up of the images, and particularly the lighting, is very convincing, the fact that it falls short of perfect works to the piece's benefit rather than its detriment.

Mcdonald is an attractive woman, but her use of makeup is spare enough that she comes across as an Everywoman rather than a Hollywood leading lady. As I've written elsewhere, the

FIGURE 7.1 *Still from Jillian Mcdonald's "Staring Contest with Brad Pitt" (Reproduced by permission of the artist.)*

catharsis Mcdonald's work provides is a kind of *détournement* of cinema for the heterosexual female gaze.[5] Often she creates a fantasy for the female fan to objectify the male body, and her accessibility invites the ordinary woman, who may not hold up to onscreen beauty ideals, to occupy her space, just as she has occupied the place of the star or starlet. Most famously, "Screen Kiss," (2005) in which the artist positions herself as a jilted fan desperate to get the attention of actor Billy Bob Thornton, is a video of various kissing scenes from fairly easily identifiable Hollywood movies. Mcdonald has inserted herself into the shot in place of the lover, sharing a digital kiss with Johnny Depp (twice), Vincent Gallo, Billy Crudup, Ben Stiller, Angelina Jolie (described as "Billy Bob's former wife"), Daniel Day-Lewis, Gary Oldman, and Ewan McGregor. For all of Mcdonald's attention to Hollywood hunks, Brad Pitt, two-time winner of *People Magazine*'s coveted title, "Sexiest Man Alive," makes an appearance only in Mcdonald's "Staring

FIGURE 7.2 *Still from Jillian Mcdonald's "Staring Contest with Brad Pitt" (Reproduced by permission of the artist.)*

Contest." Admittedly, some of her subject choices defy expectation—Vincent Gallo?—making them seem all the more
legitimate as the artist's own, real crushes. Her manipulation
of the Hollywood product taps into what I think is a
wide-spread, if latent, cultural desire: to rebel against the
images doled out by the dream factories of the Industry
and wrest control of the means of (film) production and
reception.

So, too, I think it is not incidental that Mcdonald has chosen
to intervene in a film that is a covert love letter to American
capitalism: underneath the boilerplate that even the gods
among men must die, *Meet Joe Black* still leaves us with the
sense that the rich live better lives. Parrish is a wealthy man
whose party guests include senators and congressmen, and
perhaps even the president, yet the film's moral platitudes
about a loveless life being no life at all are washed out by
Parrish's foil, the only other person whom Death takes in the

course of the movie, a wise old Jamaican woman who recognizes Death for what he is.[6] Drawing comparison to— what else?—an island vacation, she says the point of life is to "make some nice pictures to take with you." Yet, she looks as if the life she's lived has been hard, and she is dying a difficult death in a sickly lit, green-tiled hospital basement. Bill Parrish, on the other hand, symbolically fades out, walking off to the distant reaches of his waterfront property as fireworks celebrate his 65th anniversary at "the party of the year." Visually, the film gives us no reason to assume that all "nice pictures" are created equal. What Mcdonald, and other digital artists achieve, however, is the confiscation and manipulation of the pictures produced by Hollywood, thus calling into question those manufactured idols.

Curator and critic Jack Anderson discusses Mcdonald's digital manipulations and her web-based persona: "Foregrounding what is in many ways already at the foreground of enthralled public consciousness, web-artist Jillian Mcdonald meditates on celebrity culture, mining contemporary Hollywood movies before digitally reshaping their filmic narratives."[7] Drawing on the theories of Jean Baudrillard and Nicolas Bourriard to contexualize Mcdonald's contribution to contemporary art, Anderson writes, "Re-writing and re-contextualizing not the ready-made but the *already-made*, she actualizes in digital space and time her own disruptive, contrary scenarios from the already constructed signs of the screen." In many ways, Mcdonald does something similar to artists like Robert Wilson, Cindy Sherman, and others who (re)stage or recreate celebrities and film stars, but that Mcdonald does so by digitally manipulating the original source material makes her art less palatable as homage, and more obviously occupation, which I feel imbues the work with subversive potential.[8]

Acting as curator of a bizarre little wing of contemporary art, I would like to take the reader on a tour of some other "already-mades," to view a collection of cultural artifacts and *objets d'art*: artistic interventions that borrow not just any celebrity image, but the magnificent mug of Brad Pitt.

Prefab-ulous: A gallery of authorized images

Ever since Andy Warhol's silkscreens lampooned the reproducibility of the most reproduced images in our society, celebrities have haunted the work of elite members of the art community, and these overly familiar images have found new life, transposed from the movie poster and the magazine rack to the art gallery.[9] The art world today is accustomed to such subject matter, and the stakes must be raised to get a rise out of the viewer: an English footballer is posed as Christ resurrected (Michael J. Browne's *The Art of the Game*, 1997); a photo-mural depicts celebrities as if they were on the Pantheon's frieze, as "'modern day gods' adorning a 'temple of shopping'" (Sam Taylor-Wood's Selfridges mural, 2000); and Sandow Birk paints Kurt Cobain's corpse with a halo floating in mid-air, representing him as a martyr, but to what?[10]

Many have written about fame and what the celebration of these "intimate strangers" says about our culture, whether they be "representations for much more inchoate longings;" "special people" lent an illusory immortality; "cultural fabrications" that mobilize the abstract desire needed to sustain capitalism; or indications of "a shifting definition of achievement in a social world."[11] If artworks like those described above make explicit the idolatrous nature of contemporary celebrity, there is nonetheless both a mixture of sincere adulation and cynical irony visible in each. This seems to be the ambivalent posture of most treatments of celebrity in art. And in this, Brad Pitt, authorized art muse, is rather the rule than the exception: his onscreen and off-screen personae (lover *and* fighter, the hyper-masculine yet archetypal family man) perhaps suggest to the artists who represent him how to maintain the delicate balance required by his depiction in art, poised somewhere between idol and effigy.

In addition to being an aficionado of architecture and an art collector, Pitt has served as a willing muse to various contemporary artists working in diverse media.[12] Chuck Close has photographed Pitt, recreating the style of his signature large-scale, close-up oil portraits, and many high profile photographers and videographers have collaborated with Pitt on pieces, most of which were produced by magazines and translated into multipage layouts among their glossy folds.[13]

Avant-garde stage director Robert Wilson's "Video Portrait" of Pitt stands alongside the many others he has made, of people like Princess Caroline of Monaco, Mikhail Baryshnikov, and Salma Hayek. Wilson's work addresses how pivotal celebrity and cinematic culture are to our own cultural history, but it also seems to question whether the celebrity gets to have his or her *own* identity. These "portraits" hardly seem like portraits at all: on the one hand, they are made up of composites of images, references, and recognizable allusions. Divorced from context or put into new combinations, the references are, on the other hand, ultimately unsatisfying as representations of anything other than the celluloid surface of society's mirror. In Wilson's portrait, Pitt stands in socks and boxer shorts in front of a white brick wall on a concrete floor. Blue light fills the space. As it begins, it is difficult to tell whether or not the image is still, or whether Pitt is slowly, subtly moving. He holds something unidentifiable and vaguely phallic in his hand. It begins to rain in the space, and yet Pitt remains still, standing in the rain for some time as a simple music plays on what sounds like a child's toy piano. A poem read by its author, Christopher Knowles (whose voice is reminiscent of Garrison Keillor), begins like a nursery rhyme, "Apples, peaches, pumpkin pie." These discordant elements (the dramatic lighting, Pitt in his underwear in the rain) clash with the sing-song poem and its flat recitation in a manner that is disorienting. Because of the steady stream of falling rain, it becomes even more difficult to tell if Pitt is moving or if it is a trick of perception. As the poem comes to an end, the rain stops, and Pitt begins to slowly raise the object he holds in his hand—previously, it was hard to determine what it was, but as he levels it at the viewer, it becomes obvious that it is a gun, though it is light in color. He points it at the viewer for some time before he fires. It is a squirt gun filled with water. Pitt sprays in the camera's direction five times; the sexual innuendo is not lost on the viewer for all of the comic surprise of the unexpected. And then he slowly lowers the toy. The video ends.

Created in 2004, the Pitt Video, in which he has a closely shaved head, seems to draw from the substance of his recent films, in particular *Se7en* (1995), *Twelve Monkeys* (1995), *Fight Club* (1999), and *Snatch* (2000), to erect an amalgamated icon of hypermasculinity, but only in order to mock it. Pitt's sexually suggestive grasp of the object held by his side at the video's start gives way to several tense moments filled with a sense of threat when the viewer realizes that the item he has been holding in his hand is a gun—and that it is now pointed at the audience—but this is diffused with the revelation that the gun is only a child's toy, as well as a sex joke. Similar to Chuck Close's commentary on Pitt's "fair-haired boy" persona—as he described it when he did the star's portrait for a cover of *W. Magazine*—Wilson's piece illustrates the way Pitt's image is complicated by some of his darker roles, and yet remains intact.

Showcasing Pitt's ability to play dark, we might next consider his appearance in the December 2011 video portfolio, "The Hollywood Issue," produced by *The New York Times Magazine*. Named for Orson Welles's 1958 film *Touch of Evil*, this series of 13 minute-long films directed by Alex Prager featured actors from some of the best performances of 2011, reprising classic hair-raising film roles. Pitt's is one of the best and most unnerving minute-long performances of the bunch. As the film begins Pitt is seen sitting on a stool in a darkly lit studio; he is dressed like we've never seen him before, as David Lynch's *Eraserhead* (1977), wearing a similar if not exact reference to Henry Spencer's suit, a v-neck sweater over a shirt and tie. Spencer's iconic, towering, unkempt coif slightly quivers with Pitt's tensed posture. A stream of vapor billows in from off-camera left, recalling the various uses of steam that appear in Lynch's film, from the factory's steam whistle to the deformed infant's humidifier. Unnerving sounds fill the aural space: xylophone keys hit singly, a flapping of insects' wings, and a chugging sound like water coming to a roiling boil, which eventually gives way to something like a tea kettle's shrill whistle. Slowly the camera begins to track in on a tight close-up of Pitt. Giant moths fly around the figure, landing on his sweater and in his hair.[14] All the while Pitt's face slowly transforms into an awful grimace, like a silent scream. He becomes red-faced and trembling as his face morphs into a mask of agony. He looks terrible and terrifying. This is not the Brad Pitt we know.

Do we know him? What makes us think so?

These collaborative efforts on the part of Pitt and the artist seem to willfully dramatize what I imagine would be the celebrity's nightmare: stuck in a house of mirrors, he can only cast reflections about, but each thing he would produce is only another distorted, flat image, and every word he speaks is a line. Both Prager's restaging of Pitt as Henry Spencer and Wilson's discombobulating Video Portrait refuse to admit the viewer into the theater of the real Brad Pitt. In a gesture that reminds me of Perseus' trick of using her own reflection to help him destroy the Medusa, both of these artists meet the ever searching, insatiable gaze of the viewer with pure surface, an image of an image. Even Chuck Close's close-up portraits of Pitt, with all of their attention to visible crows feet and enlarged pores, or a series like Steven Klein's "Domestic Bliss" photo shoot for W. Magazine (July 2005), in which he and Angelina Jolie appear in a haunting parody of 1950s suburbia, show us nothing but façade, in both senses of the word; an actor or an actor in role.[15] This type of artistic production makes use of the media of film and still photos—modes that so often reduce celebrities to a brand or a snapshot in the Hollywood industry—but Wilson and Prager, and even the glossy magazine spreads of Close and Klein, defy the urges of the public who clamor for "more, more," and give them a version of the man that is less and less himself.

In another room: Unauthorized icons

This is by no means a comprehensive guide to all of Brad Pitt's appearances in art. Some works barely get a passing glance, while others merit their own soliloquy on my audio-tour. Admittedly, I am more interested in those that make art out of Pitt's already-made screen images than those that merely manufacture (even) more icons of this idol. Some artists have literally built the man a shrine.

Sculptor Daniel Edwards and Los Angeles-based conceptual artist XVALA (formerly, Jeff Hamilton) built a house in Oklahoma City that is considered a "large scale art work" called "The Brangelina." A stipulation comes with the purchase of the half-a-million dollar home: that the owners cede the house to, or accommodate the celebrity couple whenever they come to town. Co-creator, and self-proclaimed "tabloid artist" XVALA said, "I believe every home in America should become an 'honorary home' to our superstars, in order to connect celebrities and regular people in spirit."[16] Inside the master bedroom, a life-size sculpture of the celebrity couple in the nude is ensconced in the ceiling. Daniel Edwards's sculpture, "Brangelina Forever," reportedly contains glass fibers from wine glasses that Pitt and Jolie drank out of while celebrating an anniversary dinner. Therefore, the line goes, their very DNA (presumably, from traces of saliva) is incorporated into the piece, and by extension, into the house. The shred of hope that there may be a smear of Pitt's spit deep inside this sculpture only furthers the comparison to religious iconography, like a contact relic at the foot of a statue of an early Christian saint.

If tabloid art is, as XVALA claims, an emergent category, then British artist Alison Jackson certainly belongs among its annals. Jackson is known for her images in which she poses celebrity look-alikes in paparazzi-style candids: postmodern imitations of contemporary culture that are often so accurate it is dizzying.[17] There is no need to travel to see it: AlisonJackson. com is web-based art, like some of the work of Jillian

Mcdonald. With its (intentionally) poorly written copy and grainy or blurred images, Jackson's website is nearly indistinguishable from a tabloid site like TMZ.com.[18] In a spread called "Lucky Number 7 for Brad and Angelina," a series of photos satirizes the public's obsessive speculation about the Jolie-Pitt couple's next parenthood decision. Some photos look perfectly realistic: in one, the couple is caught shopping for baby clothes. Others push the envelope a bit more, as the pair peruses a multi-racial orphan line-up as if they were picking out macaroons in a Parisian pastry shop. The fact that sunglasses partially obscure their faces in nearly every shot works as an aid to the illusion on two levels: they hide the imperfections of the impersonators, and because celebrities often wear their shades indoors to minimize fan recognition, the images look all the more like the paparazzi-procured pictures that splash across the pages of sensationalist rags by the cash register.[19] Odd angles and overexposure, as if some of the photos were taken by camera phones, from a distance or on the sly, add to this effect, but the viewer's distance to the (ersatz) celebrity couple is maintained by the (false) frame of the paparazzo's lens.

In some sense both the Brangelina house and Jackson's images implicate the non-celebrity in the work, but the only artist we've covered so far in our exhibition who directly forces her way into the frame is Jillian Mcdonald. Mcdonald has been working in the medium of digital conquest since 2003, but the past few years have seen the global rise of the celebrity meme, which offers creators a similar opportunity to intervene in and dismantle mass-produced icons. Therefore the last stop on our tour of the imaginary Pitt exhibit is to visit a pair of images that would not be found in a gallery, though I believe they could and should be acknowledged as art: it is the work of an Austin-based graphic designer, Everett Hiller, who photoshops celebrities into his holiday party pictures.

Internet memes have already had a visible impact on the art world: in the past few years, there have been various exhibitions devoted to the topic.[20] The Internet and social media networking sites have given rise to a host of bizarre, ludic trends, but often there is a subversive motivation visible to the fads that gain the most cultural traction, including, I would argue, the celebrity meme. In the past year, for example, there was a flurry of Ryan Gosling memes, wherein this postmodern pin-up provides his take on key points of feminist debate, library science, or, most recently, the Supreme Court's decision to uphold Obama's Affordable Care Act.[21] What the impulse to manipulate the celebrity image bespeaks is a desire to transgress the border erected between the celebrities and we mere mortals, between fiction and reality, between the real and the virtual. There is a kind of mastery to be felt in these acts of digital molestation. I write on Ryan Gosling's beautiful face; I put words in his mouth; I redirect a medium over which I have previously had no control, and even as I worship at the altar of image and celebrate its power, I mock the rich and powerful at a time when the majority of people are hit by economic crisis: these untouchables become a little more touchable.

As the articles produced about Everett Hiller's party pictures often note, the cleverness of his shop-jobs comes from their subtlety, the use of candid poses and blurred images in addition to their attention to proportion and light and shadow.[22] Two of his pictures from the series produced in 2011 feature Brad Pitt.

I had seen the photo in Figure 7.3 several times before I noticed that Brad Pitt was in the left-hand side of the frame. I had not failed to notice Jennifer Aniston in the center, looking directly at the camera, smiling buoyantly. And I had even noticed the date stamp on the picture: 12 16 06. Of course, this date would put this picture at nearly two years after Brad Pitt and Jennifer Aniston's marriage crumbled, in early 2005, in what tabloids celebrated as the most public heartbreak ever.[23] Positioned with their backs turned to each other, this particular photo invokes a much more subtle commentary on the cult of celebrity and the industry that has developed around the public's desire to be informed about the private lives of the stars than the invocation of "Brangelina" in the work of

FIGURE 7.3 *From Everett Hiller's 2011 Holiday Party series at http://everetthiller.imgur.com/ (Reproduced by permission of the artist.)*

XVALA or Jackson. In Hiller's image the celebrity couple's past becomes the kind of awkward intrigue that might circulate among friends at your own holiday party:

> Have you seen Brad yet?
> Yeah. His hair looks like shit.
> [Nervous laughter.]

In the other photo (Figure 7.4), Brad Pitt is the only figure in the frame. His head appears to have been photo-shopped onto someone else's body. Wearing khakis and a cozy-looking sweater, Holiday Party Brad displays a strange Christmas gift he has just pulled from its wrappings, but the forearms are too hairy, and those aren't Brad's hands! The disorientation produced in the viewer reminds one how strange it is that we should be so familiar with the body of a man who has never once laid eyes on us.

FIGURE 7.4 *From Everett Hiller's 2011 Holiday Party series at http://everetthiller.imgur.com/ (Reproduced by permission of the artist.)*

Whereas XVALA's Oklahoma City house makes the celebrity into a kind of patron saint worshiped in every room and welcomed to take ownership of the citizen's private property on a whim, Hiller's images kidnap our society's idols, forcing them to share our eggnog, laugh at our jokes, participate in a white elephant gift exchange.

Exit through the Pitt Shop

Let's remember what Plato wrote about the Muse. Speaking to Ion, Socrates says:

> There is a divinity moving you, like that contained in the stone which Euripedes calls a magnet ... This stone not only attracts iron rings, but also imparts to them a similar power of attracting other rings; and sometimes you may see a number of pieces of iron and rings suspended from one another so as to form quite a long chain: and all of them derive their power of suspension from the original stone. In like manner the Muse first of all inspires men herself; and from these inspired persons a chain of other persons is suspended, who take the inspiration.
>
> (p. 16)

The Muse was capable of inspiring not just poets but everyone.[24] All men can be struck by the Muse, and all is equally valid as art if the Muse strikes, and all those affected are thereby linked together, like magnets in a chain, bound by their common attraction.

The important thing about fandom, as some have already suggested, may not be the celebration of the most beautiful, powerful, and wealthy members of our society as the worthiest individuals, but, in a bizarre turnabout, the equalizing force of fandom and the celebrity's ability to instill in the rest of us a sense of community.[25] This is why I believe the art that issues the most direct challenge to the industry and to our conception of celebrity is that which lets the fan share the spotlight, like Hiller's anonymous party-goers, like Mcdonald staring down the man himself. In the end, Brad Pitt may not be a mortal god, but *only* our muse, a magnet drawing together different humans: a graphic designer in his cubicle, an artist in her studio, a blogger, a photographer, a fan surfing the web.

Notes

1   *Meet Joe Black*, directed by Martin Brest (Universal, 1998).

2   In another place, we might compare a film like 1998's *Meet Joe Black* to Brad Pitt's 2011 hit *Moneyball* to see the disparity between the economic philosophies touted by each.

3   *Meet Joe Black*, directed by Martin Brest (Universal, 1998).

4   *Meet Joe Black*, directed by Martin Brest (Universal, 1998).

5   In invoking the "gaze," I am referring here to Laura Mulvey's seminal piece, "Visual Pleasure and Narrative Cinema," *Screen* 16(3) (1975), 6–18.

6   These scenes are vaguely offensive, drawing as they do, on the trope of the spiritual, exotic other. Black also calls her "Sistah," speaking to her in her native Patois. This aspect of the film is, to my mind, another way it dates itself.

7   Anderson, Jack, "Desiring the Image: on celebrity and fetishization." http://jillianmcdonald.net/press/anderson.html [Accessed December 12, 2013].

8   Mcdonald's work should also be considered for what her art says about the interface of the physical body with the virtual world. For a discussion of this trend in the work of other artists, see Susan Broadhurst, *Digital Practices: Aesthetic and Neuroesthetic Approaches to Performance and Technology* (New York: Palgrave, 2007). Mcdonald's work has even prompted others to repurpose her redactions: In a YouTube video, a visually inferior piece created by Suite 215 productions, an unknown admirer inserts himself into Mcdonald's Screen Kiss, opposite the digital artist. Disorientingly, two faces that are unrecognizable to the viewing public occupy the foreground

of familiar kissing scenes, creating a kind of *mise-en-abîme* that has cropped the cinematic idol out of the frame entirely, and puts Mcdonald in the role of crush and star.

9   The tradition of representing celebrities in art properly began in the work of pop artists like Andy Warhol (1928–1987) as well as Gerald Laing (1936–2011), Pauline Boty (1938–1966), Peter Blake (b.1932), and others, but it continued in the 1980s and 1990s in the work of artists such as Jeff Koons, Vladimir Dubosarsky, Alexander Vinogradov, and Elizabeth Peyton. For a useful overview of the history of "Art and Celebrities," see the book of the same name by John A. Walker (London: Pluto Press, 2003).

10   Sandow Birk, *The Death of Kurt Cobain*, 1994.

11   The quotes above come from: Richard Schickel, *Intimate Strangers: The Culture of Celebrity* (New York: Doubleday & Co., 1985), viii; David Giles, *Illusions of Immortality: A Psychology of Fame and Celebrity* (New York: St. Martin's Press, 2000), 6; Chris Rojek, *Celebrity* (London: Reaktion Books Ltd, 2001), 10, 188; and Leo Braudy, *The Frenzy of Renown: Fame and its History* (New York: Oxford University Press, 1986), 10.

12   For example, Pitt is a frequent attendee and buyer at contemporary art shows and biennials. He recently chartered a private jet to take him to the art exhibition Documenta in Kassel, Germany, on a single day off from filming his latest movie, *World War Z*. http://galleristny.com/2012/06/brad-pitt-took-a-private-jet-to-documenta/.

13   Pitt worked with American photographer and videographer Steven Klein on a video for *W. Magazine*. He has also collaborated with British photographer Nick Knight for *Vanity Fair* on a video in which he recites a poem by André Breton and with Peruvian fashion photographer, Mario Testino, in a fashion shoot for *V. Magazine*. For a discussion of some of Pitt's collaborations with fashion photographers, see Fashion blog Niwdenapolis.com, "Brad Pitt as an art subject," dated 9/26/07. http://www.niwdenapolis.com/2007/09/brad-pitt-as-art-subject.html. [Accessed June 30, 2012]. Pitt has even had his own photographs (of Jolie) grace the cover of *W. Magazine*, November 2008.

14   Although there are several nests and cocoon-like structures in
      the original film, and even a moth-hole-filled blanket, this is
      Prager's own addition, which reveals her careful reading of
      Lynch's film.

15   I wonder if Close's portraits aren't legible to fans retrospectively
      —appearing as it did in February of 2009—more as a portrait
      of Pitt *as* Lt. Aldo Raine (with his uncharacteristically short-
      cropped hair and the outlines of a 1940's mustache visible,
      though a scruffy goatee is beginning to grow in as well), from
      Quentin Tarantino's *Inglourious Basterds* (2009), which
      premiered six months later, the only feature film Pitt debuted
      that year.

16   Martin Newman, "Art: Daniel Edwards' Brad Pitt and Angelina
      Jolie Sculpture," *Mirror*, December 8, 2009.

17   Jackson's work first drew widespread attention with her 1999
      images of the late Lady Di and Dodi Al-Fayed posing with "a
      mixed-race love child" (John A. Walker, *Art and Celebrities*,
      London: Pluto Press, 2003), 152. It has been said that
      Jackson's early work sought to create a kind of catharsis
      for the viewer by filling in the gaps and completing unfinished
      celebrity narratives, like the romance between the former
      Princess and Al-Fayed which was cut short by their deaths.
      I think also of her picture of "Marilyn Monroe" and "Jack
      Kennedy," shot through a partially closed door, subtly
      emphasizing the voyeurism of the tabloid industry. Usefully,
      these images sought to scratch the public's urges in a manner
      that called into question investment in the private lives of public
      figures.

18   For example, on the website alisonjackson.com [Accessed
      June 29, 2012] pop star look-alikes of Katy Perry and Rihanna
      pose for a sexy photo-shoot in the back of a car; there is a
      vague suggestion that a lesbian relationship has been uncovered
      but far more likely from the staging of the narrative "Dream
      Tea Party Pals," in which they picnic together in full make-up
      and are obviously aware of the camera's presence as they feed
      each other strawberries in "Saucy Snaps," is that this piece is
      just an approximation of the kind of publicity stunt to which
      we've grown accustomed. Likewise, Jackson's version of Lady
      Gaga is caught urinating into a pot in the middle of a store and

building her latest outfit out of items found in a dumpster. The sensationalism of the images she creates is hardly a dead giveaway, since we've been conditioned by tabloids to expect the most salacious and inappropriate of subject matter. Either of these stories, it seems to me, might actually be featured in a tabloid.

19 In some ways, Jackson's work is in line with the kind of occupation of the celebrity impersonation that we see in the work of artists like Cindy Sherman (American, b. 1954) and Yasumasa Morimura (Japanese, b. 1951), both of whom have cast themselves as celebrities in their work, even dressing up in imitation of particular scenes from films.

20 For example, "Memery: imitation, memory, and internet culture" at Massachusetts Museum of Modern Art in North Adams, Massachusetts (3 April 2011–31 Jan. 2012); and "For the Lulz," at Tin Sheds Gallery, Sydney, Australia, (15 July–6 Aug. 2011).

21 A very comprehensive list of Ryan Gosling memes can be seen at http://www.readwriteweb.com/archives/hey_girl_i_know_you_think_this_meme_thing_is_just_temporary_but_im_not_going_away.php One of the most celebrated, Feminist Ryan Gosling, created by gender studies graduate student Danielle Henderson, http://feministryangosling.tumblr.com has also been published as a book by Running Press (2012).

22 See, for example, bitrebels.com (http://www.bitrebels.com/entertainment-2/facebook-prank-photoshop-celebrities-in-your-party-photos-10-pics/); twistedsifter.com (http://twistedsifter.com/2012/03/photoshopping-celebrities-into-holiday-party/); 3/1/12, 2/23/12 (http://gizmodo.com/5887800/the-best-holiday-party-that-never-was. Buzzfeed.com (http://www.buzzfeed.com/cityofglass/man-photoshops-celebrities-into-his-holiday-party-4eor). Hiller has multiple galleries on imagur.com displaying several years' worth of holiday parties: http://everetthiller.imgur.com/ [Accessed April 1, 2013].

23 When Brad Pitt's marriage with actress Jennifer Aniston was destroyed by his affair with Angelina Jolie, the prevalent narrative was that the "girl next door" had been thrown over for a seductress. Women bought t-shirts declaring their support and sympathy for Aniston. The company that made the shirts,

White Trash Charms, at one point reported that Team Aniston was vastly outselling Team Jolie.

24 In Plato's *The Ion*, Socrates emphasizes that the God proves this "when by the mouth of the worst of poets he sang the best songs" and that those affected by the Muse "compose their beautiful poems not by art, but because they are inspired and possessed." (p. 15).

25 See Cheryl Harris and Alison Alexander (eds.) *Theorizing Fandom: Fans, Subculture and Identity* (Cresskill, NJ: Hampton Press, Inc., 1998). Several essays stress the various ways that "fan discourse works to create a specific kind of community that becomes more important than the object of fandom itself" (p. 6).

26 Plato, "Ion" in *Criticism: Major Statements*, Fourth Edition. Charles Kaplan & William Davis Anderson, eds. Bedford St. Martin. Boston, MA 2000.

DECON STRUCTING BRAD PITT

A VISUAL ESSAY

BY

NANCY A. BERNARDO

CAN ONE
SIGN WITH

A PERFUME?

HE SPEAKS
IN TONGUES
OR IN A
LANGUAGE

BECAUSE THERE CAN BE A YES WITHOUT A WORD

follow the madman down the road of his exile

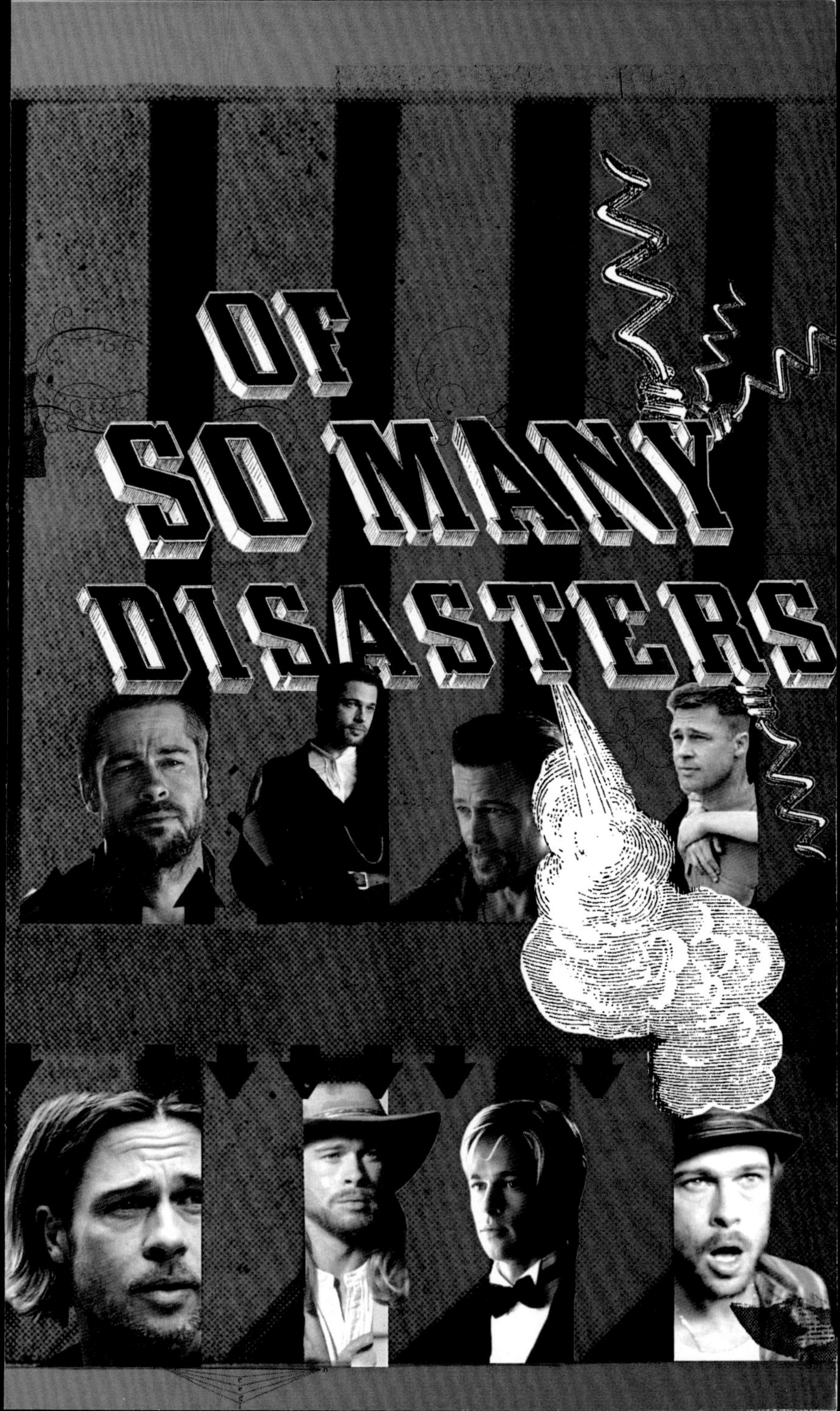
OF
SO MANY
DISASTERS

BOTTOMLESS CHAOS

proximity

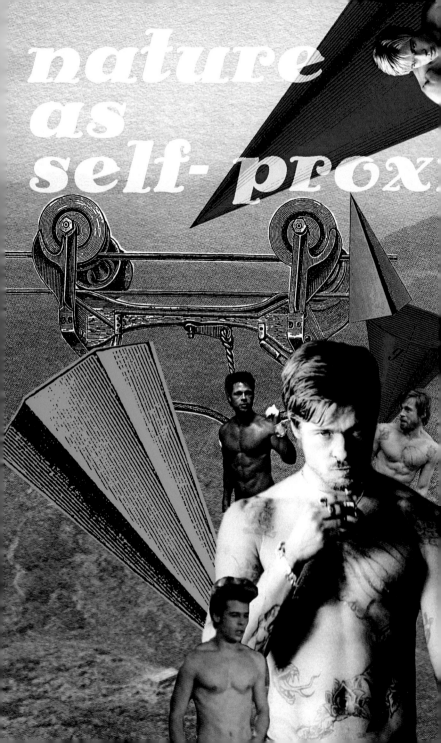

Can one sign with a perfume?
—Jacques Derrida, "Ulysses Grammaphone"

he speaks in tongues or in a language that is foreign to
every other human language
—Jacques Derrida, *The Gift of Death*

because there can be a *yes* without a word
—Jacques Derrida, "Ulysses Grammaphone"

follow the madman down the road of his exile
—Jacques Derrida, "Cogito and the History of Madness"

In the face of so many disasters
—Jacques Derrida, *Specters of Marx*

this order is founded upon a bottomless chaos
—Jacques Derrida, *The Gift of Death*

Nature as self-proximity
—Jacques Derrida, *Of Grammatology*

CHAPTER EIGHT

Oedipus Cop

Fran Pheasant-Kelly

At first glance, the relationship between David Mills (Brad Pitt) and William Somerset (Morgan Freeman), the two male protagonists of David Fincher's bleak neo-noir, *Seven* (sometimes written as *Se7en*) (released in 1995), appears to conform to the inter-racial cop–buddy formula. Widely acknowledged as an alliance that privileges male platonic bonds above all other relationships, and a model that initially evolved in films of the Second World War period, the buddy movie comprises a same-sex relationship "composed of humour, tacit understanding and, usually, equality of toughness between men."[1] However, its format altered during the late 1960s and early 1970s, partly in response to the growth of feminism, and thereafter, according to Harry Benshoff and Sean Griffin, "often wistfully recreated earlier eras where 'men were real men' and/or pessimistically suggested that American culture was coming undone because American masculinity itself was in decline."[2] In relation to the latter, Benshoff and Griffin suggest that "the fact that the heroes of many of these films often die in the final reel is one indication of this pessimism," which arguably reflected the national mood following failures and losses in the Vietnam War.[3] This negativity marked the onset of a now well-recognized and chronologically broadened crisis in masculinity, with Sally Robinson claiming that, "from the late sixties to the present, dominant masculinity appears to have suffered one crisis after another."[4] She further notes that, "white masculinity most fully represents itself as victimized by inhabiting a wounded body."[5] Certainly, *Seven* iterates a mood of darkness and nihilism, and lacks the optimistic closure generally associated with Hollywood, though, in part, its generic format as a neo-noir dictates this sense of gloom.

Even though the 1960s' resurgence of the buddy film was partly triggered by a burgeoning feminist movement, such films often included a female character—albeit usually to confirm the buddies' heterosexual status (thereby avoiding any intimation of homoeroticism between them—a censorship issue in Hollywood films at that time). Indeed, the token female (and/or homosexual) is a defining characteristic of the buddy genre because, as Cynthia Fuchs suggests, male–male relationships are paradoxical and so "must always deny and fulfil . . . 'male homosocial desire', the continuum from homosexuality to homophobia and back again."[6] Dyer further contends that the buddy relationship is

> constructed by a disavowal of the very thing that would appear to bind the men together—love. The elements that effect this relationship—badinage as a way of not expressing serious emotions, silent communication as a means of not articulating or confronting feelings, toughness as a sign that one is above tenderness.[7]

In short, any significant alliance between two men has historically strived to suppress its homosexual potential, often, as Fuchs goes on to comment, by displays of masculinity that are excessive in nature. Otherwise, "these films efface the intimacy and vulnerability associated with homosexuality by the 'marriage' of racial others, so that this transgressiveness displaces homosexual anxiety."[8] *Seven*'s teaming of Brad Pitt as Mills with Morgan Freeman as Somerset typifies such a coupling and, as Dyer explains:

> The set-up—older, orderly black cop and younger volatile white one: initial hostility developing into buddiness—was, when it first appeared, a reversal of stereotypes: In Western tradition, it is black men who are irrational and uncontrolled and white men their opposite. However, by the time of *Seven*, this reversal had become almost the norm.[9]

Yet, even as Dyer acknowledges the cop/buddy relationship between Somerset and Mills by likening it to the *Lethal Weapon* series, he also highlights deviations from its formula. For example, he observes how

> *Seven* . . . is short on action sequences and almost barren of wisecracking humour and the joys of virile sparring . . . Moreover, though their gradual liking of each other is touchingly sketched, their relationship, always eclipsed by the detail and horror of what they are dealing with, is never the heart of the film.[10]

Taking a different approach, David Greven contends that *Seven* corresponds to the criteria of what he terms, "the double-protagonist film."[11] According to Greven, this proposed new form features "a complex negotiation for power between two protagonists, each played by a star, both of whom lay legitimate claim to narrative dominance."[12] Greven goes on to specify that "the double-protagonist films cannot be called buddy films: the men in them are not, for the most part, buddies."[13] However, while the association between Mills and Somerset begins in an antagonistic fashion, with constant rivalry between them, they eventually become accepting of each other, and certain scenes frame them as equals. In many ways, their relationship corresponds more with that of a father and son, displaying oedipal tendencies in its early conflicts, thus departing from the "double-protagonist" schema. Mark Browning too acknowledges that "in terms of the ages of the characters and the relative stages of their careers, one retiring, one just starting out here, there is a father–son element."[14] Indeed, alongside the buddy film, such father–son alliances were common in films of the 1980s and 1990s, Susan Jeffords identifying these as a conscious projection of masculinity that centered on family values, and which constituted an emergent "sensitive man" image.[15] According to Jeffords, the popularity of the father–son motif was a response to the concurrent political climate. She explains:

> Whereas the Reagan years offered the image of a "hard body" to contrast directly to the "soft bodies" of the Carter years, the late 1980s and early 1990s saw a re-evaluation of that hard body, not for a return to the Carter soft body but for a re-articulation of masculine strength and power through internal, personal and family-orientated values.[16]

She therefore attributes the fathering image that became increasingly apparent throughout the 1980s to Reagan, identifying this narrative feature in a wide range of genres and claiming that specific aspects of such father–son narratives reflected the transition from Reagan to Bush. For example, she argues that these transition films "in which the son learns to operate independently of the father and in which he in turn protects the father, externalized the deep-seated anxieties . . . about the passage from Reagan to Bush."[17] She goes on to state that by the early 1990s, interest in the father–son plot dwindled and was once more overtaken by the buddy movie.

Arguably, *Seven*, released in 1995, signals the intersection of these two formats, its revisionist buddy politics perhaps marking the transition from George H.W. Bush to Bill Clinton. Following Jeffords' line of travel, the dual cop–buddy and father–son dynamic evident in the relationship between the film's protagonists may have reflected anxieties surrounding an incoming younger president. These two dimensions duly influence the course of the narrative. For while there is a grudging mutual acceptance between Mills and Somerset, commensurate with the buddy format, the film simultaneously traces an oedipal trajectory, suggested narratively by Mills's planned replacement of Somerset. Throughout the film there are visual and narrative indications of a father–son scenario. Ultimately, however, Mills is unable to achieve a coherent masculinity, failing in respect of the law and incapable of taking the "father's" place. Instead, his impulsive actions and irrationality lead him to face imprisonment.

Engaging with Dyer's study of *Seven*, Freud's account of the Oedipus complex, as well as Jeffords' analysis of masculinity, this chapter analyses the failed oedipal trajectory of Pitt's character and suggests *Seven*'s narrative outcome as a continuation of white masculinity in crisis.

Seven as Oedipal trajectory

The film's plot follows the impending retirement of Somerset and his replacement by Mills, their changeover complicated by a series of murders that re-enact the seven deadly sins. The imminent displacement of Somerset by Mills is not only accentuated literally by a sign painter who removes Somerset's name from his door, but is also signaled in an early scene when Mills opens his office door to see Somerset still at his own desk. "Be out of your way in a second," says Somerset apologetically as he quickly clears the desk before moving his possessions across to a smaller adjacent table.[18] Mills therefore literally takes the place of Somerset, his incongruity in the role marshaled by his reluctance to answer the telephone and his awkwardness in placing his possessions on the desk. Mills's displacement of Somerset is also apparent in the way that he constantly attempts to compete with Somerset. This conflict extends to Mills's wife, Tracy (Gwyneth Paltrow), who confides in Somerset about her pregnancy—in turn, Somerset makes personal confessions to Tracy about his prior relationships.

Though Mills's and Somerset's respective connections to Tracy subvert the conventions of the classic oedipal scenario, in which, normally, the son competes with the father in his desires for the maternal figure, arguably, Tracy here serves as a maternal figure. Somerset also displays paternal qualities, while Mills's juvenility is constantly emphasized. Indeed, an earlier version of the script has Tracy and Somerset as lovers, and as Browning observes, "Tracy even wipes sleep from Mills's eyes as if he still needs mothering."[19] In describing the oedipal scenario, Freud explains how:

> [a]t a very early age the little boy develops an object-cathexis for his mother, which originally related to the mother's breast . . .; the boy deals with his father by identifying himself with him. For a time these two relationships proceed side by side, until the boy's sexual wishes in regard to his mother become more intense and his father is perceived as an obstacle to them. His identification with his father then takes on a more hostile coloring and changes into a wish to get rid of his father in order to take his place with his mother.[20]

By suggesting a similar oedipal situation, the film quickly establishes a tension between the two men, primarily through certain differences apparent in the *mise-en-scène*. Fundamentally, Somerset is precise and fastidious in appearance and behavior. His orderliness manifests in the way that he dresses carefully, medium close-ups of him revealing a meticulously ironed shirt, and subjective close-ups disclosing his possessions lined up in orderly fashion. We observe him remove a fleck from his jacket that he has carefully laid out. His later examination of a crime scene where we see extreme close-ups of his fingers precisely reposition plastic fragments within the lino from which they were cut further signify his measured and purposeful figure behavior. Another clue to Somerset's methodical nature emerges in the close-up of a metronome that is positioned adjacent to his bed and which he activates to aid his concentration. The regular tick of the metronome highlights Somerset's obsession with exactitude. As Browning notes, the ticking metronome, "impos[es] control and meaning on the chaos that surrounds him as well as captur[es] his key qualities—a sense of timing and timely action."[21] In addition to his orderliness, there are subtle hints of his fatherly nature evident during an earlier murder investigation when he asks a colleague, "kid see it [the murder]?"[22] "Who gives a fuck?," responds his colleague, and though "the kid" may have been of concern merely as a valuable witness, the spectator at once gains insight about Somerset's paternal tendencies.[23]

In marked contrast, Mills's hyperactive figure behavior is antithetical to that of Somerset, and he constantly displays a juvenile and rebellious attitude. In Somerset's initial encounter with Mills, the latter's qualities are first suggested by the fact that he chews gum and his clothes are disheveled. In fact, his overall characterization is haphazard, impulsive, and uncontrolled. For example, he repeatedly rolls his head to one side as if alleviating pent-up tension. In a sequence that parallels Somerset getting dressed, we see Mills lying in bed with his wife, Tracy. Rather than the regular ticking of the metronome, however, the background sound is an intrusive one of blaring sirens and continuous rain, consistent with the film's neo-noir tendencies. Mills dons a crumpled shirt (without showering), and removes a tie (which is already knotted from its previous wearing) from a clothes hanger. He smoothes down his hair with his hand, and, as the phone rings shrilly, snatches the receiver and writes a note on the palm of his hand. As Tracy turns to kiss him, she removes a speck from his face, further implying his childlike tendencies.

Distinctions are apparent, too, in the way that Mills and Somerset examine the first murder scene: Mills immediately jumps to the wrong conclusion because the victim is morbidly obese, announcing "if this isn't a coronary, well, I don't know," therefore basing his opinion merely on a superficial scanning of the scene rather than precise analysis.[24] While Somerset quietly studies the evidence, Mills also talks incessantly to the

point that Somerset asks him, "Could you please be quiet?"—
speaking to Mills as if to a talkative child.[25] On Mills's
discovery of a bucket beneath a table at which the dead man is
seated, Somerset enquires, "What's in it?" before Mills peers
into the bucket, his sudden reaction of disgust to the vomit
causing him to pull away violently.[26] "Any blood in it?"
Somerset presses, further indicating his analytical, systematic
nature compared to Mills's less methodical approach. Somerset
then instructs Mills to question the neighbors—the implication
being that he wants to get rid of him because his talkativeness
is too distracting.[27] These various opening scenarios thus
establish that Mills is dominated by superficial primary drives
and emotions, corresponding to the oedipal child, whereas
Somerset always remains in control. Indeed, while Somerset
comments, "We have to divorce ourselves from emotion,"
Mills retorts, "I feed off my emotions."[28] Yet, despite Somerset's
superior experience and wisdom, Mills claims equality with
Somerset, telling the latter, "My belt says detective—just the
same as yours."[29] Nonetheless, he is always a step behind
Somerset, who suggests to the police captain (Lee Ermey) that
"this should not be his first assignment" and then informs
Mills, "it's too soon for you."[30] While implying that Mills is
not up to the task, Browning suggests that this comment may
also indicate that Somerset is being "paternally protective."[31]
Indeed, there is an implied correlation between being a "cop"
and having a meaningful masculine identity, suggested when
the police captain comments to Somerset, "How will you feel,
you're not gonna be a cop any more?"[32] This association has
repercussions at the end of the film when Mills acts on his
emotions and breaks the law. He is therefore unable to take
Somerset's place (with implications of a flawed masculinity).

The opposition between Somerset and Mills is conveyed not
only through their differences in age, ethnicity, and figure
behavior, but also through Somerset's appreciation of culture.
This becomes apparent in his visit to the library where he
searches for clues within a number of classical literary texts
concerning the seven deadly sins (since the murders begin to

follow a pattern that coheres to them), including works by Dante and Chaucer. The library has an elegant interior with archways, low-key illumination, and precisely laid out tables. In fact, an overhead shot emphasizes its uniform layout, which further suggests a connection with Somerset's orderly character. Somerset even comments to the guards, "I'll never understand, all these books, a world of knowledge at your fingertips. What do you do? Play poker all night."[33] Furthermore, diegetic classical music accompanies the sequence as Somerset surveys first, the book titles, which are rendered in extreme close up— Chaucer's *Canterbury Tales* and Dante's *Divine Comedy*—and then certain phrases contained within the books, including "opened up his windpipe" and "to tear his flesh.[34] These scenes cross-cut with Mills's analogous examination of forensic photographs and coroners' reports of the obesity murder scene, the sequence also centering on key phrases similar to those studied by Somerset. Therefore, though the two men are set up as opposites, there are also parallels suggested between them.

In addition to the obvious differences in *mise-en-scène*, the cinematography in the above sequence varies in its filming of the two men: in relation to Somerset, it is fluid and kinetic, the camera deploying slow panning long shots and circling close-ups of him, with wipes and fade-ins to heighten its fluidity. In fact, the cinematography seems almost synchronized with the diegetic classical music that plays in the background and contributes towards Somerset's cultured characterization. In contrast, a number of extreme close-ups of Mills as he reads the coroner's reports are forensic in nature, deploying flat lighting and montage editing, and which cut to extreme close-ups of the forensic reports themselves. In short, Somerset uses literature to access the murders whereas Mills focuses on graphic forensic imagery, their respective approaches (and characterization) materializing in the *mise-en-scène* and cinematography.

Yet, they follow similar paths to solve the murders, leading Browning to argue that rather than "opposites, they can be seen as older and younger versions of the same character."[35] Even as there are parallels between the two men, effectively suggesting them as buddies, there is also a constant rivalry. This becomes especially evident when Tracy telephones Mills (who has now taken over Somerset's desk and telephone) and asks to speak to Somerset, inviting him to dinner. Browning here notes that "the irony is there is common ground between the two, sensed almost immediately by Tracy, who, in an action that makes her more plot device than fully rounded character, invites Somerset to dinner."[36] Having accepted the invitation, Somerset passes the telephone back to Mills, and before he can say goodbye to her, she has already replaced the receiver. The implication for Mills is that she is more interested in speaking to Somerset than to him. This subtle relationship that privileges Somerset over Mills persists throughout the film and there is an emotional connection between Somerset and Tracy—for example, at the dinner table, they laugh together at the vibration effects of the subway on their apartment, much to Mills's frustration. Somerset also understands her dilemma concerning her pregnancy, conceding that he had been in a similar situation. In fact, he embodies the "sensitive masculinity" articulated by Jeffords. Thus, while normally, neo-noir might position Tracy (perhaps in combination with the effeminate John Doe [Kevin Spacey]) as a variant of the *femme fatale* because she causes the downfall of the hero, she also serves as a maternal figure, favoring Somerset over Mills in the revelation of her pregnancy. This tension fuels the possibility of an oedipal relationship between the two men where there is rivalry for the maternal figure, even if it assumes an inverted form. As Thurschwell explains, "[The child] realises there is someone else, the father, in competition for his mother's love. He begins to develop rivalrous and antagonistic feelings towards his father when he sees that his mother's attention is also directed towards this other person."[37]

Nonetheless, while Tracy's character is crucial to the narrative outcome, she has limited screen time and is marginalized visually and narratively, functioning only in relation to the three main male protagonists: Mills, Somerset, and Doe. Dyer suggests that the reason for her limited appearance is because "we must not forget her or lose a sense of her importance for Mills, but we must not be reminded too insistently of it, otherwise we will too easily guess her involvement in the denouement."[38] Certainly, high-key lighting, a *mise-en-scène* of pale colors, together with her blond hair and gentle characterization consistently place her as an angelic figure, causing her horrific murder to be even more shocking. On the one hand, therefore, her limited screen time and mode of death might shore up claims for the misogyny and female tokenism of the film's "buddy" aspects. In a sense, the film surely seems to encapsulate the backlash against feminism, by domesticating and then killing her. On the other hand, Tracy arguably occupies a unique role, located at the intersections of overlapping discourses and cultural paradigms in a genre that usually accords women a pivotal sexualized/dominant position. Yet, if Tracy is neither sexualized nor dominant in character, she does play a critical part, and the entire film, especially its impactful twist, hinges on her characterization and narrative function. Ostensibly, she serves a dual purpose in the narrative's overlap of father–son and cop–buddy models, functioning first to substantiate Mills's heterosexuality, and second, as the maternal figure of competing father and son characters in an inversion of the classic oedipal scenario. Accordingly, Somerset and Tracy engage in polite conversation while Mills gambols on the floor with the dogs, which he refers to as "the kids."[39] "He was the funniest guy I had ever met," Tracy tells Somerset, as the camera cuts to Somerset's viewpoint to disclose Mills still rolling around on the floor, the use of long shot making him appear diminished in stature and contributing further to the infantile analogy.[40]

Substantiating this father–son scenario, there is a persistent sense that Somerset is guiding Mills, more than in just a professional sense with Mills repeatedly cast as a child. "These murders were forced attrition," Somerset informs Mills.[41] "Forced what?" enquires Mills to which Somerset responds by explaining the meaning of the word.[42] Somerset also helps Mills by leaving clues about the murders with indications that Mills appears to learn from Somerset. In one such example, Somerset finds the words "gluttony" inscribed in grease behind the refrigerator in the obesity murder scene together with a sheet of paper, its handwritten text stating, "long is the way and hard that out of Hell leads up to light."[43] "It's from Milton. *Paradise Lost*," Somerset informs his superior while we see Mills in the background note this down.[44] Following his subsequent search through the literature, Somerset gives further clues to Mills, and we see in close-up his handwritten note instructing Mills which texts might be useful. Even as Somerset is reading through the literature (suggesting his diligence), there is a parallel edit to Mills settling down in front of the television, watched by Tracy. Witnessed from her viewpoint, the spectator observes Mills through window bars, these alluding to a later interchange between Mills and murderer John Doe as they journey out to the site of Doe's death in the film's finale. The viewing of Mills from "behind bars" also anticipates his subsequent incarceration. A close-up of Tracy, also seen as if "behind bars," implies her feelings of captivity too, both within the apartment and the city (which she confesses to Somerset that she hates).

As Somerset finalizes his library search, he photocopies the material and folds it carefully before placing it in an envelope, also seen in close-up, and which he later places on Mills's desk. Thereafter, we see Mills struggle with the complexities of Dante, shouting and swearing as he throws the book that he is reading, "Fucking Dante, goddamned poetry-rhyming faggot piece of shit!"[45] (The regular use of profanity is a distinctive feature of his persona.)

Despite their differences, Mills and Somerset eventually approach the case as a team—and one evening after dinner at the Mills' apartment, they begin to overcome their differences and combine their expertise. "Just going to get another beer. Beer?" asks Mills, but Somerset asks for wine, another subtle indication of the social gulf between the two.[46] As they discuss the details of the case, Mills offers his knowledge on Dante: "You read them?" asks Somerset, seeming surprised and pleased that Mills had followed up his suggestions.[47] Their ensuing discussion illustrates a developing correspondence between them, more in keeping with the buddy film, and they also demonstrate a grudging respect for each other's points of view. Indeed, as Browning notes, "the implication of the worldly wise persona also misses things too and the pair are more efficient when they work together."[48] After they arrive at the joint conclusion that a photograph of the murder victim's wife, Mrs Gould, is significant (because her eyes have been drawn around), they interview her. Somerset pushes Mills in questioning her, whispering to him "it's got to be now" (and thereby further indicating his guiding role).[49] They discover that a painting is upside down and visit the Gould's apartment to investigate further where they discover a message "help me" in fingerprints on a wall behind a painting hung upside down. While they wait for the fingerprint analysis, they slump on a sofa outside, their banter revealing further differences between them but also their increasing affinity. "I wish I still thought the way you do," Somerset tells Mills admiringly, commenting on the latter's idealism, which contrasts with Somerset's cynicism: "so many corpses roll away un-revenged," adds Somerset pessimistically.[50] Thereafter, they fall asleep, a medium close-up revealing Mills lying across Somerset much like a child might do.

Therefore, even though they maintain their differences, they begin to work together as a team, though their heterosexuality remains subtly signaled. In one example, as they wait in a café for the results of an illegal search of the library's users (to track down readers of Dante and Chaucer), Somerset sits adjacent to Mills. While narratively, this is to keep free a seat opposite for the imminent arrival of a contact, Mills protests, asking Somerset, "Could you at least sit across from me? I don't want people thinking we're dating."[51] The irony of this statement rests on the fact that Pitt is now a keen supporter of same-sex marriage.[52] Somerset then confides to Mills that "by telling you this, I'm trusting you more than I'd trust most people," and then he divulges information about illegal FBI monitoring of library user records given to him.[53] Almost immediately, he tells Mills to "get a haircut," again as a father would to his son.[54] A second narrative irony here is that Somerset himself is clearly involved in a dubious means of surveillance, which again alludes to the emerging similarities between the two men.

When the list of library users arrives, it includes titles by "Marquis de Sade" and "Saint Thomas Aquinas," both of which Mills reads out loud and mispronounces, Somerset again correcting him. The library search yields the name of a possible suspect, John Doe, leading them to his apartment. Here, as Doe shoots at them, Mills threatens to break into his apartment. Somerset warns Mills that such an action could jeopardize a prosecution, and in a heated discussion between the two men we now hear Somerset swear and become agitated (previously, it has been only Mills who has sworn). There is therefore continued cross-over between their personalities as the film progresses, and when Mills becomes suspicious after Doe turns himself in, Somerset comments, "for the first time ever, you and I are in total agreement."[55]

The growing parity between the two men is further indicated when they prepare to escort Doe to the site of the remaining bodies, each performing the same ritualized actions, first, of shaving their chests in order to attach radio wires and then donning bulletproof vests. They even laugh and joke, their relationship now seeming more akin to the buddy formula. Yet, a side-on close-up of Mills standing adjacent to Somerset, so that his profile is superimposed against that of the latter, implies Mills as a younger version of Somerset. Arguably, such framing suggests that Mills now identifies with Somerset—as Patricia Thurschwell notes, "In the Freudian schema, when the baby settles for identifying with the father, rather than wanting to kill him, he also internalizes the threatening, punishing aspect of the father."[56] In the final scene, when it becomes apparent that Doe has decapitated Mills's pregnant wife, Doe reveals Tracy's pregnancy to Mills as a further act of cruelty. "Oh, he didn't know," says Doe fraternally to Somerset, suggesting to the spectator and to Mills that Tracy had confided to Doe that Somerset also knew about the pregnancy.[57] Close-ups of Mills's face disclose his mental anguish as he is torn between an impetus to kill Doe, and the paternal logic of the super-ego (represented by Somerset). "If you kill him, he will win," reasons Somerset. Despite Somerset's cautions, Mills is consumed with anger and shoots Doe, thereby displaying a failed oedipal trajectory.[58] This flawed masculinity seems incongruent with Brad Pitt's star persona, yet corresponds with certain other films of his corpus in which there is similar undermining of his masculine identity (for example, David Fincher's 2008 film *The Curious Case of Benjamin Button*). Arguably, its deviation from Pitt's star persona is a result of Pitt's desire to be taken seriously as an actor.[59] Indeed, in an interview with David Fincher, Judy Sloane reports that Fincher "rewrote stuff for Brad because the Mills character was originally tailored for everything Brad Pitt was trying not to do, which was be the heartthrob, the young, good-looking guy."[60]

The film ends with Mills locked in a police car: "whatever he needs," says Somerset protectively to the police captain as Mills is driven away, again iterating a fatherly attitude towards Mills and illustrating how the film's narrative fluctuates between the two men as buddies and as father and son.[61] Released in 1995, the film thus illustrates the overlap between the two forms, Mills's actions exemplifying an on-going crisis in masculinity, initiated after Vietnam, inflamed by feminism and gay rights, and perpetuated in more recent times by 9/11.

Notes

1   Richard Dyer, *The Matter of Images: Essays on Representation*, (London and New York: Routledge, 2002), 103.

2   Harry Benshoff and Sean Griffin, *America on Film: Representing Race, Class, Gender, and Sexuality at the Movies* (Oxford: Wiley-Blackwell, 2009), 281.

3 Harry Benshoff and Sean Griffin, *America on Film: Representing Race, Class, Gender, and Sexuality at the Movies* (Oxford: Wiley-Blackwell, 2009), 281.

4 Sally Robinson, *Marked Men: White Masculinity in Crisis* (New York: Columbia University Press, 2000), 5.

5 Sally Robinson, *Marked Men: White Masculinity in Crisis* (New York: Columbia University Press, 2000), 6.

6 Cynthia Fuchs, "The Buddy Politic," in *Screening the Male: Exploring Masculinities in Hollywood Cinema* (New York: Routledge, 1993), 195.

7 Richard Dyer, *The Matter of Images: Essays on Representation*, (London and New York: Routledge, 2002), 103.

8 Cynthia Fuchs, "The Buddy Politic," in *Screening the Male: Exploring Masculinities in Hollywood Cinema* (New York: Routledge, 1993), 195.

9 Richard Dyer, *Seven* (London: BFI Publishing, 1999), 24.

10 Richard Dyer, *Seven* (London: BFI Publishing, 1999), 25.

11 David Greven, "Contemporary Hollywood Masculinity and the Double-Protagonist Film," *Cinema Journal* 48.4 (2009), 22.

12 David Greven, "Contemporary Hollywood Masculinity and the Double-Protagonist Film," *Cinema Journal* 48.4 (2009).

13 David Greven, "Contemporary Hollywood Masculinity and the Double-Protagonist Film," *Cinema Journal* 48.4 (2009), 28.

14 Mark Browning, *David Fincher: Films That Scar* (Denver: Praeger, 2010), 59.

15 Susan Jeffords, *Hard Bodies: Hollywood Masculinity in the Reagan Era* (New Brunswick, NJ: Rutgers University Press, 1994), 13.

16 Susan Jeffords, *Hard Bodies: Hollywood Masculinity in the Reagan Era* (New Brunswick, NJ: Rutgers University Press, 1994), 13.

17 Susan Jeffords, *Hard Bodies: Hollywood Masculinity in the Reagan Era* (New Brunswick, NJ: Rutgers University Press, 1994), 67.

18 *Seven*, directed by David Fincher (New Line Cinema, 1995).

19 James Swallow, *Dark Eye: The Films of David Fincher* (London: Reynaulds and Hearn, 2003), 77; Mark Browning, *David Fincher: Films That Scar* (Denver: Praeger, 2010), 59.

20 Sigmund Freud, *The Ego and the Id and Other Works: The Standard Edition of the Complete Psychological Works of Sigmund Freud*, Vol. 19 (London: Vintage, 2001), 31–2.

21 Mark Browning, *David Fincher: Films That Scar* (Denver: Praeger, 2010), 58.

22 *Seven*, directed by David Fincher (New Line Cinema, 1995).

23 *Seven*, directed by David Fincher (New Line Cinema, 1995).

24 *Seven*, directed by David Fincher (New Line Cinema, 1995).

25 *Seven*, directed by David Fincher (New Line Cinema, 1995).

26 *Seven*, directed by David Fincher (New Line Cinema, 1995).

27 *Seven*, directed by David Fincher (New Line Cinema, 1995).

28 *Seven*, directed by David Fincher (New Line Cinema, 1995).

29 *Seven*, directed by David Fincher (New Line Cinema, 1995).

30 *Seven*, directed by David Fincher (New Line Cinema, 1995).

31 Mark Browning, *David Fincher: Films That Scar* (Denver: Praeger, 2010), 57.

32 Mark Browning, *David Fincher: Films That Scar* (Denver: Praeger, 2010), 57.

33 Mark Browning, *David Fincher: Films That Scar* (Denver: Praeger, 2010), 57.

34 Mark Browning, *David Fincher: Films That Scar* (Denver: Praeger, 2010), 57.

35 Mark Browning, *David Fincher: Films That Scar* (Denver: Praeger, 2010), 58.

36 Mark Browning, *David Fincher: Films That Scar* (Denver: Praeger, 2010), 59.

37 Pamela Thurschwell, *Sigmund Freud* (New York: Routledge, 2000), 48.

38 Richard Dyer, *Seven* (London: BFI Publishing, 1999), 30.

39 *Seven*, directed by David Fincher (New Line Cinema, 1995).

40 *Seven*, directed by David Fincher (New Line Cinema, 1995).

41 *Seven*, directed by David Fincher (New Line Cinema, 1995).

42 *Seven*, directed by David Fincher (New Line Cinema, 1995).

43 *Seven*, directed by David Fincher (New Line Cinema, 1995).

44 *Seven*, directed by David Fincher (New Line Cinema, 1995).

45 *Seven*, directed by David Fincher (New Line Cinema, 1995).

46 *Seven*, directed by David Fincher (New Line Cinema, 1995).

47 *Seven*, directed by David Fincher (New Line Cinema, 1995).

48 Mark Browning, *David Fincher: Films That Scar* (Denver: Praeger, 2010), 56.

49 *Seven*, directed by David Fincher (New Line Cinema, 1995).

50 *Seven*, directed by David Fincher (New Line Cinema, 1995).

51 *Seven*, directed by David Fincher (New Line Cinema, 1995).

52 Katherine Thomson, "Brad Pitt Donates $100,000 to Fight Gay Marriage Ban," *Huffington Post*, September 17, 2008, http://www.huffingtonpost.com/2008/09/17/brad-pitt-donates-100000_n_127263.html [Accessed February 4, 2013].

53 *Seven*, directed by David Fincher (New Line Cinema, 1995).

54 *Seven*, directed by David Fincher (New Line Cinema, 1995).

55 *Seven*, directed by David Fincher (New Line Cinema, 1995).

56 *Seven*, directed by David Fincher (New Line Cinema, 1995), 48.

57 *Seven*, directed by David Fincher (New Line Cinema, 1995).

58 *Seven*, directed by David Fincher (New Line Cinema, 1995).

59 Cynthia Pearlman, "Brad Pitt's Seven Deadly Sins," *Chicago Sunday Times* September 17, 1995.

60 David Fincher quoted in Judy Sloane, "David Fincher," *Film Review* (February 1996), 34.

61 *Seven*, directed by David Fincher (New Line Cinema, 1995).

CHAPTER NINE

Anger of Achilles

Rick Hudson

In his numerous film roles Brad Pitt has often played "heroic" masculine characters that have, at the very least, had a troubled relationship with conventional notions of the heroic male. He took on the role of a mopey, troubled, angst-ridden undead in *Interview with the Vampire* (1994); a mopey, troubled, angst-ridden detective in *Se7en* (1995); and the anarchic Tyler Durden in *Fight Club* (1999). However, while these roles may be interpreted as subverting the hegemonic masculinity usually portrayed in mainstream cinema, these subversions constitute little more than "designer" rebellion: rebellion articulated through consumer choice.[1]

Nevertheless, Pitt's portrayal of Achilles in *Troy* (2004) was perhaps the role in which the actor most profoundly subverted notions of conventional masculinity and heroism. Paradoxically, while *The Iliad* is perhaps the ur-text from which all western heroic narratives evolve, and Achilles is perhaps the ur-hero from which all action heroes descend, it was this film's authenticity to its literary source material and Pitt's authenticity to the literary Achilles that led to this film being such a successful critique of conventional heroic narratives.

This film does not attempt to re-brand either its plot or its heroes in line with contemporary morality or film conventions. In *Troy*, as in Homer's *Iliad*, we are presented with quite alien notions of heroism and morality which jar with our own. We are presented with a heroic narrative that questions heroism; a heroic narrative which does not justify itself within an over-arching morality, but in which men are pitted against each other in political conflict; a heroic narrative in which protagonists are neither celebrated as heroes or castigated as villains; a heroic narrative in which vanity and guile triumph over courage and honor; a heroic narrative in which mighty men are subject to peevish moods and whims that have devastating consequences for others: "Sing, O goddess, the anger of Achilles son of Peleus, that brought countless ills upon the Achaeans. Many a brave soul did it send hurrying down to Hades, and many a hero did it yield a prey to dogs and vultures."[2] This chapter argues that Pitt's (and *Troy*'s) most subversive act is to remain faithful to a 3,000-year-old piece of literature rather than embrace contemporary mores and fashionable values.

In his very short article "Rebel Consumerism," E.J. Park satirizes—in a style that pastiches the writing of Chuck Palahniuk—the 1999 movie adaptation of the novel *Fight Club*, mocking the film for commodifying rebellion and anti-consumerism:

> If you're going to be Tyler Durden, you have to have the right look, the right style, the right kick-ass vibe. At Urban Outfitters, you can buy a wardrobe of descent for less than six hundred dollars. All the products have that fuck you attitude, which is to say they all appear to be worn-out and retro-fitted. Shopping at Urban Outfitters gives you that instant "rebel" credibility. Tyler may mock Gap, but he's not going to mock a store that sells Atari T-shirts for twenty-eight bucks. Hell, just visit the nearest Urban Outfitters, and you'll see Tyler Durdens and Marla Singers everywhere.[3]

Tyler Durden is, of course, the anarchic antagonist/protagonist of *Fight Club*, played by Brad Pitt. As in many of Pitt's roles we are presented with a hero/villain whom we are encouraged to identify as a subversive and anti-establishment figure. However, as Park argues, many of these roles are merely "cooler" portrayals of hegemonic masculinity and hidden variations on a consumerist mind-set.

If we are going to consider Pitt's heroic film roles, then it may be worth considering the possibility that his portrayal of Achilles in Wolfgang Petersen's movie *Troy* (2004) has been his most dissident heroic role. The irony here is that this film is an adaptation of *The Iliad*, the text from which all western heroic fiction has evolved, and Achilles himself could be argued to be the original figure from which all action heroes descend.

It would be disingenuous to claim that *Troy* is a completely faithful adaptation of *The Iliad*, but then it does not claim to be so. Nevertheless, the film could be said to be authentic *in spirit* to the eighth-century BC poem, and it is this belief that this chapter seeks to explore.

Ostensibly *Troy* is nothing more than a spectacular sword and sandals movie and an epic adventure yarn. It is a Hollywood blockbuster movie that features an attractive cast and huge highly choreographed battle scenes. However, *Troy* differs significantly from many Hollywood action movies in that it does not project contemporary morals or ethics onto the characters or narrative but instead presents us with heroes who are motivated by and display classical virtues—strength, honor, courage, fortitude and guile—which they see as useful and rewarding rather than "good." These virtues are to be prized and demonstrated because it is through these that the heroes may gain *Kleos* (κλέος, "glory, fame") which they believe to be the only form of immortality available to them. The film draws our attention to, perhaps even overstating, the fact that the heroes all crave to garner reputations for themselves that will live on after their death. Indeed, the film opens with off-screen narration by Odysseus (Sean Bean):

> Men are haunted by the vastness of eternity. And so we ask
> ourselves, "Will our actions echo across the centuries? Will
> strangers hear our names long after we are gone and wonder
> who we were, how bravely we fought and how fiercely we
> laughed?"[4]

Indeed, many of the heroes, and particularly Achilles, place
gaining such *Kleos* above their loyalty to the side to whom they
are supposedly aligned or any morality that we would recognize.
It would be wrong to say that *Troy* does not feature heroes and
villains. Indeed, in the classical sense all the principal characters
are heroes in that they are great warriors who seek to forge
terrible reputations. In the contemporary sense, however, we
are presented very clearly with both heroes with whom we are
invited to identify, Achilles and Odysseus, and villains we are
led to despise, Agamemnon (Brian Cox) and Menelaus (Brendan
Gleeson). Importantly though, the "good" heroes perform acts
of great cruelty and brutality which can equal that of the
supposed villains. In this sense, *Troy* demonstrates a significantly
authentic relationship to *The Iliad* as can be demonstrated by
specific scenes and aspects of the film.

In the opening scene, Achilles fights as Agamemnon's (the
High King of the Greeks) champion in single combat with the
champion of a king who resists Agamemnon's rule. While
Achilles swiftly kills his opponent, he is eager to display his
disdain towards Agamemnon by turning up late to the conflict
and then, after the fight, refusing to acknowledge Agamemnon
as his master, saying "He is not my king" and refusing to take
the symbolic scepter of authority and deliver it to Agamemnon
himself.[5] This opening scene establishes two things: first, it
establishes Achilles as a "free agent" or "maverick" hero,
something of a staple of Hollywood cinema. Second, and more
importantly for the purposes of this chapter, it establishes that
while Achilles is a hero, he demonstrates great vanity, and this
vanity will, rather than just make him a "likeable rebel"
character in the audience's eyes, also cause great and terrible
suffering as the narrative progresses.

The scene then shifts to Sparta where a banquet is in progress. Menelaus, the King of Sparta and Agamemnon's brother, is host to two envoys from the city of Troy, the princes Hector (Eric Bana) and Paris (Orlando Bloom). The two states have been at war for years and now celebrate the brokering of a peace. However, Paris and Menelaus' wife, Helen (Diane Kruger), have fallen in love and after the celebration Paris smuggles Helen onto the Trojan ship to take her home. During the journey home Paris reveals to Hector what he has done. Furious, Hector berates his brother saying that he has already destroyed the peace that had only just been established. Hector maintains that Paris's acts will inevitably lead to war, and when Paris claims that he will fight for Helen, Hector retorts that war is "nothing glorious, nothing poetic."[6] While this might appear to be a little ironic, considering that the film is based on an epic poem about war, it is not a statement that is in conflict with the spirit of The Iliad. Rather, it is in sympathy with it: plague-ridden battlefields, terrible cruelties, and treachery are prominent features of the original source material.

On hearing of his wife's desertion, Menelaus goes to his brother Agamemnon for aid in recovering Helen. Under the guise of brotherhood Agamemnon agrees to assist Menelaus, however, it suits his political purposes to do so. If the Spartans with all their Greek allies defeat Troy, then Agamemnon will have undisputed control of the entire Aegean. Agamemnon's adviser, Nestor (John Shrapnel), counsels the king to take Achilles and his followers, the Myrmidons, as part of his invasion force as they will make a significant military contribution to the invasion. Agamemnon is unwilling, wary of enlisting "a man who fights for no flag."[7] However, the king is persuaded and dispatches Odysseus to convince Achilles to join the king's fleet as "there is only one man he [Achilles] will listen to," and this is Odysseus.[8]

Odysseus meets with Achilles, and we witness that Achilles has a respect for Odysseus that he holds for few other men. During this meeting we see another example of Troy remaining faithful to its ancient roots because both heroes represent a particular virtue: Achilles is the embodiment of courage, while his friend is the personification of guile. Although Achilles is aware of Odysseus's capacity for trickery, he succumbs to it all the same when Odysseus appeals to Achilles's desire for *Kleos*: "This war will never be forgotten. Nor will the heroes that fight in it."[9]

Achilles then goes to his mother, Thetis (Julie Christie), to seek her advice on whether he should go to Troy with Agamemnon's army. Initially, Thetis appears to persuade Achilles not to go, saying that if he stays at home he will meet a wonderful woman and have wonderful children. But after saying this, rather surprisingly to our contemporary minds, she nonetheless encourages him to go to his death, saying that if he stays at home "his name will be lost" after his children's death.[10] If he goes to Troy, however, people "will write stories about your victories for thousands of years . . . Your glory walks hand in hand with your doom."[11] This scene reinforces the alien quality of the culture that is being presented to us: it is inconceivable to us that a mother would encourage her son to go to his inevitable death for the sake of becoming a legend, and yet this is what Thetis does.

When the Greek fleet approaches Troy, Achilles's ship races ahead of the bulk of Agamemnon's forces: this is partly a means by which Achilles can yet again express his derision for the king but also born of a desire to gain greater *Kleos*. He urges his Myrmidons on with the cry: "Immortality! Take it, it's yours!"[12] Much to Agamemnon's chagrin, Achilles lands on the beach ahead of the other Greeks; they establish their own strategic position by taking over the temple of Apollo rather than attack Troy itself or wait for their allies to join them. In the taking of the temple, Achilles exhibits behavior that is inimical to our familiar notions of heroism: he orders his men to sack the temple, beheads the statue of Apollo, murders the unarmed priests, and takes the priestess, Briseis (Rose Byrne), as a captive. When Hector leads a failed attempt to retake the temple, the Trojan prince's life is spared by Achilles, not out of mercy, but because there is no glory for Achilles in killing Hector without an audience: "Why kill you now, Prince of Troy, with no one to see you fall?"[13]

When the main body of the Greek army has landed and established themselves on the beach, several attacks and counter-attacks take place. However, the next significant event is when Paris challenges Menelaus to a duel to determine ownership of Helen and the outcome of the war itself. Paris is besotted with the idea of war as glamorous and fighting for the woman he loves; however, in reality, he is not only beaten but humiliated by Menelaus. Paris runs from the fight and ends up sniveling at the feet of his brother. It is only through Hector's intervention that Paris survives as Hector kills Menelaus.

However, the narrative neither rewards courage nor punishes cowardice. In particular, heroism does not win love: despite Paris's cowardice Helen does not desert him but states instead that she is repelled by the supposed "heroic" behavior of her former husband and men like him. This attitude is reasserted several times in conversations between the heroes who are shown to have wives or lovers. Hector's wife, Andromache (Saffron Burrows), pleads with the prince for him to flee the city, and Briseis displays nothing but total revulsion for Achilles's combat prowess and martial skills.

The heroic conventions we are familiar with are transgressed further when Achilles withdraws the Myrmidons from the field and refuses to fight in order to spite Agamemnon. The hero states that he wants Agamemnon to "groan to have Achilles back."[14] Achilles's further isolation from the main Greek army results in him giving the order for his men to sail away from Troy altogether. However, while Achilles is asleep, his cousin, Patroclus (Garrett Hedlund), leads the Myrmidons into battle in the hero's armor, and Patroclus is killed by Hector, who mistakes the young Myrmidon for Achilles.

Despite Achilles arguably being responsible for the death of Patroclus, Achilles is enraged by the news of his death. He strikes the loyal subaltern that brings him the news and throws Briseis to the ground. Determined to have his revenge, he challenges Hector to single combat. Achilles's wrath is so great that, not only does he kill Hector, but he also ties his opponent's body to his chariot and drags it around the city walls.

Perhaps one of the most significant paradoxes about this heroic narrative is that, of all the classical virtues that are demonstrated within both *Troy* and *The Iliad*, it is guile that triumphs. Odysseus is perhaps the most likeable of all the heroes; however, he demonstrates throughout the film that though he is a friend of Achilles, he is also prepared to manipulate him when required. Odysseus's greatest act of guile is, of course, the devising of the wooden horse which will enable the Greeks to enter Troy.

The sacking of the city is brutal and terrible and many of the heroes commit horrific acts and meet awful ends. As the city burns, Paris rushes through the flames to save Helen, and Achilles desperately seeks Briseis. Agamemnon murders Priam, the king of Troy (Peter O'Toole), and is in turn killed by Briseis. Briseis is then seized by Agamemnon's guards but is rescued by Achilles. Paris misinterprets Achilles's actions and shoots the hero down with his bow, first crippling him in his heel and then killing him with further arrows.

Although ostensibly a spectacular action narrative, *Troy* is very much more than a conservative and reactionary narrative which celebrates war, conventional heroic masculinity, and simplistic morality. The plot of both *Troy* and *The Iliad* itself presents us instead with a piece of fiction which highlights the terrible and appallingly destructive reality of war. Neither is it a simplistic narrative in which good, humble warriors are exploited by callous and self-serving commanders. Indeed, the characters we are invited to empathize with the most—Achilles, Odysseus, and to a lesser extent Paris—are shown as men who are essentially good, but are equally venal, mercenary, self-interested, driven by pride, and seekers of personal glory over the greater causes that they supposedly serve. Each one of them is subject to flaws of character. The wrath and vanity of Achilles propel the narrative of *The Iliad* and *Troy*, his wounded pride and rage at the death of Patroclus are both unfounded, as his cousin's death is a consequence of Achilles's actions, and also the cause of thousands of other deaths and the prolongation and increased savagery of the Trojan War itself. Odysseus, although a highly likeable character, is shown to be treacherous and perfectly willing to manipulate events and his supposed friends and allies if it serves his personal and political agenda to do so. And while Paris is the most romantic character in this story, his romantic notions are as much a character flaw as Achilles's anger. It is Paris's romantic dreaming and conceptions of love that break the truce between Troy and Sparta, thereby causing this terrible war.

Both *Troy* and *The Iliad* portray a world in which heroism is greatly valued but is not rewarded in narrative terms. Principles and virtues which we recognize do not win the principal characters either honor or love. The principal female characters, Helen and Briseis, are shown to be appalled by supposed "heroic" virtues. Despite his cowardice, Paris still gets the girl: Helen does not desert him. The hero who is rewarded the most in terms of *Kleos* is the one whose primary virtue (in Greco-Roman terms) is guile: craftiness, treachery, deceitfulness. It is Odysseus who manipulates his friends and allies, and commits the ultimate act of guile in all European literature, the planning and construction of the wooden horse itself. It is Odysseus who survives and gains the greatest glory, it is Odysseus who wins *Kleos* and Odysseus who will go on to have further adventures in which he not only garners greater *Kleos* but is also eventually rewarded with the greatest prize obtainable by any Greek hero, *Nostos*: the heroic homecoming. Characters who demonstrate courage, virtue, and honor—such as Hector, Priam, Ajax, and Achilles—are only rewarded with death, indignity, and humiliation.

In remaining true in spirit to *The Iliad, Troy* not only puzzles us with a system of values and notions of heroism that are quite alien to those of the contemporary Hollywood action movie, but it also prompts us to question the notions of heroism that we have come to accept in our regular diet of action and adventure. If all western heroic narratives descend from *The*

Iliad and all western action heroes are the literary progenies of Achilles, then surely we must question the integrity of contemporary action narratives and the characters that populate them as well as the values that inform them if these stories have veered so widely from the text which spawned them: a text which is a heroic epic about war which is horrified by war and belies our notions of heroism. Indeed, unlike Homer's other great work, *The Odyssey*, there is no joy, nor celebration of war and heroism in *The Iliad* at all. As Hammond observes, while *The Odyssey* celebrates heroic deeds and acts of war, often in song, "[t]here are no such singers in the sterner world of the *Iliad*—only the keeners set beside the bodies of the dead."[15]

Perhaps counter-intuitively, Pitt's most significant contribution to the film was not merely in lending his name to Achilles, but rather in his accurate delivery of the role of Achilles. Although, and this is somewhat speculative, it would have been preferable in the eyes of some actors to Hollywoodize Achilles and portray the hero in a much more conventional and palatable manner—as a maverick loner hero—Pitt's performance remains more authentic to the Achilles of *The Iliad*. In Pitt's portrayal we are presented with a hero who, while admirable for his physicality and as a wish-fulfillment superman, is difficult to like as he reneges on our contemporary idea of a hero. Pitt's Achilles is very much like Homer's: impulsive, capricious, viscous, arrogant, and self-absorbed. Pitt is willing to portray a classical hero who demonstrates ancient Greek virtues which are in his own interest and further his glory—bravery, savagery, and pursuit of glory—rather than sanitize Achilles into a more comfortable and digestible figure who conforms to and validates our notions of what a hero should be and what we, in the twenty-first century, consider to be virtues.

Notes

1   See E. J. Park, "Rebel Consumer," in *You Do Not Talk About Fight Club: I Am Jack's Completely Unauthorized Essay*

Collection, ed. Read Mercer Schuchardt (Dallas, TX: BenBella, 2008), 117–18.

2   Homer, *The Iliad* (London: Penguin, 2001), 1.

3   E. J. Park, "Rebel Consumer," in *You Do Not Talk About* Fight Club: *I Am Jack's Completely Unauthorized Essay Collection*, ed. Read Mercer Schuchardt (Dallas: BenBella, 2008), 117.

4   *Troy*, directed by Wolfgang Peterson (Warner Bros, 2004).

5   *Troy*, directed by Wolfgang Peterson (Warner Bros, 2004).

6   *Troy*, directed by Wolfgang Peterson (Warner Bros, 2004).

7   *Troy*, directed by Wolfgang Peterson (Warner Bros, 2004).

8   *Troy*, directed by Wolfgang Peterson (Warner Bros, 2004).

9   *Troy*, directed by Wolfgang Peterson (Warner Bros, 2004).

10 *Troy*, directed by Wolfgang Peterson (Warner Bros, 2004).

11 *Troy*, directed by Wolfgang Peterson (Warner Bros, 2004).

12 *Troy*, directed by Wolfgang Peterson (Warner Bros, 2004).

13 *Troy*, directed by Wolfgang Peterson (Warner Bros, 2004).

14 *Troy*, directed by Wolfgang Peterson (Warner Bros, 2004).

15 M. Hammond, "Introduction," in Homer, *The Iliad* (London: Penguin, 1987), ix.

CHAPTER TEN

Becoming Brad

Bob Batchelor

Even as he sips a glass of ice water in his suite at the Mayfair Regent Hotel, Brad Pitt smolders . . . And it's precisely that slow-burning sensuality, first glimpsed in his steamy appearance as the sexy hitchhiker . . . that has put him on top of Hollywood's list of hunky heartthrobs to watch.

—LISA ANDERSON, 1992

History is meaningless without leaders and heroes . . . Heroes are mirrors of the times and inspirations for our future.

—MARSHALL FISHWICK, 2004

From a peculiar amassing of media savvy, marketing acumen, and interesting role choices, Brad Pitt emerged as a budding star. "Smolders" served as an all-encompassing label on young Pitt in his early career. The word suggested that he possessed deep-seated qualities beyond mere beauty or charisma. It also held the implication that Pitt's roots plunged deeper than his pretty boy guise; he was natural, fire-like, which merged with his status as an all-American guy who enjoyed drinking beer and "normal" stuff. His early role in the 1991 blockbuster, *Thelma & Louise*, portrayed Pitt as an attractive, wayward cowboy who became a lynchpin in the Americana and modern popular culture of the day. Henceforth, whether Pitt played a killer or villain or appeared splashed across the tabloids with a starlet on his arm, audiences yearned for more. Coming of age in an era just prior to the dawn of the Internet, but still in a time of expanding technology pushing mass communications, Pitt emerged at the right time.

This chapter considers Pitt's improbable rise from obscurity to his standing at the top of Hollywood's power elite. Through his story, I hope to make sense of modern celebrity and the factors that enable one to become larger than life, not just significant like other celebrities, but an immense icon on the grandest scale. Currently, Pitt, along with his partner Angelina Jolie and friend George Clooney, ranks among a select group of the world's most preeminent celebrity icons, yet guessing that he might achieve this prominence would have been almost unimaginable when his acting career launched in the late 1980s. Almost.

Looking at Pitt's early career and tracing the webs that connect that era with today, we can gain insight into the world of mega-celebrity and its role in contemporary culture. Like many stories, Pitt's begins with both adversity and a dream—his deeply personal yearning for a one-in-a-hundred-million shot at stardom whose tale begins as just one of innumerable Hollywood hopefuls searching for that bit of magic.

Take one: Creating a hero

Hollywood needs heroes. We might speculate that the desire is more substantial than that—perhaps *culture* needs heroes. Whether in Homer's ancient travels telling the story of the

Trojan War, or embodied in the latest superhero action flick in eye-popping 3D, hero narratives play a critical role in human culture, ingraining legends to the point that people use heroes and iconic figures to interpret or make sense of their own lives. Such tales enable people to address issues by channeling culture's grand narratives on micro scales and in everyday contexts. As the scholar Thomas Mickey explains, "We interact with one another through symbol. It is the symbol, mostly language, to which we give meaning. In the process we become part of a social order greater than ourselves (a family, a community, an organization)."[1] Similarly, Chris Rojek asks, "Why do so many of us measure our worth against figures we have never met? Why is the desire for fame so widespread among ordinary people?"[2]

Film and television stars are in a unique position in a world of celebrity worship. Viewers watch them on the screen playing heroes or antiheroes, but then they also obsess over how actors and actresses negotiate the "real world." The constant evaluation and media bubble celebrities live in creates an intricate and constant exchange based on perceptions the public crafts both from a great distance from celebrities' lives and out of intimate and ubiquitous representations on home screens and fondled print matter. Ultimately, stars become symbol-laden ideas that people load up with their own notions, connotations, and expectations—all within a mass media system designed for just such exchanges.

Still, part of the hero narrative is the struggle to overcome adversity. This story arc both fuels popular culture and taps into an urge for everydayness, or an ordinary life out of which greatness can arise. Brad Pitt also fits well into this narrative. His tale begins in 1987 as a college dropout (just two credits short of a degree), who sets sail for Los Angeles in a beat-up car with $325 in his pocket, launching a rags-to-riches narrative that seems straight out of central casting, but there is also real drama in Pitt's climb. Unlike Clooney, who had famous relatives to turn to for advice, Pitt had no one to lean on or look to for support. In fact, both young men struggled for a long time as bit actors before breaking the star barrier, even overcoming the desire of producers and agents to turn them into products playing "pretty boy" roles based more on their looks than their talent. The harsh reality of late 1980s Hollywood hit home quickly for Pitt; he struggled to find roles, working as a driver shuttling strippers around and donning a giant chicken suit outside a restaurant to lure customers. Eventually, however, the face could not be ignored. Pitt began acting lessons and took the typical route, first finding extra roles and then working on the soap opera *Another World*. The guest appearance roles start adding up, including *Dallas*, *21 Jump Street*, and *Growing Pains*—all hit shows that bolstered the young man's standing. Both Pitt and Clooney could have essentially sustained careers in the land of guest roles and sit-coms, rather than hold out for more significant careers.

In 1991, the little-known actor Brad Pitt bloomed in *Thelma & Louise*, a watershed film that grew into a touchstone movie of its age. The film symbolized an important political point as the 1980s rolled into the new decade. J. D. the young drifter served as a sexual liberator for Thelma (Geena Davis), an unfulfilled housewife with a controlling husband. Although hardly a household name prior to this point, Pitt suddenly became a sex symbol and the public grew more intrigued, thus launching the traditional media and tabloid press to satiate the frenzy around Pitt, whom many saw as the next big thing. Then, in seemingly short order, Pitt landed significant starring roles in Robert Redford's *A River Runs Through It* (1992), *Interview with the Vampire* (1994), and *Legends of the Fall* (1994). The cumulative consequence of these films was to quickly transform Pitt from chicken suit to rising star. As he starred in these films and built his career, Pitt also negotiated a relationship with the media and found its favor with well-honed interviewing skills and a laidback personality. For example, in his first big *Rolling Stone* interview, Pitt and writer Chris Mundy roam around pubs in London and Glasgow, enabling Lundy to depict the actor as down-to-earth, interacting with the star-struck patrons.[3]

In short, being in the right era at the right time served Pitt well. He landed a minor role in a major blockbuster, and it helped propel him into Hollywood's stratosphere. From that launch, the tabloids and entertainment journalism industry took interest, which he then fed by playing the role of young heartthrob. Coming full circle, he played heroic roles in a series of films that accentuated, punctuated, and validated his real-life persona. In other words, the heroic onscreen roles authenticated the image Pitt and the media built around him as a person. The fans who first took notice of Pitt in the late 1980s and early 1990s grew up with him via the burst of early films, tabloids, teen magazines, and entertainment television. Similarly, the Internet would later grow Pitt's celebrity exponentially.

Take two: That magic dust

A question that might seem pretty direct, but is in fact fraught with complexity, is: "Why Brad Pitt?" The trajectory from college dropout to bit actor to minor roles and then a television and film star had been played out countless times. Yet Pitt took those initial modest steps and then parlayed a rather minor role in *Thelma & Louise* into an amazingly successful career. What is it about Pitt as an individual and the fortuitous circumstances around him that enabled this megastar turn to occur? Obviously, Pitt's charisma and charm were evident, dating back to his earliest television appearances. Even his parents, siblings, and college friends realized that growing up he already possessed traits that drew people to him. It is simply impossible to disregard Pitt's natural beauty as an element of his success. However, something else also sparked that moves beyond mere splendor, which is almost impossible to identify outside the parameters of mysticism, because Hollywood is full of stunningly beautiful people. Perhaps the only way to categorize this would be to call it "that magic dust"—a rare combination of timing, looks, affect, and luck that sprinkles down on some celebrities, turning them into something grander than they ever imagined. An even luckier few—Jolie, Clooney, Tom Hanks, Tom Cruise, and a small group of others—emerge from the realms of entertainment stars to become iconic.

Yearning to answer the question, "Why Pitt?," we can turn to others who given the right circumstances *could* have become Pitt-like megastars, such as Rob Lowe, John Stamos, or Christian Slater. What is it that separates such successful actors from the genuinely iconic? Director Neil Jordan, who teamed Cruise and Pitt in *Interview with the Vampire*, hinted at this "magic dust" part of the equation, as well as the role talent plays, explaining Pitt by saying, "I think he's great, and I think he actually knows he's great. People are either stars, or they're not. They either project it, or they don't. The minute Brad walked into *Thelma & Louise* he did that. He was a star from then on."[4] The ineffable is couched in terms of confidence and actuality, but even beyond that it still fundamentally remains a mystery.

Another aspect of the magic certainly pertains to longevity. For example, one could argue that many film stars are able to move up to superstar status. Few, however, are able to maintain that level over a long period. Then, when one adds in how the iconic star grows beyond his or her chosen medium to kind of an über-celebrity, it seems almost impossible to fathom. Pitt and Jolie, as two of today's iconic celebrities, carry a significance that exceeds their stardom as movie stars. Jolie rarely makes films any more, and she has not had a legitimate star vehicle in recent memory. As a matter of fact, her iconic standing is even more problematic than Pitts', certainly as she has moved into political activism. One might speculate that as each has transcended the bounds of most superstars, their combined status has propelled them as well.

Take three: From star to icon

It would be dishonest to say that luck and timing did not also play important roles in Pitt's transition from star to icon. The young actor started getting meaningful parts in an era marked by pre-Internet innocence, but Pitt still benefited from the era's cheap tabloid press and the so-called entertainment news industry filling evening television hours. His good looks and beautiful girlfriends more or less guaranteed his place in the nation's grocery store aisles and their sensationalist tabloids. As Pitt's star rose, a technology explosion simultaneously revolutionized mass communications, and he would again benefit as the Internet demanded content, and celebrity news and entertainment pieces seemed as if they were made just for such opportunities.

Technology—from increasingly high-definition television to the omnipresent Internet—has wiped away barriers that at once divided culture into high and low forms. All culture is popular culture, and the access technology offers enables nearly everyone to engage with culture however and whenever they want, regardless of economic status, social standing, or any other societal categories. Ray B. Browne aptly defines this state of affairs, explaining that popular culture is "the everyday world around us: the mass media, entertainments, diversions, heroes, icons, rituals, psychology, religion—our total life picture."[5] Pondering Browne's definition in light of heroic figures such as Pitt, it becomes clear that some icons are able to slip more easily into the public's collective consciousness and take up residence there, essentially becoming more powerful and influential as a result even if this influence remains diffuse and spectral.

As a force that permeates contemporary life (perhaps a kind of cultural Higgs-Boson particle, dubbed by the media the "God particle" for its role in holding together all matter), popular culture exists in the impulses that draw members of the global community to a particular person, thing, topic, or issue that arises out of the juncture of mass communications, technology, political systems, and economic institutions. As the foremost figures in this new federation of celebrities and icons, Pitt, Jolie, Clooney, and select others meld these disparate impulses across global mass media, political, and socio-economic institutions. They hold power as cultural entities, as well as real-life political influencers, using their vast fame to intervene and engage in global causes. In a society marked by around-the-clock connectivity, the popular culture industry has concurrently moved from its roots as emerging from the masses to a genuine people's culture that represents—as well as produces—what audiences and consumers hold most treasured. The Internet and unlimited access via handheld devices make this an era of hyper-popular culture, in which people not only expect but demand continual entrée to mass communications. As Elizabeth Currid-Halkett explains, "It's not that Brad Pitt isn't talented. He is, of course, one of the most highly regarded film stars of his generation. But we are far less interested in any talent he possesses compared to our obsession with him as a person."[6] What people demand is a celebrity North Star to orient their cultural and personal lives around, and in turn, hyper-popular culture reproduces these expectations and guarantees their delivery in megastars such as Pitt who serve as cultural touchstones that enable people to make sense of their worlds. Examining the public's hopes and aspirations as they relate to celebrity culture, Karen Sternheimer argues, "Rather than simply superficial distractions, celebrity and fame are unique manifestations of our sense of American social mobility: they provide the illusion that material wealth is possible for anyone."[7] Here we see how the heroic narrative and entertainment capitalism are melded and then served back to people as they create their worldviews. The resulting emotional tie audiences create (and crave) from iconic figures is captured by Barbara O'Dair's description of Pitt as "the closest thing we've got to a storybook hero: he of the solid stock, killer smile, quiet ambition [. . .] rebel with a homebody heart, a tantalizing meld of devil and angel, an altar boy in a ripped T-shirt, with a wicked grin."[8]

Take four: Authenticity

In prior attempts to dissect Pitt's life and career, one aspect that has been overlooked is the skill set he acquired studying the media and advertising at the University of Missouri. One does not have to read through interviews from Pitt's early days to understand that the lessons he learned at Missouri stuck with him as he marched toward Hollywood stardom.[9] What is difficult to ascertain is how much of the image-making and reputation-building in these early clippings resulted from the tried-and-true template used by entertainment reporters and magazine writers and what percentage derived from Pitt understanding how to stay on message and build his burgeoning brand. In other words, how much credit does Brad Pitt deserve for developing Brand Pitt?

Consistent themes extend across Pitt's early interactions with the media. Most prevalent are the young actor's rags-to-riches story and countless quotes, anecdotes, and examples of how he is more than just a pretty face.[10] As a result, reporters tended to paint Pitt as a normal guy, emphasizing his charm and ruggedness. For example, in a 1995 profile in *People* magazine, Pam Lambert and Tom Cunneff noted how the young actor "likes to downplay his looks, often sporting a grunged-out wardrobe and hiding beneath a knitted cap."[11] It is as if Pitt's determination not to be labeled based on his looks demanded that readers comply and identify him as an exceptionally unexceptional person/actor who stands for authenticity in an otherwise plastic world.

Undoubtedly, the public's early stockpile of positivity for Pitt, echoed and cemented over and over again across mass media channels, enabled him to avert crises when his high-profile relationships with actresses went south. As his star rose, a cavalcade of women added to the glare without damaging his reputation (and in some cases adding to his legend), ranging from playing house with the then-teenage Juliette Lewis to a reported on-set romp with Geena Davis. Later, the list would include Gwyneth Paltrow and Jennifer Aniston, both rising stars, and then most publicly with the rumors of infidelity while filming *Mr. & Mrs. Smith* (2005). Throughout this series of high-profile relationships, Pitt has maintained his standing with audiences and observers, transitioning from a devilish heartthrob to an upright partner and father.

While it may seem that Pitt easily maneuvers his marketing ship amid a fickle public sea, the keel of celebrity marketing is relatively hidden and precisely engineered. As the film scholar Mark Browning declared about Clooney, "Modern stardom is a branding exercise."[12] Certainly the maxim may be applied to Pitt as well, but one wonders at what point does the star realize this and respond accordingly. Do we believe the "aw shucks" media portrayal of a young Pitt or Clooney when we simultaneously realize that actors are paid to play roles and backed by an industry that demands that stars appear just like us, not anointed gods and goddesses? In contemporary culture, the constant (if primarily virtual) exchange between stars and fans is viewed as a necessary aspect of celebrity. Modern consumers usually realize that they are being sold products. The public not only lives this notion daily but also experiences it via sounds (actor's voices and voiceovers), smells (perfume lines built around celebrities), and feeling (clothing endorsements and commercials). Browning points to the overt role of marketing, explaining that it is all contrived within "an age of media agents, PR consultants, and complex and sophisticated media campaigns, leaked stories, and off-the-record comments . . . stories that swirl around stars are part of a carefully managed 24-hour media discourse."[13] At the center of the exchange resides the star and his or her fans, yet those on the periphery are there as part of the capitalist infrastructure. The monetary stakes are enormous, whether it is the funding for a film or the ad campaign for a product line.

The public even forgives Pitt's slip-ups (there have not been many), which demonstrates how the reputation-building work and feelings of authenticity that resulted early in his career continue to pay dividends. For instance, Pitt had to draw on this reserve in late 2012 after his now-infamous Chanel No. 5 commercial aired. Although he faced widespread criticism and left many viewers shaking their heads in disbelief, the Chanel ad in no way marred Pitt's image. In the ad, Pitt stood off-center, hands in his pockets, halfway between radiance and shadow as the light moves behind him. Sporting shoulder length hair and a smartly trimmed goatee, he looks directly into the camera and murmurs in a low voice: "It's not a journey. / Every journey ends, but we go on . . . / . . . Chanel No. 5 / Inevitable." A bottle of the perfume is then superimposed over a shot of the earth at night, dots of glimmering humanity and sunlight bouncing off the northern horizon. The product is only shown for a moment. Then, in a tight close-up, the actor delivers the final line, his brow furrowed, suggesting intensity and thoughtfulness. Whether using Pitt to sell a female product worked or not is beside the point. What matters again is how Pitt was deployed to stand for a kind of zero level of authenticity. The YouTube version of the ad attracted some 7.8 million views through early 2013 and thousands of articles talked about the work. Pitt recites his lines with a straight face, and a *Saturday Night Live* skit spoofed the earnestness of the ad (as did countless people on the Web). More than 12,000 spoofs representing countless views ensured that people were talking about (and laughing at) the Pitt Chanel ad long after it initially aired on television.

One imagines that Chanel and Pitt meant the commercial to be taken seriously. It was precisely the serious comportment of Pitt that drew the most laughs and criticism. And yet, the joke would seem to be on those who mocked him: the viral spread of the ad and its spoofs served precisely to spread the image of Pitt yoked to the brand of Chanel. The authenticity here emerged in Pitt's ability to spread virally: contemporary advertising takes such mechanisms seriously. In other words, even the spoofs kept both Pitt and the perfume on people's minds, which was the exact intent of the ad. It is almost post-postmodern in the way this incident went past irony to a different (perhaps darker) form of sincerity and authenticity. The Chanel commercial was brazen about the fact that Pitt was selling a product that has absolutely no relation to the seller. Pitt's association with authenticity functioned crucially here, precisely by serving as something as-if serious to then parody.

Conclusion

Early Brad Pitt emerged from the Mid-West, like a modern-day Jay Gatsby, with an undeniable feeling that his life would contain something more. After years of hard work and struggle, he finally breaks through to become a superstar, and suddenly millions of people have seen him and want to know more. If the story had not actually happened, it would take Hollywood to create it. Karen Sternheimer wisely encapsulates the idea, saying, "Celebrities seem to provide proof that the American Dream of going from rags to riches is real and attainable."[14] But there is more to Pitt's rise to glory than merely capitalizing on the Horatio Alger-notion of the American Dream. The young actor used his understanding of media and advertising to create an image for himself based on authenticity and everydayness. Whoever Pitt would become as he moved into the glare of the celebrity spotlight, his charm and Midwestern values seemed real—or at least did real publicity work—to those around him.[15]

Returning to the epigraphs that begin this exploration of Pitt, one cannot help but note how the young actor defied the labels that many people placed on him—sexy, heartthrob, and the next big thing—a risky move that could have derailed his career. Yet he emerged as a heroic figure in a broader culture that demands such larger-than-life, yet lifelike, characters. Pitt's career trajectory is unique among his era of iconic megastars based on how he carefully blended his professional and real life personas. As a result, audiences find Pitt beautiful and likeable at the same time, believing that he exudes authenticity in a world lacking it. Pushing past the "hunk" label and its initial limitations, Pitt grew first into a major film actor and then into a megastar beyond the medium of film— yet he also reaches constantly back down to a perhaps paradoxical ground level of authenticity which he sustains, and which sustains Pitt, and his audience's belief in him, in turn.

Notes

1 Thomas J. Mickey, *Sociodrama: An Interpretive Theory for the Practice of Public Relations* (Lanham, MD: University Press of America, 1995), 9.

2 Chris Rojek, *Celebrity* (London: Reaktion Books, 2001), 10.

3 Chris Mundy, "Brad Pitt," *Rolling Stone*, December 1, 1994. http://www.bradpittpress.com/artint_94_rollingstone.php [Accessed October 1, 2012].

4 Quoted in Chris Mundy, "Brad Pitt," *Rolling Stone*, December 1, 1994.

5 Ray B. Browne, "Popular Culture as the New Humanities," in *Popular Culture Theory and Methodology: A Basic Introduction*, eds. Harold E. Hinds, Jr., Marilyn F. Motz, and Angela M. S. Nelson (Madison, WI: University of Wisconsin Press, 2006), 75.

6 Elizabeth Currid-Halkett, *Starstruck: The Business of Celebrity* (New York: Faber and Faber, 2010), 31.

7 Karen Sternheimer, *Celebrity Culture and the American Dream: Stardom and Social Mobility* (New York: Routledge, 2011), xiii.

8 Barbara O'Dair, "Preface," in *Brad Pitt*, ed. Holly George-Warren (New York: Little Brown, 1997), 6.

9 For examples of Pitt's media savvy, see his interactions with reporters in Tom Green, "Unpretentious Brad Pitt," *USA Today*, October 22, 1992; Catherine Dunphy, "Ozark Lad Goes Fishin' with Redford," *Toronto Star*, October 9, 1992; and Chris Mundy, "Brad Pitt," *Rolling Stone*, December 1, 1994.

10 The themes used to examine Pitt appear in hundreds of articles, represented by Green, Dunphy, Mundy, and Lisa Anderson, "No Pit Stops for Brad." *Toronto Star*, published August 31, 1992.

11 Pam Lambert and Tom Cunneff, "A Legend to Fall For," *People*, January 30, 1995, Academic Search Complete, EBSCOhost http://www.people.com/people/archieve/article/0..z0104953.00. html [Accessed January 24, 2013].

12 Mark Browning, *George Clooney: An Actor Looking for a Role* (Westport, CT: ABC-CLIO, 2012), xi.

13 Mark Browning, *George Clooney: An Actor Looking for a Role* (Westport, CT: ABC-CLIO, 2012), xi.

14 Karen Sternheimer, *Celebrity Culture and the American Dream: Stardom and Social Mobility* (New York: Routledge, 2011), xiv.

15 Celebrity biographer Andrew Morton outlines the early stages of the Jolie–Pitt relationship and declares some aspects of Pitt's actions "a subtle public-relations operation" to come out of the break-up with Aniston without damaging his own reputation. See Andrew Morton, *Angelina: An Unauthorized Biography* (New York: St. Martin's Press, 2010), 237–50.

CHAPTER ELEVEN

A Star Is Born

Andrew Horton

In 2012, Angelina Jolie released her film, *In The Land of Blood and Honey*, which deals with the bloody Bosnian wars of the 1990s. In numerous interviews when the film opened, Brad Pitt stood alongside Jolie, smiling and commenting that in many ways his own career as a lead actor started in the former Yugoslavia. It was there that he starred in *The Dark Side of the Sun* (1988), a film shot in Montenegro before the Yugoslav wars. Moreover, Pitt added that coming to Yugoslavia to make this film "was my second time on a plane. It was my first time out of the country. I had to get a passport. It was a great, great time for me. We started in Belgrade and shot mainly in Montenegro."[1] At age 25, Pitt was clearly enjoying both getting outside his "box" (the United States) and experiencing a foreign culture while also growing as an actor to play a lead character in a feature film. Consequently, three years before his role as J.D. in *Thelma & Louise* (1991), Pitt was learning about acting and filmmaking, and about living in a culture beyond the United States—and these experiences would prove formative in his future pursuits as an actor, a celebrity, and beyond. Having myself played a key role both in helping cast Pitt for this film and in revising the film's screenplay, my account offers various behind the scenes insights into the early origins of Pitt's stardom.

Casting Pitt

How did Brad Pitt become the lead actor in an independent feature, with Chicago based producers, shot in Yugoslavia? The producers of *The Dark Side of the Sun* in 1988 were aware that besides having worked and taught in Yugoslavia and Greece, I was actively involved both as a screenwriter and as a film scholar. In completing my book on the director George Roy Hill—whose films include *Butch Cassidy and the Sundance Kid* (1969), *The Sting* (1973), and many other popular films—I got to interview and know quite well Hill's casting director at Warner Brothers, Marion Dougherty. Dougherty was *the* star of her profession and was well known for helping give so many stars their first real breaks, including "James Dean, Al Pacino, Dustin Hoffman and Warren Beatty, and who suggested Carroll O'Connor for the role of Archie Bunker in the long-running hit television show *All in the Family*."[2]

Angelo Arandjelovic, producer of *The Dark Side of the Sun*, asked if I would help rewrite the original script and help find actors to play the main American roles: the main character, Rick; his father; and Frances, the young American whom Rick falls in love with. Agreeing to help, I got in touch with Dougherty who was busy on several films but helped connect us with a younger casting director, Gail Levin. Levin came up with a variety of actors, and Arandjelovic and Bozidar Nikolic, the director, eventually chose Cheryl Pollak, who had done some TV series such as *21 Jump Street* and several films including *My Best Friend Is a Vampire* (1987), to play Frances; they chose Guy Boyd—whose credits included the TV shows *The Twilight Zone, Miami Vice*, and *Moonlighting* as well as movies such as *No Man's Land* (1987)—to play Rick's father.

Then it was time to cast Rick. A variety of young actors were introduced to Arandjelovic and Nikolic, including River Phoenix and Brad Pitt. Phoenix, ironically, was the candidate with the most credits to his name, having done numerous TV appearances and films such as *Stand By Me* (1986) and *The Mosquito Coast* (1987). Pitt, in contrast, only had "un-credited" roles in several films and a few TV appearances, including some *Dallas* episodes. According to Angelo, however, Pitt was particularly friendly; when the two met for coffee later after the official meeting, Pitt expressed how strongly he wanted the role and the chance to work overseas. And so it was Pitt who was chosen because he most deeply impressed them. Apparently when Pitt got the word, he was so happy that he left the office doing somersaults down the sidewalk!

The success of casting all three can be seen in the performances themselves. Cheryl Pollak is lively and talented in her role playing an actress, and she performs the emotions of being caught in a struggle with the unsympathetic guys in her acting group and her growing passion for Rick. Guy Boyd also expresses a range of emotions well in scenes including a fistfight with the actors who beat up Rick, and pleading to Rick to stay literally "under cover," lest he die.[3] Then there is Brad Pitt as Rick! Words cannot adequately describe this performance—you must see it to believe it.

Reviewers constantly speak of Pitt as not just an actor, but as a personality and star as well. For example, the *New York Times* critic Dennis Lim captures how the spirit of the young Pitt whom we see in *The Dark Side of the Sun* has extended throughout his entire career:

If there is one facet of Brad Pitt that could be considered somewhat obscure, it may be—oddly enough—his acting career. For much of his two decades in the spotlight . . . Mr. Pitt has been a star first and an actor second. His every move . . . often with a hard-to-miss entourage that includes Angelina Jolie, and their six children—provides endless fodder for the celebrity media. But the Brad Pitt on screen remains surprisingly elusive.[4]

Of course, Pitt was not yet a star when making *The Dark Side of the Sun*, but what comes through so clearly to most viewers seeing the film for the first time is that Pitt appears to be fully having fun on camera, convincing us that he really is a young American falling in love in a foreign country with a beautiful landscape behind him. As Marjorie Johns explains,

> [The] joyful fatalism with which Rick approaches his certain doom is liberating and there are worse films being made every day by big studios, never mind by impoverished fringe nations like the former Yugoslavian states. And it has a proper movie ending as Rick rides to his death, quite literally, into the sunset.[5]

A fair commentary indeed, for Johns gets at the darkly triumphant non-Hollywood happy ending that was always central to this unusual dark romance.

Revising the script

FADE IN on a close up of a dark motorcycle helmet reflecting bright sunlight as a young man's voiceover says, "I want to live," pauses briefly, and then shouts in a tearful voice, "I WANT TO LIVE!"[6] And then follows the line, "Sometimes I wish I had never been born."[7] The film's title, *The Dark Side of the Sun*, appears as the image zooms along a beautiful seacoast highway with a cut to the motorcyclist in close-up but with no view of the face within the helmet. Suddenly, the masked driver comes to a screeching halt and walks over to a mother dog that has been run over, with a suckling puppy clinging to her. The cyclist picks up the little pup, holds it up close, and then puts it safely within his leather jacket as he resumes his ride. Soon a dozen roaring motorcycles with rough-looking riders zoom past him. The masked rider is Pitt playing Rick, a young American on a special journey on the Montenegro coast of what is now the former Yugoslavia. And the completed script was my assignment at the time in 1988.

My early scripts that were made into films happened to have been shot in the former Yugoslavia. Thus when Angelo Arandjelovic, who formed the Abj Chicago Film Company, got in touch with me in 1988, he said he had seen and enjoyed the 1983 award-winning Yugoslav feature film, *Something In Between*, which I had co-written with the film's director, Srdjan Karanovic. Arandjelovic explained that he was a friend of Bozidar Nikolic, an award-winning cinematographer whom I had met and whose films I admired greatly, and that Nikolic had come up with the first draft of a script, *The Dark Side of the Sun*, they wished to produce. Arandjelovic then explained he and Nikolic felt the script needed revision before shooting and asked if I would be willing to do a rewrite. I was interested because I appreciated the variety of fine films Nikolic had worked on, including *Who Is Singing Over There?* (1980), *Balkan Spy* (1984), and *A Film With No Name* (1988). I read a rough draft of the script, and knowing that Nikolic would direct and do the cinematography, I agreed to take on the project. I also agreed to help them when it came time to cast the American characters, since I had Hollywood contacts.

The script's story? Start with the genre that we would have to call a family drama and coming-of-age romantic drama. The narrative of the original story concerned a young twenty-something American, Rick, who has a rare skin disease that requires him to be completely covered and masked; even brief exposure to sunlight for a few days could lead to his death. Pitt's Rick, then, is entirely clad in a black leather full-body (including head) suit, so as to protect his frail flesh. Let us be very clear, here: in other words, *for much of the film the actual visage of Pitt is not seen!*

As we open the story, Rick has been living on the coast of Montenegro for two years. His wealthy businessman father is committed to finding a cure for his son, and all efforts with medical science have failed we learn early on—and so Rick's past two years have been spent seeing a local "natural faith healer" who supposedly has his own powers to accomplish miracles. Add to this scenario Rick's mother, who is also with them but is in a nearly catatonic state of illness herself; she spends all day in bed or wheelchair and unable to speak or otherwise communicate.

Cut to an international theater competition in the harbor town, Budva, that is attended by a young American traveling theater group whose lead actress, Frances, captures Rick's heart when he happens to see their performance one evening. As Rick gets to know Frances—in his masked outfit, of course—Frances becomes attracted to this new masked friend even though she can't exactly "see" him. This situation leads Rick to decide to remove his mask, knowing the oncoming fatal results but believing that a few days of real life and love are worth more than a lifetime in the dark. And so Rick removes his mask and dives into real life—while no one whom he's known for those two years recognizes who he is until he tells them. This goes for Frances, too, as Rick (Rick qua *Pitt*!) strikes up a friendship with her, not revealing that he is in fact the masked rider—and thus playing a double game of getting to know her as just another American abroad.

When Frances learns that Rick is a "friend" of the masked man, she makes it clear that she wants to meet him again—so Rick reappears in his mask, saying his other friend told him to come, and scenes play out with the couple falling in love . . . and finally spending the night together. At this point Rick's skin is blistering and deteriorating, leading towards his inevitable end, and thus he finally makes the decision to ride his motorcycle to his own death just at the moment that Frances discovers that her masked lover is Rick. But Frances is too late to stop him: Rick cycles off to his own ending having at least experienced a few brief days of real life, and love.

The challenge for me as screenwriter was to rewrite this tale with a non-Hollywood, dark ending.[8] There was also a particular challenge in this script, given that the audience can't see and thus identify easily with Rick until some 40 minutes into the film—he is masked, despite the "real voice" that we hear (and, at least at this point, that we know so well) in dialogue and voice-over. One of my additions was to start the film with seeing Rick stop to save a young puppy, so that we get his caring side immediately.

In addition, my rewrite needed to revise the familiar "fish out of water" story-form, as these young Americans are falling in love in a foreign environment and culture. My work on *Something In Between* had explored a similar narrative, following an American young woman who falls in love with two Yugoslav men who happen to be best friends. Thus, everything and everyone in the script is "something in between," including in between Europe and America, communism and capitalism, the Balkans and Europe, romance and tragedy, war and peace, comedy and drama, and the list goes on. With *The Dark Side of the Sun*, I also tried to bring out both more comedy and romance and sharper drama and cultural conflicts between Yugoslavs and Americans than were present in the original script, drawing frequently from my background of having lived, worked, taught, and traveled in Greece and Yugoslavia for over twenty years at that point during the 1960s and 1970s.

Finally, I also did my best in the rewrite to further develop the father/son relationship. Rick's conflicts are clear. What kind of a life has he had, completely covered up day and night? Should he decide to "live" for a few days, and not spend his lifetime in the dark? But I also wrote in more of the father and the agony that he has been going through dedicating his life to trying to heal his son while at the same time caring for a wife who has become an invalid herself. This helped focus the narrative more clearly on Rick's double conflict of being caught between the love that he knows that his father has given him, and the new love that he feels for (and from) Frances.

On the set

As we have noted, Pitt said that the making of *The Dark Side of the Sun* was "a great, great time for me"—even though it was an "un-Hollywood" film produced on a total budget of around $650,000, rather than the millions that Hollywood films require.[9] We should further emphasize that although it was technically a Chicago-based production, many of those involved in terms of crew and actors were Yugoslavs.

So what did Pitt enjoy about making this film? Start with the stunning landscape of the coast of Montenegro. The sea, the fine beaches, the surrounding mountains, the lovely small coastal island village of Sveti Stephan, and the main coastal towns of Kotor and Budva—together these add up to something of a paradise of a location, and one can imagine the first-time-abroad Pitt taking in this setting. Pitt also seemed to enjoy playing his role as Rick. Director Bozidar Nikolic smiled when he related what happened as they shot the beach scene in which Rick takes off his mask and protective suit and celebrates his new freedom by jumping into the sea with joy for the first time in his life. In the film, we see Pitt's lively pleasure as he splashes like a happy child—but there is also a surprise, for a small dolphin swims right up to Pitt, and he laughs and actually starts playing around with the dolphin. *This was not in the script!* And when the dolphin at one point hit Pitt, they stopped the shot and Nikolic discussed the situation with the actor, explaining that dolphins are very much a part of that bay and they could reshoot the scene after waiting for the dolphins to pass. But Pitt made it clear that he was up for going back out into the sea with them! The result is such a satisfying and enjoyable scene—again, uncontrived—that it conveys how Rick has opened up his life to a sort of unbridled, youthful freedom. Once more, this is Pitt as both an actor and as a real young fellow from Shawnee, Oklahoma, having a hell of a good time.

Arandjelovic also speaks of how easy-going yet totally professional Pitt was on the set, "For he always showed up on time when many of the crew and cast were often late and there was nothing he was asked to do that he did not do eagerly."[10] He did not even complain during hard moments such as having to keep chemicals on his face longer than was safe to do so since the filming crew was often running late for a shot. "I was very impressed with Brad," comments Arandjelovic, "because he was so responsible that it was just hard to believe and he was clearly having fun too."[11]

I offer one final indication of how important this first starring role and its foreign context were for Pitt. Very simply, here are the opening and closing lines from a poem that Pitt wrote for his director, or "Bota," as Bozidar is called:

> Follow the brilliant man
> above men and make-believe . . .

> And I shall be brilliant
> Just like him.

> Thank you, Bozidar, for such an incredible experience!
> —Brad Pitt, Yugoslavia, 1989

While these may strike readers as fairly simple lines, they are worth considering as representative of the scope of Pitt's aspirations. The poem is a note of thanks, but also a wish to be not just a star, but brilliant "above men and make-believe." The closing couplet says everything, really, given the career that Pitt has had since the late 1980s and the friendship between Brad and Bozidar, which was renewed in 2011 when Pitt came full circle returning to the former Yugoslavia with Jolie as she worked on *In The Land of Blood and Honey*. Brad and Bozidar continue to stay in touch, and have even considered the possibility of working together again in the future (Figure 11.1). For Pitt, his first leading role in *The Dark Side of the Sun* was no mere stepping-stone, but rather pays tribute to the long arc of his career, showing how a star was born.

FIGURE 11.1 *Photo of Andrew Horton, Bozidar Nikolic, and Brad Pitt on the set of* The Dark Side of the Sun *(Reproduced by permission of Andrew Horton.)*

Notes

1   Jeff Giles, "Brad Pitt: The E.W. Interview," *Entertainment Weekly* (September 23, 2011), 42.

2   Dennis Hevesi, "Marion Dougherty, Hollywood Star-Maker, Dies at 88," *The New York Times* (December 7, 2011).

3   *The Dark Side of the Sun*, directed by Bozidar Nikolic (Fox, 1988).

4   Dennis Lim, "Don't Forget, He Acts Too," *New York Times*, December 30, 2011, www.nytimes.com/2012/01/01/movies/ awardsseason/brad-pitt-discusses-moneyball-and-tree-of-life [Accessed January 10, 201].

5   Marjorie Johns, "Dark Side of the Sun," *Movie Archive Reviews* http://www.citizencaine.org/movies/50filmchallenge/dark-side- of-the-sun.shtml [Accessed January 11, 2014].

6   *The Dark Side of the Sun*, directed by Bozidar Nikolic (Fox, 1988).

7   *The Dark Side of the Sun*, directed by Bozidar Nikolic (Fox, 1988).

8   What I worked to do was to open up the characters and develop them more, an approach that I have always followed in screenwriting and script teaching as expressed my book *Writing the Character Centered Screenplay*.

9   Jeff Giles, "Brad Pitt: The E.W. Interview," *Entertainment Weekly* (September 23, 2011), 42.

10 I wish to thank Bozidar and Masha Nikolic and Angelo Arandjelovic for personal email and phone interviews during 2012 while writing this chapter.

11 See note 10.

CHAPTER TWELVE

Brad Pitt for Mayor

Thomas M. Bayer

The campaign

New Orleans will elect a new mayor on April 22, 2010, and the Brad Pitt for Mayor Campaign Steering Committee is asking you to vote for Brad Pitt. After extensive polling, focus group discussions and soul searching, the steering committee, headed by Tulane University's Dr. Thomas M. Bayer, has decided upon thirteen reasons why the Crescent City would be best served with Brad Pitt as Mayor.[1]

Reason #1—He's Qualified
Rather than having to make vague and unpersuasive connections between clearly unrelated qualifications such as, say, franchise executive and governing abilities, the qualifications of our candidate are plainly obvious: as the worldwide audience of Homer's *Troy* can attest, Mr. Brad Pitt clearly has the stomach for the job, not to mention the shoulders to carry the burden of governance.
Reason #2—NOLA ♥'s Brad Pitt
By bestowing the great office of Mayor of our city upon Mr. Pitt, we, the citizens, are afforded the opportunity to say

thanks for the many wonderful things this gentleman has already done for us. What better way to show our heartfelt appreciation than to present to him the mayoral office, the patronage trough, the cornucopia of our great city, that which we hold so dear and is ours to bequeath?

Reason #3—Lagniappe

If we elect Brad Pitt mayor, Angelina Jolie would be the First Lady of New Orleans.

Reason #4—Technology and Gastronomy

Instead of technology executives vying for malfunctioning anti-crime camera installation contracts and lap dances, movie moguls from everywhere will lobby the mayor to get a table on Galatoire's ground floor for the Friday before Mardi Gras all-afternoon lunch.

Reason #5—Publicity

Publicity and photo opportunities will chase our Mayor, instead of the Mayor chasing publicity and photo opportunities.

Reason #6—Urban Planning

We will not have to rename a street to honor his name, as Pitt Street already exists.

Reason #7—City Council Relations

Stacy Head will be nice to the new Mayor.

Reason #8—Economics

Instead of executive travel expenses depleting our budget, the city's coffers will be filled through generous personal appearance fees earned by Mr. Pitt as our elected leader and ambassador.

Reason #9—Convention Business

New Orleans will become the magnet for conventions of professional women's organizations worldwide. The warm glow of pink Cadillacs will illuminate our Southern nights. This mass of sensually charged femininity will attract male visitors eager to contribute their economic stimulus.

Reason #10—Jazz Fest

Instead of being greeted by the ubiquitous presence of Shell (God bless them!), visitors to Jazz Fest will be welcomed at the main entrance by our Mayor enthroned on the King of Rex Float, officiated by his Secretary of Music, Quint Davis.

Reason #11—Rebuilding

Rather than relying on Aussie eloquence and narrative creativity or malfunctioning federal and state agencies, Mr. Pitt, as our chief executive will, instead, lead us, the local Pittwomen and Pittmen, in the fight against blight, crime, poverty, and lack of humor. Dressed in period costumes and assisted by experienced producers, set builders, make-up artists, and camera operators, this cast of thousands will launch our Renaissance epic in weekly reality sequels.

Reason #12—Transparency

Instead of having to sue for the release of public records, or to attempt to restore accidentally deleted emails, we can learn everything about our first executive from the pages of the *National Enquirer* and *People Magazine*.

Reason #13—Integrity

Rather than governing our city to achieve fortune, fame and a book deal, our candidate already has achieved fortune, fame and MOVIE deals.

The following is a personal account of events that spiraled into a national and international, media-fueled phenomenon ignited by the "Brad Pitt for Mayor" of New Orleans campaign.

The background

During the winter of 2009, four years after the catastrophic Hurricane Katrina, the dissatisfaction of the population of New Orleans with the incompetence and callousness of the government of the current mayor, C. Ray Nagin, had reached a new level of frustration. Cronyism, contentiousness, waste, corruption and a shameless, undisguised lack of care for a city that had faced near annihilation just four years earlier were the hallmarks of his administration. New Orleans had lost nearly 80 percent of its residential housing when the shoddily constructed federal levies failed to contain the floodwaters caused by Hurricane Katrina, and the city's population had been uprooted and cast across the entire United States. The disruption to the social fabric and unique character of the city is impossible to fathom for outsiders: neighborhoods shaped by generations of the same families living in close proximity and relying on each other were violently swept away. Death, decay, and unimaginable stink replaced parks, playgrounds, schools, neighborhood businesses, churches, and homes. Also destroyed was the community-based social safety net that had been so vital to the survival of the city's poor.

Yet, running parallel to the mayor's useless and often incoherent actions and his utterly inept recovery "czar", Ed Blakely, were highly effective private initiatives without which the city's struggle to rebuild would have been infinitely harder. One of the most visible of these endeavors was the Make It Right Foundation created by Brad Pitt. Apparently, after reading Michael Braungart and William McDonough's *Cradle to Cradle: Remaking the Way We Make Things*, Pitt became intensely interested in sustainable, "green" architecture and its associated life philosophy. He also had developed a bit of a crush on New Orleans—easy to understand for those of us who call this magical and exotic place our home. After reading and hearing of the catastrophic destruction the city had suffered, he decided to buy a home here and start a foundation with the specific mandate to construct environmentally sound houses in one of the most devastated neighborhoods of New Orleans, the city's Lower Ninth Ward.

The inception

In February 2009, at the Crescent City Brewhouse, during one of the weekly afternoon socials of a loosely organized group of long-time friends, the conversation had turned to the upcoming mayoral election. The usual heterogeneity of the gathering, encompassing, among others, a member of the Jackson Square artist colony, a prominent retired federal prosecutor, a brew master and several academics from Tulane University, engendered a spirited debate. Numerous names were brought up as viable candidates, passionately promoted by some and equally passionately discarded by others. None seemed to have the merits to justify her or his election to this all important office. None had demonstrated the level of commitment to our beloved city, which we deemed necessary to earn our undivided support. I suggested that, perhaps, we needed to expand our search beyond the familiar names, and, as an example, mentioned Brad Pitt. At the time, no one, including myself, took this suggestion seriously, but instead we considered it merely as a model for the kind of broader thinking that we needed to employ. In fact, Constantine Georges, the former prosecutor, informed us that Mr. Pitt, unfortunately, did not meet the five-year residency requirement for candidacy.

Later that evening, however, when I recounted the discussion to my partner and academic colleague, Laura Kelley, a Brad Pitt candidacy began to take on increasing appeal. Certainly, as Laura pointed out, he would win the female vote hands down. Encouraged by this astute observation, I set aside candidacy requirements for the time being and ordered ten t-shirts from an internet company with the logo "Brad Pitt for Mayor" prominently printed on the front. Five were blue, the remainders red. Two were for us, and the rest for eight yet to be hand-picked friends with the mandate to wear them for as many public occasions as possible.

Our first opportunity was the Mardi Gras Marathon on February 25, 2009. Before the race started, while we maneuvered through the crowd to get to our starting position, we were greeted with enthusiastic cheers. When quizzed by out-of-town runners, unfamiliar with Brad Pitt's local involvement, we would bring them up to speed regarding the "campaign." Locals, overhearing us and, as usual, quick on the uptake, would chime in and offer their own input. Everyone, it seemed, was enjoying the idea. During the race, friends and other spectators along the course, support personnel, and participants also retorted with wit and tongue-in-cheek support. In fact, one of the 13 Reasons Why Brad Pitt Should Be Our Next Mayor was inspired by a woman's knowing comment that Brad surely had the "stomach for the job and the shoulders to carry the burdens of governance."

We wore the t-shirts on numerous other occasions during the Carnival season. Since New Orleans is actually quite small, we managed to achieve a certain recognition factor. However, it became evident that the idea was not growing legs quite yet. New Orleanians love to dress up, costume, or dress funky at any opportunity, and a couple people wearing a t-shirt displaying a home-made "Brad Pitt for Mayor" logo was amusing, but clearly not enough. Beyond the small original group, no one else had joined the campaign. We had also not tried that hard, hoping, instead, for a more organic development.

The breakthrough came on May 2, 2009, the second Saturday of New Orleans annual Jazz Fest. Before going to the festival, we meandered down Magazine Street together with a visiting friend, Zoe Panarites, a former neighbor who was now a city attorney in Palm Beach, Florida. The three of us wore "campaign" shirts to try to get some attention later on at the Fest. While we were inspecting the window display of a local t-shirt shop called Storyville, the proprietor, Josh Harvey, came out to compliment us on our shirts and asked if he could get my permission to use the idea for a t-shirt to sell in his shop. Since occasionally people had asked where they could buy our shirts, I was thrilled by the opportunity to be able to point them to a source. Josh offered me a percentage of sales for the use of the idea, but, instead, we decided that 10 percent of gross sales would go to Brad Pitt's Make It Right foundation.

Consequently, that afternoon at Jazz Fest, we were able, for the first time, to direct people to where they could buy campaign tees. Josh Harvey's talented sister and chief designer significantly improved our rather homespun design, and within a week the shirts were available at Storyville (Figure 12.1).

From this point forward, events took on their own somewhat surreal momentum. Jason Sanchez, a local financial advisor and regular member of our Friday social, mentioned our "campaign" to one of his clients, Tina Dirmann, a freelance journalist from Los Angeles. Tina contacted me, loved the story, and decided to try to place it. I thought at the time that her enthusiasm should not be curbed by such details as qualifying criteria and did not mention the topic.

Interestingly, the US print media was not interested at first, but Tina was able to place the story in the London daily, *The Mirror*.[2]

And with that the "campaign" soon went viral: within less than 2 weeks, nearly one and a half million internet/media sites had latched onto the story, and, finally, the US media

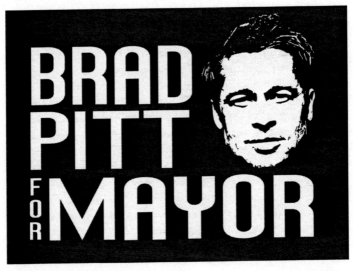

FIGURE 12.1 *"Brad Pitt for Mayor"* © *Storyville New Orleans (Reproduced by permission.)*

also jumped on board. From this point on, if I wanted a quiet moment, I had to turn off my landline or go to a neighborhood bar. Journalists from untold different countries, looking for an inside scoop, would call to bombard me with pointed questions concerning the mayoral campaign and our platform. International time differences or a fellow human's need for sleep were irrelevant to their noble search for truth. Claims of personal interviews that had never taken place came from as far away as the Indian subcontinent. A number of remarkably zealous journalists had even managed to convince their editors that a personal trip to New Orleans was essential to interview the chief protagonist of the campaign and cover this story properly. I remember one particular afternoon, when Josh Harvey and I gave two separate interviews to two reporters working for two competing newspapers from Spain, Mercedes Gallo of *El Correo* and Carlos Fresneda from *El Mundo*.

I am indebted to the TV series *West Wing*. Effortlessly propelled by events and seemingly overnight, I became the quasi spokesperson of what had already been described by the media as a grassroots movement. My standard and often repeated stump speech emphasized Brad Pitt's outstanding personal efforts, trumping those of any of the other candidates, towards the improvement of our city; the chance for New Orleans to become under his leadership a center for green industry and a model for environmentally sustainable living; the huge advantages his administration would yield to our nascent movie business and our general ranking as a convention and tourist destination; and similar obvious benefits, all soundly reasoned. Years of lecturing for hours without notes yielded their benefit. I made a point of including comments taken from the obviously humorous list of 13 reasons that I had composed for Josh Harvey to be used on the website of his store. Those caused varying degrees of amusement, but they made little impact on journalists' ardent faith in the existence of a rapidly growing grassroots movement committed, for all the right reasons, to install Brad Pitt as the mayor of New

Orleans. The story was so good that it should be true. The linkage of noble cause, celebrity sex symbol, and exotic locale was irresistible. Wishful assumptions became facts, and not once was any part of our campaign rhetoric questioned. It was fascinating to observe objectivity set aside in favor of make-believe. Many of the journalists were involved, as I am, in green causes, however we may define these. We all recognized, and still do, that Brad Pitt was, indeed, in the ideal position to direct the spotlight of public attention onto New Orleans as well as promote dialogue on green architecture and associated issues on an international level. I suppose in the minds of many, the New Orleans mayoral campaign was merely the journalistic hook to which a green agenda could be attached. It seemed like an unwittingly conceived plot that no one wanted to reveal. Reality mixed with bubbles of make-believe too good to burst. Josh Harvey could not print tees fast enough to meet demand, and the weekly financial contributions his business made to Brad Pitt's Make It Right foundation were growing.

Locally, Chris Rose, one of our prominent columnists for the local newspaper, the *Times Picayune*, conducted a lengthy interview and photo shoot with me dressed in a "Brad Pitt for Mayor" t-shirt. The "campaign," became the lead story for the "Living" section of the paper's Sunday, July 21 edition. Our satirical newspaper, *The Levee*, devoted its entire July 2009 issue to the topic. Finally, the thing—whatever it was—had grown legs that were getting longer by the day.

From my subjective position, I had the general impression that among the local population there was an unquantifiable number that took the campaign in earnest—so it seemed—debating the pros and cons of a Pitt administration. Others, however, commented with tongue firmly in cheek. Regardless of opinion, the sincere appreciation of the tremendous work Brad Pitt was doing for our city was the leading common denominator. A "Brad Pitt for Mayor" website—still active as of this writing—had been set up to facilitate communication with and among the "constituency" (as it were). While occasional critical concerns about the Make It Right project were voiced, there was uniform praise for our leader.

One day, Josh Harvey and I received an invitation from Tom Darden, the Executive Director of Brad Pitt's Make It Right Foundation, to come to the foundation's New Orleans' headquarters on Lee Circle. We were both rather concerned that we were about to face a lawyer presenting us with a "cease and desist" order. After all, we had been using an image of Brad Pitt for ostensibly commercial purposes without any explicit permission to do so. We stepped out of the elevator into the reception area, tense and nervous, and stared down a lengthy hallway covered with countless newspaper clippings of the mayoral "campaign." Greatly relieved, Josh and I rewarded ourselves with a self-congratulatory, discreet high-five. Tom Darden showed us around and introduced the staff. We were clearly among friends. We were congratulated, thanked for our efforts, and praised for our ingenuity and humor. We could not have been more pleased and left feeling like the proverbial "million bucks."

I made occasional attempts to find out what motivated people to buy campaign shirts. An older gentleman pointed out that due to Brad Pitt's personal wealth, he would never become part of our local culture of corruption. What a radical novelty for New Orleans! Personal wealth has never been a deterrent of corruption in our city. A very tall and curvaceous visitor from Canada who had read about the "campaign" informed me that she had always wanted to have Brad Pitt's head between her breasts. Another woman, quite petite but purchasing an XL-size shirt, intended to wear it as a night gown so that she would have Mr. Pitt in her bed. In general, among all age groups, women's replies reflected Brad Pitt's sex appeal. Among the local gay population, Brad Pitt was popular for his support of gay marriage and also his looks. A member of the local film community supported the cause because of the benefits to her industry. Sustainable architecture was often mentioned, as was Brad Pitt's engagement in green causes. "He is such a nice guy!" was also among the more frequent replies.

Brad Pitt's persona had a wide array of different types of attractions from which individual t-shirt buyers could select those with which they chose to identify. There was something there for everyone.

On June 30, I received an email from Michelle Krupa, the political reporter of the *Times Picayune*, informing me that she would like to refer to the Brad Pitt for Mayor campaign in her column this Saturday, though under a bit of a dark cloud. The article would state unequivocally that Mr. Pitt did not meet the city's electability requirements. Michelle asked if I saw this technicality as destroying the campaign? She was also curious if I had a way around the residency requirement, such as a charter change, before next winter's primary. The fact that the paper's editorial staff deemed the topic worthy of commentary by a specialist reporter reconfirmed that, indeed, the campaign was taken seriously on some level. Michelle's explicit concern over the potentially harmful effects of her article to the "campaign" echoed the level of endearment the notion of Mr. Pitt as our next mayor had achieved among the city's population. Judging by the sales of t-shirts—not the most scientific criteria—her column had no measurable effect on the popularity of whatever it meant to an individual to support "Brad Pitt for Mayor." By all indications, "Brad Pitt for Mayor" had become something separate and distinct from the reality of Brad Pitt as the mayor of New Orleans.

The climax of the spectacle was, without doubt, Brad Pitt's comments regarding the mayoral campaign on the *Today Show* on August 13, 2009.[3] With a "campaign" shirt in hand, Ann Curry posed the crucial question: "If chosen, would you run?" "Yeah" Pitt replied, chuckling. "Would you serve?" "Yeah, I'm running on the gay marriage, no religion, legalization and taxation of marijuana platform. I don't have a chance." He was obviously enjoying this entire affair.

He was also wrong. As a newcomer to New Orleans, he evidently did not realize that this platform would have made him, most likely, the leading contender. Or perhaps he did. It certainly endeared him to the hearts of many.

As the city was in the midst of a real mayoral campaign with a number of prominent citizens battling each other for supporters, individual candidates' perceptions of the composition and size of the "Brad Pitt for Mayor" faction resonated in the contest. Concerning constituency size, the figures we mentioned reflected simply the activity on the Facebook page and ever growing t-shirt sales. At its peak, around late August/early September, there were well over 10,000 followers from all parts of the world on the Facebook page, and due to the international publicity, t-shirts were bought not just by locals, but also by visitors from all parts of the U.S. as well as tourists from around the globe. The juxtaposition of thousands of "campaign supporters" who had absolutely no stake in the local mayoral election and the solicitous email from one of the real candidates, obviously aware of the residence restrictions, asking me to convey his utmost sincerity in all matters green to the vast army of Brad Pitt followers brought the complex nature of the events to the fore. On a local level, the press and, by inference, the media-consuming public was, as best as we could judge, still enamored with the story and had an appetite for more. Yet it also became apparent that certain limitations should be imposed. Reality was encroaching on make-believe, and the borderline between the two began to become less distinct. Even the best-intended fun can have serious repercussions. Our city's desperate want for a competent and caring mayor was very real, and our much-tested citizenry needed no distraction from the importance of the upcoming election. We concluded that without someone intentionally adding fuel to the story, it would meet its natural demise.

It was, in fact, the *Today Show* that had effected a change in our perception of events. The dialectic between celebrity of any sort and media requires that they provide for each other. Since it has become quite the custom among today's celebrities to be involved in social causes, such engagements alone no longer suffice to maintain media attention and distinguish one celebrity from another. As a result, to keep the public's interest alive—the determining variable of celebrity status—the media require a constant flow of new and differentiated stories. It is the function of celebrities to provide these, and their status survival depends on their ability to produce such commodities for the media. Brad Pitt's main asset to the Make It Right Foundation is his ability to direct spotlights that shine on him to the foundation and thus promote its cause. His celebrity status and all that comes with it are the coin he brings to the table. Since the start of the Ninth Ward project shortly after Katrina, there had been intermittent promotional events staged by Make It Right to refresh media attention and energize public support. Most notable among these undertakings was the "Pink Project" starting as 429 pink geometric shapes spread over the 14-square block site where ultimately the real Make It Right homes would be constructed. The project motivated thousands upon thousands of people to donate a total 12 million dollars towards the cost of building the actual homes and brought global awareness to the good work of Brad Pitt personally and his foundation. By comparison, our mayoral campaign's direct financial contribution to Make It Right—10 percent of gross revenue of campaign t-shirt sales—was minuscule. The indirect benefit of the campaign, however, while difficult to quantify, must have been considerable. Moreover, unlike the "Pink Project," the mayoral project was staged at no cost whatsoever to Make It Right or Brad Pitt personally. In the fierce and pricey contest for media and public attention, this was quite a coup.

The "Brad Pitt for Mayor" campaign caught on because it constituted, rather unplanned, an episode that satisfied certain requirements of Brad Pitt's celebrity status and his own passion for sustainable architecture; the needs of the media for marketable products; and the public's constant demand for new stories. For a period of time, the union of "campaign"; the recent dramatic history and exotic character of New Orleans; issues of race and poverty; and Brad Pitt's individual convictions and celebrity status together with his role in relation to his foundation made up an irresistible media commodity.

Due to the lack of quantifiable data, it is impossible to determine the ripple effects of Brad Pitt's activism. But they must be considerable and of robust longevity. During a summer 2013 visit to the Galapagos Islands, one of the local nature guides on our vessel wore a "Brad Pitt for Mayor" t-shirt on several land excursions. A friend had sent it to him two years ago with links to the story. Ecological issues are a constant and very real concern for the unique archipelago, and the guide had adopted Brad Pitt as his personal symbol for raised ecological consciousness. The t-shirt apparently stimulated curious inquiries that quite naturally led to the desired topic: tourism's impact on the fragile ecology of the Galapagos Islands. Also, an exclusive and very chic eco resort in the fashionable Mexican town of Tulum sells "campaign" shirts in its boutique to raise money for Brad Pitt's Make It Right Foundation as well as awareness of the region's unique and highly vulnerable geology. During my travels, I often wear a "campaign" shirt as well. Inevitably, someone will either ask me what the t-shirt means or mention her or his recollection of the "campaign." Again, the t-shirt presents an easy conversation opener and a natural lead into discussions on green topics. Even to this day, the occasional campaign t-shirt can be spotted around town. While I cannot presume to know the motivation of the wearers, I am certain that they, like me, elicit a certain curiosity.

Finally, in response to the singularly most frequent question asked of me: no, I have never met Brad Pitt. It was better that way. A direct personal contact would have been misconstrued as some personal ambition to meet a celebrity and taken away from the spirit of the enterprise. But I do know where he eats. In retrospect, I am convinced that had Brad Pitt met the residency requirements for candidacy and had indeed entered the contest for the mayoral office, he would have won in a landslide. However, the position never had any compelling benefit for him to be even remotely interested in entering the fray. Federal indictments are unlikely to be on his wish list. Still, he showed himself to be a good sport and, as I had hoped, he played along.

Notes

1   "Thirteen Reasons Why Brad Pitt Should Be the Next Mayor of New Orleans," *Storyville* online, May 2, 2009, http://www. storyvilleapparel.com/brad-pitt-for-mayor-10285.html [Accessed January 11, 2014].

2   Tina Durmann, "Brad Pitt Asked to Stand for Mayor of New Orleans," *The Mirror* online June 12, 2009, http://www.mirror. co.uk/3am/celebrity-news/brad-pitt-asked-to-stand-for-mayor-399532 [Accessed January 11, 2014].

3   *Today Show*, August 21, 2009 http://www.youtube.com/ watch?v=lpP2_8GH0CU [Accessed January 10, 2014].

CHAPTER THIRTEEN

Gay for Brad

Edmond Y. Chang

The Brad Pitt Theory: The concept that all men, no matter what sexual orientation they practice, are gay for Brad Pitt.

—URBAN DICTIONARY

I like seeing Brad Pitt hanging out, that's cool. I like these guys, I like their work. And he's so attractive. If there was a line to be crossed ever.

—JIM CARREY

Who would I go gay for? Brad Pitt. Now he's a bit older, he's a bit of a looker.

—JOHN KEY, 38TH PRIME MINISTER OF NEW ZEALAND

I mean, who doesn't have it? I had the chance to meet him and he's very nice, very sweet. I mean, great body, great face. I was like, alright!

—JAVIER BARDEM

"Who would you go gay for?" So asks the popular party game, truth-or-dare provocation. For self-identified straight men, the answer more often than not is Brad Pitt. Brad Pitt with a healthy side of "if I *had* to choose," and "I'm straight-as-an-arrow but," and "no homo" qualifying. A cursory online search reveals the prevalence of this straight-male-pattern-gayness, or this "Brad Pitt Theory." From star athletes to politicians to celebrity heartthrobs to everyday dudes, everyone seems all too willing to jump Brad Pitt's bones. According to *On Top* magazine, pun intended, singer Robbie Williams would go gay for Brad for *free* even. House-beat-thumping, body rocking, booty shaking, self-identified-49% homosexual, Williams says, "It's 2 million pounds for Santa, but it's a freebie for Brad Pitt." But why specifically Pitt, and what bent logic makes men willingly heteroflexible? In other words, wherefore gay for Brad? Let us count the ways.

First and perhaps the most cited reason men would sway for Brad is because they want to be *like* Brad. Going from his humble beginnings in Oklahoma and small-town Missouri to college drop-out to "Sexiest Man Alive" (twice) to A-plus-list celebrity, he is the perfect storm of idealized good looks, charisma, rags-to-riches success, creativity, individuality, philanthropy, and humility. He is the boy-next-door. He is Horatio Alger. He is the hero, the man that men aspire to emulate in their own lives. Brad is their brother, their father, their best friend, their wingman, and their totem animal. According to Nilo Otero, assistant director of *Legends of the Fall* and *Seven*, "He's a man's man who seems to be a woman's man too. He's a classic American lover. He's a man that women can love and like at the same time."[1] Brad represents and embodies an attainable masculinity and a contained femininity. He is neither too hard nor too soft, too butch nor too Ken doll. Even the myriad of adjectives used to describe Brad are a healthy mixture of butch and femme: hot, handsome, blue-eyed, boyish, chiseled, charming, tall, tousled, down-to-earth, sexy, sweet, versatile—actor, that is.

Perhaps Brad's 1991 breakout role in *Thelma & Louise*, ostensibly a "chick flick" *par excellence*, forever enshrined the shirtless scalawag J.D. as the sensitive but bad boy "outlaw" that appeals to both men and women. J.D. is a trickster, and like Brad, knows when to tease, please, play it rough, or keep things tongue-in-cheek. He soliloquizes:

> Ladies, gentlemen, let's see who wins the prize for keeping their cool. Simon says, everybody down on the floor. Now, nobody loses their head, then nobody loses their head. Ah, you, sir, yeah, you do the honors, take that cash, put it in that bag right there, you got an amazing story to tell your friends. If not, you got a tag on your toe. You decide.[2]

This oft-quoted "Simon Says" speech reveals the smoldering desirability and flexible masculinity of Pitt that is a little dangerous and a whole lot titillating. The hair dryer, cowboy hat, tawny torso, and twang don't hurt, either.

It is Brad's body, at first blush, that makes women want him and men want to be like him. Brad's body, his Hollywood hair and jawline, and his lanky muscularity is part of a long line of what Yvonne Tasker calls "spectacular bodies," or an "active construction of the body invoked within muscular mythology [that] offers the kinds of possibilities for change to which the small ads in men's magazines appeal, the promise that, as reward for time and energy invested, a new image will look back at us from the mirror."[3] And really, it's about Brad's abs. Abs of stone, iron, or steel that are the envy of every man, woman, and child. And really, really, it's about Brad's iliac furrow, the V-shape at the waist that undergirds the abs—like flutes in marble carved by Michelangelo himself—the groove of muscle and skin that follows the crest of the hip bone down to the pubis. Also called the athlete's belt. Adonis's belt. See the above scene in *Thelma & Louise.* Hercules's girdle. See *Troy* (we don't need no stinking Spartans). Apollo's belt. Poseidon's fanny pack. See the pelvis-de-resistance: *Fight Club.* They are his synecdoche of sexiness.

The second popular touted rationalization for the men's club for Brad is akin to the first: they want to sleep with the women Brad has been with—actually or fictionally: Juliette Lewis, Robin Givens, Christina Applegate, Geena Davis, Elizabeth Daily, Gwyneth Paltrow, Claire Forlani, Tom Cruise (too bad his Lestat refused to be gay for Louis), Jitka Pohlodek, Demi Moore, Jennifer Aniston, Helena Bonham Carter, Thandie Newton, Diane Kruger, Robin Wright, and the mother-of-all Bradmances, Angelina Jolie. On or off screen, the list is long and winding—and again, intertwining fact and fantasy. If men aspire to be like Brad, in part, it is because they believe it will win them love, affection, and intimacy with women who like Brad. But if they cannot get with said women, then at least they can send in Brad as their fantasy body double, their manly, manly avatar and imagine they share in the experience. It's like when straight men say that they watch porn only for the women and supposedly identify with or ignore the pesky men involved. This imagined threesome, this Sedgwickian erotic triangle, allows men access—a sexually-transmitted circuit—to these ideal women as if by being gay for Brad, having sex with Brad, then, technically, they are having sex with Gwyneth or Jennifer or Angelina. (Or Tom.) Being gay for Brad then means being straight for hot models, celebrities, and fictional characters. It's like *bro*mosis.

Reason three is about seizing the gay. This is where things get slippery when wet: if self-identified straight men can imagine having sex with Brad to have sex with hot women, then what happens if we keep Brad as the main course and skip the lady sides? In other words, as if in some erotic bidding war, outing yourself as Bradsexual begins with admitting to like Brad, to wanting to be like Brad, then moving on to proving how comfortable you are in your own sexuality to admit that he is an attractive man, to finally, upping the ante to the possibility of a full-on hard-on for Brad. To come out of this blond, blue-eyed, and buff closet would seem like a bold admission, but being gay for Brad does not mean losing face, losing power, or losing privilege. Brad is a safe choice and an obvious one. On the one hand, this coy willingness allows men to prove their open-mindedness, their sensitive side, and their security in their selves. They can flex their manhood by simultaneously claiming Brad Pitt as a pretty boy, therefore feminized and therefore in a weaker position, and on the other hand, as a paragon of manly but not too manly men. Being gay for Brad allows men to traffic in masculinity. In other words, *bro*mosis becomes *Brad*mosis. Having sex with Brad means there is a chance that some of his cool, his suave, his swag, his eminent Bradness will rub off on you. To have sex with Brad is an exchange of masculinity rather than the loss of it. Moreover, to make it with Brad—to top Brad, even—would mean topping Paul Maclean, Tristan Ludlow, Jeffrey Goines, Louis de Pointe du Lac, Mickey O'Neil, David Mills, Rusty Ryan, Aldo Raine, Achilles, and Tyler Durden combined. It would mean getting a piece of *A River Runs Through It, Legends of the Fall, Twelve Monkeys, Interview with the Vampire, Snatch, Seven, Ocean's Eleven, Inglourious Basterds, Troy*, and, of course, *Fight Club*. And then some. This exchange of masculinity, of sexuality is about the bragging rights to shout to the rafters, queer or not, that you hooked up with one of the sexiest men in the world and therefore get to be crazy, sexy, cool by association.

But let's take things a logical step further. Reason number four: a Brad in the ass is worth two in the bush. Singer Robbie Williams, above, admits that he would sleep with Brad Pitt for free—and then jokes, "How much would I have to pay him?"[4] In a sense, assuming Brad is straight-identified, *he* would need incentive to go gay for Williams. Though not exactly rough trade, one way to read Williams's indecent proposal is that he is willing to subordinate himself to Brad, to play the submissive role, to pay for the privilege and the prestige. To put it indelicately but deliciously, bottom for Brad. The most hardcore of Bradsexuals then would go all the way, not only pitch for Brad but catch as well. Simon says, "Ah, you sir, you do the honors, take that, I'll put it in that right there, you got an amazing story to tell your friends."[5] Sex with Brad is a floating signifier, an act of transubstantiation, where the taking in of Brad is the taking in, drinking deep of all things that Brad Pitt represents, embodies, and performs. The softer side of Brad makes men feel like they are large and in charge, but the harder, tougher, rougher side of Brad demands a flip-flop of role, position, and possibility. With this feat of queer magic, men gay for Brad admit that they would not mind necessarily, if it came down to it, if there were beers or Barry White or any kind of friction involved, given the chance, they could imagine being topped by Brad Pitt. After all, in the heterosexual fantasy of playing at queer, if you are going to get fucked by someone, that someone better be worth it, an upgrade, and ultimately, someone who can enhance and augment your property values. Taking it like a man, then, takes on a whole different meaning.

Finally, the gay for Brad transformation culminates, climaxes in not so much a rationale but an act of transcendence. It is more than want. It is wish fulfillment. The fully-fledged Bradsexual is not satisfied with simple inversion, with switching sides, so to speak, but with conversion, transmogrification. They do not just want to be *like* Brad Pitt or be *with* Brad Pitt. They want to *be* Brad Pitt. Identification becomes transmutation. Congress becomes congruence. The fetish collapses back into the self. It is an impossible and magnificent act of narcissism. In essence, it is the unspoken wish at the center of every straight-identified man's favorite Brad Pitt movie, *Fight Club*. After all, the narrator asks, "If you wake up at a different time in a different place, could you wake up as a different person?"[6] Gay for Brad men then want to wake up a different person, a different man, not some loser alter-ego. A different man, a better man. A man who wrestles with women and bears, who can fight, speak, save; who is both a lone wolf and a leader; who has the freedom to be crazy, angry, kind, even queer. All wrapped up in a magnificent package, a vigorous and virtuous body, and immune to the critiques that would shatter lesser men. To be Brad Pitt then is to circumvent any circuits of queerness by becoming the very object of queerness itself. To be Brad is to be always already having sex with Brad, the final autoerotic fantasy.

In the end, where does all of this hunky hubbub leave us? Hot, sticky, sweaty, panting, and wanting more, for sure, but still safely nestled in the protective arms of everyday masculinity and sexuality. To be gay for Brad, to be queer for Brad is hardly transgressive. There is no real risk, no palpable peril. Rather, to be gay for Brad is a measure of how well straight-identified men are able to navigate a world of shifting expectations, political correctness, and genuine redefinitions of genders, sexualities, desires, and ideals. To avow gayness for Brad is to disavow homophobia and heterosexism. It is a hat trick much in the same way that *Fight Club* allows men to watch, consume, and in some ways desire the men on the screen and in the close company of one another. But the homosociality, the homoeroticism of *Fight Club* is recuperated by violence, by rugged individualism, by boys-will-be-boys. Ironically, the film resonates with straight-identified men because it mourns the perceived loss of traditional, productive, unapologetic he-men. Durden's in-film exhortation:

> Man, I see in fight club the strongest and smartest men who've ever lived. I see all this potential, and I see squandering . . . Advertising has us chasing cars and clothes, working jobs we hate so we can buy shit we don't need . . . We've all been raised on television to believe that one day we'd all be millionaires, and movie gods, and rock stars. But we won't. And we're slowly learning that fact. And we're very, very pissed off.[7]

But what the film does with this perceived loss is to simply rescue it, reinvigorate it, and repurpose masculinity and violence as radical resistance, using the master's tools to take down the master's house all the while being the master himself. Even as Durden shakes an angry fist at the sky, it is Brad Pitt whom the audience sees and admires, the very millionaire movie god who they are supposed to deny.

But they cannot deny the Brad, for the spell is too strong. It might be possible then to recover a little bit of promise and queer possibility from all of this manly theater. After all, you cannot have something until you can imagine it. Being gay for Brad, even a teensy bit, is at the very least being able to imagine the potential for queerness. In a sense, like the recent popular and critical furor over men who are gay-for-pay, being gay for Brad is what Jeffrey Escoffier defines as "situational homosexuality," or other forms of man-on-man behavior "that cannot be explained by contemporary notions of *gay identity* . . . men who have casual or opportunistic sex with men."[8] In other words, rather than worry over whether or not men who are queer for Brad can be easily labeled as straight or gay, how might we see this situational queerness as a place to leverage change in standards of sex, gender, and desire. For some, might Brad be the gateway gay? The energy is there, the vim, and in a curious way, the conviction. One online blogger sums up why he is gay for Brad:

> How cliché, I know. The thing is, it's cliché because it's true. Guys want to be more like Brad Pitt. He plays badass characters, and he seems like a chill dude in real life. He's swimming in money and his hobbies include banging Angelina Jolie. Not to mention that I'm convinced that Tyler Durden is the epitomy [*sic*] of fucking cool. Argue what you want about the ethics/morals/philosophies of *Fight Club*, but don't try and tell me that you don't wish you could be as flippantly badass as Brad Pitt is in that movie.[9]

Methinks he doth protest too much.

So, who would you go gay for? Brad, Johnny, Sean, Matt, George, Hugh, Ben, Gerard, Christian, Justin, Benedict? Or in the immortal words of the enigma that is Benjamin Button, "You can be as mad as a mad dog at the way things went. You could swear, curse the fates, but when it comes to the end, you have to let go."[10] Maybe next time the answer to the question will be closer to home.

Notes

1   Quoted in Pam Lambert, "A Legend to Fall For," January 30,
    1995, http://www.people.com/people/archive/
    article/0,,20104953,00.html [Accessed January 9, 2014].

2   *Thelma & Louise*, directed by Ridley Scott (MGM, 1991).

3   Yvonne Tasker, *Spectacular Bodies: Gender, Genre, and the
    Action Cinema* (New York: Routledge, 1993), 9.

4   "Robbie Williams Would Go Gay for Brad Pitt," *On Top
    Magazine*, December 29, 2011, http://www.ontopmag.com/
    article.aspx?id=10497&MediaType=1&Category=22 [Accessed
    January 11, 2014].

5   *Thelma & Louise*, directed by Ridley Scott (MGM, 1991).

6   *Fight Club*, directed by David Fincher (20th Century Fox,
    1999).

7   *Fight Club*, directed by David Fincher (20th Century Fox,
    1999).

8   Jeffrey Escoffier, "Gay-for-Pay: Straight Men and the Making of
    Gay Pornography," *Qualitative Sociology* 26(4) (2003), 532.

9   Audie Sumaray, *Bleeding Color*, Personal website, http://
    bleedingcolor.com/post/114097106/guys-i-would-go-gay-for-
    brad-pitt [Accessed January 9, 2014].

10 *The Curious Case of Benjamin Button*, directed by David
    Fincher (Warner Bros., 2008).

Coda:

Failure

Brian A. Sullivan

Failure seems like an odd term to associate with Brad Pitt. His box office success, price per film, and charitable endeavors would certainly suggest that he is actually a huge success. While the success of real-world Brad Pitt is generally settled, the successes and failures of the characters he portrays are anything but. Pitt could easily embrace a uniform role of the eye candy, nice guy, or hero. By his box office success alone, he could always win at the end of his films. Yet there is an interesting diversity in his characters—stoner, vampire, detective, imaginary friend/fiend, genetic mutation, and assassin being some of the more exciting choices he's made. Contrast his roles with the perpetual hero of Arnold Schwarzenegger in the 1990s or the eternally nice guy Tom Hanks and we see an actor who wants to portray a broad range of experiences.[1] Prior to *Se7en*'s premier Pitt admitted, "I wanted to [. . .] play someone with flaws."[2] Within that one sentence we can see Pitt's embrace of characters that fail. Flaws mean failures, and failures make us human.[3] A tour through some of Brad Pitt's on-screen failures shows how these roles embrace failure as a rejection or reinforcement of societal values.

Various roles in Pitt's canon can simply be described as failures in the eyes of polite society: Floyd from *True Romance* is a stoner living on his friend's couch, while Jeffrey Goines in *Twelve Monkeys* is both a patient in an asylum and a member of a "terrorist" organization. Michel Foucault's *Madness and Civilization* would probably have some interesting things to say about him. In *Fight Club*, Tyler Durden is an outright rejection of middle-class values. All of these characters fail to live as productive members of society and rebel against society in a variety of ways. In that vein, *Snatch* provides one of Pitt's best explorations of failure as a rebellion against "traditional" success. As an Irish Gypsy, Mickey is a member of a group that deliberately lives outside of mainstream society. Mickey's and his family's failure to live in a fixed residence, pay taxes, or follow the rule of the law, puts them in a unique sphere for exploring failure. In the film, Mickey refuses to deliberately lose a boxing match twice, failing to deliberately fail in both fights. Yet through this failure he achieves monetary gain and exacts revenge on the people who killed his mother. It is an interesting contrast that a character who purposely fails his role in society uses this failure to his advantage, and then uses the money to continue his rejection, his marginalized life.

Pitt's on-screen failures sometimes seem to reinforce capitalist values. The very nature of capitalism deems that success is dependent on failure.[4] The narrator's enlightenment (success) in *Fight Club* is seemingly dependent on his willingness to destroy Tyler, to use Tyler's failure for personal gain. This dynamic is one of the movie's failures. The final act of *Fight Club* is about the destruction of the debt economy, yet its characters perpetuate the stakes of unfettered capitalism. Gilles Deleuze and Félix Guattari's *A Thousand Plateaus: Capitalism and Schizophrenia* would probably have some interesting thing to say about that.

In *Burn After Reading*, Pitt plays a gym employee, Chad, who gets caught up in an escalating blackmail scheme. The interesting thing about Chad as a character is his intentional and unintentional embrace of failure. He embodies the role of the goofball jock in a dead-end job. While it is not an ambitious lifestyle, he seems to fully embrace his place as a member of the Hardbodies crew. Even though he fails to be ambitious in his career choices, he is happy playing this role as the smiling, good-looking, personal trainer. Chad's happy-go-lucky career failures are contrasted by his blackmailing failures. In his role as blackmailer he misinterprets financial statements as government secrets, and he fails numerous times to extort money from Osborne Cox (John Malkovich). This would seem to be the set-up for a heroic moment in the final act of the film. Instead, in spite of his disarming smile, he is killed during his brief confrontation with Harry Pfarrar (George Clooney). Chad's failures seem to be both a caution against ambition and a reminder that failure sometimes has permanent results.

As a movie husband, Pitt's roles provide good fodder for discussing familial failure and violence. In some instances violence is used as a point of reconciliation as when Pitt's failure to fulfill his husbandly duties in *Mr. & Mrs. Smith* is mended after an over-the-top shootout in the couple's house. *Se7en* takes violence and family to the extreme when the serial killer is stopped at the cost of Detective Mills's (Pitt's) wife's life. His success as a detective and his failure as a husband are tied up into one violent event. Similarly, the friendship (marriage) of Tyler Durden and the narrator is both formed and undone through violence.

The Curious Case of Benjamin Button also embraces both failure and computer-generated graphics (CGI) as a means to both reject and reinforce normative familial bonds. In *The Queer Art of Failure*, Judith Halberstam argues that the use of CGI in animated films for children is directly linked to themes of failure, rebellion, and a reimagined society.[5] While *The Curious Case of Benjamin Button* is not a children's film and does not solely use CGI, but instead uses an advanced method of motion capture combined with CGI, it does allow for new families to be formed through failure.[6] Telling the story of a man aging backwards, Pitt was given sole acting credit in the film, even though a significant portion of it was Pitt's digitally old face on other actors' bodies.[7] Benjamin's failure to age traditionally creates an interracial, multigenerational family in the pre-Depression South. This nontraditional family dissolves as Benjamin's age coincides with Brad Pitt's age. Once overt CGI is no longer necessary, Benjamin's adopted mother dies and he embraces life in a nuclear family. The absence of digital effects signals "traditional" familial success for Benjamin. As Benjamin becomes younger than Pitt and digital effects become necessary again, the nuclear family falls apart as Benjamin abandons his family and travels the world.[8] In this film the nuclear-biological family succeeds and fails depending on the use of digital effects.

As this tour continues it becomes apparent that getting a comprehensive look at failure in Brad Pitt's roles becomes more daunting—in part, because such an imaginably successful person has in numerous ways also failed and portrayed failure as a central aspect of his artistic persona. Earlier in this volume, in Chapter 2, Abele connects Pitt's portrayals of Romantic Heroes to an idealism that is unafraid to fail, while Pheasant-Kelly in Chapter 8 and and Hudson in Chapter 9 explain how several of Pitt's significant roles succeed precisely because Pitt performs a sense of failed masculinity in crisis. Off-screen, Pitt also endured a highly visible break-up with Gwyneth Paltrow, divorced Jennifer Aniston in one of the most highly publicized divorces in recent memory, and currently lives in an unconventional familial arrangement that has received incessant, and as White demonstrates in Chapter 6, often outright ignorant press coverage.

As I continue to write I realize that, along with completely—until now—ignoring his lack of Oscar wins, I have forgotten to mention several other roles that perform similar acts of failure: *Babel, Tree of Life, World War Z, Meet Joe Black, Interview with the Vampire*, and many others. It seems that this short essay could be expanded to encompass its own book, something like *Deconstructing the Failures of Brad Pitt*. Even then it would reach a point where publication with missing elements or failure became the only options. Even if Pitt were perfectly successful, the attempt to analyze, to understand, and to explain Pitt—the stories that we tell about him—would themselves fall short, always representing him as simultaneously more, less, and other than he is. Hence, the failures—personal, professional, and hermeneutic—described in this essay haunt not only this anthology but also the larger circulation of images and texts about Pitt.

Looking back on this book as something of an alien offspring of Pitt, it itself has so many shortcomings: it couldn't keep up with the Pitt performances as they rolled out—there is nothing in the book about *12 Years a Slave*, nothing about *The Counselor*. Even Pitt's more recent roles got relatively short shrift. Which reminds us that Brad Pitt is so much more than these pages could possibly contain. And yet, despite his character's failures and the failures of culture to encompass his celebrity, Brad Pitt keeps accepting roles, keeps acting, keeps going: he remains in play. Pitt's continuation means that this partial chapter can only end in failure, much like this book—because we can never fully grasp, but only endlessly deconstruct, something like the totality of Brad Pitt.

Notes

1   David Foster Wallace, "The (As It Were) Seminal Importance of Terminator 2," in *Both Flesh and Not: Essays* (New York: Little, Brown and Company, 2012), 183. Wallace notes that Schwarzenegger would only return to the *Terminator* franchise as the good guy lest his image as an action hero be tarnished.

2   Cindy Pearlman, "Brad Pitt's Seven Deadly Sins—'Sexiest Man Alive' Explains Film—and Errors of His Ways," *Chicago Sun-Times*, September 17, 1995.

3   Costica Bradatan, "In Praise of Failure," *Opinionator*, December 15, 2013. http://opinionator.blogs.nytimes.com/2013/12/15/in-praise-of-failure/ [Accessed December 16, 2013].

4   Judith Halberstam, *The Queer Art of Failure* (Durham, NC: Duke University Press, 2011), 88.

5   Judith Halberstam, *The Queer Art of Failure* (Durham, NC: Duke University Press, 2011), 29.

6   Yacov Freedman, "Is It Real [. . .] or Is It Motion Capture?: The Battle to Redefine Animation in the Age of Digital Performance," *The Velvet Light Trap* 69(1) (2012), 46. http://search.ebscohost.com/login.aspx?direct=true&db=lfh&AN=72288516&site=ehost-live&scope=site [Accessed January 2, 2012].

7   Yacov Freedman, "Is It Real [. . .] or Is It Motion Capture?: The Battle to Redefine Animation in the Age of Digital Performance," *The Velvet Light Trap* 69(1) (2012), 46. http://search.ebscohost.com/login.aspx?direct=true&db=lfh&AN=72288516&site=ehost-live&scope=site [Accessed January 2, 2012].

8   Jody Duncan, "The Unusual Birth of Benjamin Button," *Cinefex* 116 (Jan. 2009): 93. Duncan reports that the special effects company Lola VFX supplied the effects to make Pitt appear younger.

Postscript?

Madness

Robert Bennett

To Christopher Schaberg who inspired me to commit the unspeakable to print.

To Rob Wallace, the music guy: don't ever let them give you electro-disciplinary shock therapy; on you, it would never hold.

And for Brad Pitt: because he may just act, but he has been in there with us twice—and he brought his A game, too.

For everyone else—in or with—fly the singular freak flag of whatever rationality you may be!

Finally, for Chris because I can find my way in all by myself, but only you know how to get me out.

Brad Pitt, I'm with you in Rockland (RKL)

Check around your seat for any personal belongings and use extreme caution when opening overhead bins, as heavy articles may run wild in flight.

Remember how Chris's Preface suggested that this book involves personal attachments and narrative threads? Here's the truth: all my attachments are unhinged, my threads are frayed beyond recognition, and narratives are just plane crashes waiting to happen. It is not that certain belongings are *personal*, but rather that heavy enough articles are *nothing but*. If you want personal, I can do personal; for I, too, have been in Rockland.

Where to begin the ending, or end the beginning? Welcome to my world—the world of deconstruction's never-ending catch-22s. For _Deconstructing Brad Pitt did not begin as a simple call for academic papers (CFP) about Brad Pitt—as I stated in my Foreword any more than it resulted from the second CFP for this book.[1] As far as the back-story to this book is concerned, these two CFPs are red herrings. (Origin stories usually are.) You see, deconstruction generally cares less about your city of origin than it does about the vehicle that got you there in the first place—or about where you are headed next or after that, or even beyond that (though not so much in your so-called final destination). You see, deconstruction works in the texts, spaces, and experiences that dwell in-between beginnings and ends; in other words, it plays the middles, thrives in the margins, and explores everything outside the frame (and it turns out we were always in a frame, too). So instead of concluding this book, my Postscript aims to reconfigure and reevaluate the emergent field of Brad Pitt Studies from an altitude of 36,000 feet.

Certainly CFPs can precipitate and momentarily crystallize dynamic conversation, but the archaeology of Brad Pitt Studies resists origin narratives (though this volume itself does contain several variations on the genre). Even the two distinct CFPs that seem to have set this project in motion, do they not also have prior backstories perhaps larger than even this book itself? Or as Brian A. Sullivan's Coda on "Failure" might suggest, did this entire project not succeed at least in part because it initially failed rather dismally? What did Tyler say the "first step to eternal life was"?[2] Something about needing to die first? Might a Postscript, too, turn away from definitive conclusions to instead begin the inevitable process of unraveling the very book within which it resides?

If nothing else, Chris and I have arrived at this project with very different personal baggage. Chris's Foreword explains some of his own backstory, so mine follows here. Just don't expect us to be traveling with the "exact same suitcase"—like Tyler Durden and Edward Norton—just because we both happen to study Brad Pitt.[3]

BPI-RKL (Fall 2001–Spring 2013)

The Captain has turned on the fasten seat belt sign.

Brad Pitt International to Rockland, the state mental health institution where Allen Ginsberg and Carl Solomon "scream[ed] in straitjacket[s]" while "losing the actual game of the pingpong of the abyss."[4] Have you ever flown that one? Which direction and with whom? By yourself or with your other selves? Or maybe with Brad Pitt and Edward Norton? How about with the barrel of Tyler Durden's gun blocking your pipes. Done that. Three times.

So let's drop the metaphors and be excruciatingly clear: I *have* sat on a plane while clinically insane three different times in my life, and each time when Edward Norton has offered me *that* peach I have eaten it while lying etherized upon my seat-back tray, and strange as it may have tasted, I have swallowed it pit and all: (1) a Tel Aviv (TLV)-JFK-SLC in the Fall of 1987; (2) a Bozeman (BZN)-SLC-SEA commuter in the Spring of 2013; and (3) the SEA-BZN direct return a few days later. For I, too, have tasted of madness. And I, too, have been destroyed by it. And sometimes madness can even destroy you more than once. Just ask Edward Norton. Because he has, on three different occasions, helped measure out my sanity—one coffee spoon at a time, and this, too, is no less painful than having Brad Pitt's eyes and paranoid innuendos bore into your skull at cruising altitude.

You see, it can happen anywhere, anytime, anyhow, and in more ways than you can imagine—even (or especially) on a plane. Remember what Tyler said, "people do it every day."[5] One minute you're of one mind, and the next moment . . . tick . . . time . . . tock. Accelerates. Tick . . . tick, tick-tick-tick: Wake up! And just like that, you are your seatmate's own strange self.

I very well may be over-identifying with *Fight Club*'s *mise-en-scène*, but doesn't this itself just demonstrate my point? We all come at this whole Brad Pitt thing burdened with different personal backstories, and at times these stories in turn dig so deeply into the story proper that the backstories themselves begin to inform and shape and alter how we read Brad Pitt (or anything else for that matter). For example, Chris's analysis of plane crash scenes in *World War Z*—in his Chapter 3 "On Crashing"—completely changed my own understanding of that film, of Pitt, and even of how planes shape my own analysis of madness. I used to think of Tyler primarily in terms of exploding skyscrapers and my own personal experiences with madness; now Tyler's mad innuendos increasingly remind me of crashing planes or of Norton and Pitt precariously negotiating their alternative rationalities on a plane. But our understandings of texts, even the text of Brad Pitt, do indeed alter each other and evolve over time in startlingly unpredictable ways. (Curiously, this book has already begun to influence itself, and it is still being written as of this writing.) In fact, I had even personally forgotten how many times that I had gone (or been) crazy *on a plane* until I read Chris's innovative analysis. You think that one would not forget such things— going crazy on a plane—though at some point, I guess, the plane really isn't the first thing on your mind.

JFK-SBA-RKL (Spring 2005–Spring 2014)

Lost baggage should immediately be reported to Baggage Service.

My Foreword may have offered few clues that my involvement in Brad Pitt Studies might have a backstory, let alone a personal one—so let me henceforth make amends.

I became interested in Brad Pitt long before I had any real awareness of him at all. Let me explain. I wrote my dissertation, *Deconstructing Post-WWII New York City* (now Routledge, 2003), to explore how New York City writers, musicians, and artists—Allen Ginsberg first and foremost among them— used provocative cultural "representations of skyscrapers to deconstruct" real "skyscrapers'—and hence corporate America's—traditional function as the socio-spatial center of American cities" because these artists believed passionately that corporate "skyscrapers impose not only their physical presence but also their dehumanizing techno-rational and corporate ideologies onto the urban spaces and subjects that they dominate."[6] Then one normal, ordinary Tuesday morning as I went to file my final copy of my dissertation with the university, I was hauntingly interrupted—you see, deconstruction always, routinely, incessantly, incisively, profoundly, belatedly, imperceptibly, presciently, ambiguously and unambiguously, repeatedly, repeatedly, unpredictably, repeatedly, blatantly, and provocatively interrupts (even ruptures) all texts, practices, and events—as airliners so similar to the ones Chris analyzes exploded into the same corporate skyscrapers that Allen Ginsberg's saxophone raged about in my dissertation. And in that moment of singularity in which time felt like it had stopped altogether, on the day that became known as "9/11," I ran with my dissertation flapping in hand to the Graduate Division offices, because if the world was coming to an end, I had no intention of going without my Ph.D.

I should have stopped cold in my tracks, however, pausing mid-crisis to recompose a new Preface—however brief and faltering—to acknowledge if not my own, then at least my dissertation's, unique relationship to those events. I now offer this Postscript again as penance for that Preface which never was.

Lost in my studies of skyscrapers, I knew nothing about Brad Pitt beyond having seen and liked *Thelma & Louise* and *A River Runs Through It*. I did not even know about *Fight Club* until my students alerted me of its existence, and even then had no idea that Pitt performed in it. In that first post-9/11 semester, however, *Fight Club* seemed to be all that my students really wanted to talk about, and they routinely lined up after each class begging me to see *Fight Club* and incorporate it into my syllabi. They repeatedly reiterated that it would make so much sense in my classes: on the Cultural History of American Skyscrapers (I get that); on Jazz Literature (the Ginsberg connection was recognizable to me if not them); and on Native American Literature (run that one by me again?).

It would take me years to fully understand the connections that my students hinted at between my own work and *Fight Club*. Over time, however, some of the pieces began to fall in place. 9/11? Check. Crashing Planes? Check. Exploding skyscrapers? Check. A keening cry against global capitalism? Check. Allen Ginsberg? Check? Carl Solomon! Carl Who? Who. .. who ... who ... That was it! For *Fight*

Club, too, was about all those who have been "destroyed by madness":

> who poverty and tatters and hollowed-eyed and high sat up
> smoking in the supernatural darkness of cold-water flats
> floating across the tops of cities contemplating jazz
> who bared their brains to heaven under the El and
> saw Mohammedan angels staggering on tenement roofs
> illuminated[7]

Only unlike Ginsberg's friends running mad through the "negro streets at dawn," Carl Solomon was *in* Rockland, like I have been *in* the Utah Valley Psychiatric Hospital or *in* the Billings, Montana Psychiatric Center. So I, too, have been in Rockland with Ginsberg and Solomon. I had just never made the connecting flights from Rockland's insanity to *Fight Club* to planes, so I had never really focused on how you can be in Rockland and on a plane at the same time.

After catching that flight, however, my personal investment in Brad Pitt Studies got real personal, real fast, and from more than one direction. You see, like Ginsberg's "Howl," *Fight Club* also offers a trenchant exploration of a generation of exceptional minds destroyed by madness, sometimes even on a plane. I had finally found *my* missing link between "Howl" and *Fight Club*. So there was no question that I would write my chapter for this book on Brad Pitt's performance of Tyler Durden's madness. I never told Chris this at the time, but the main reason why I took his screwball suggestion about studying Brad Pitt seriously was because I was already crazier than he was: I already had a previous on-going research agenda about Brad Pitt even if I knew precious few of his films at that point. I just didn't know what to do or where to go with my studies. I guess that I should have simply told Chris that he had me at Brad. (Though you can read a more trenchant take on that line of inquiry in Edmond Y. Chang's Chapter 13, "Gay for Brad.")

Now I may stand alone here but I maintain staunchly, if perhaps also shrilly, that the *truest* celluloid heir to Ginsberg's

"Howl" is not James Franco's, not Tom Sturridge's, and not Daniel Radcliffe's lukewarm impersonations of the Beat poet—but rather Brad Pitt's fiercely engaged performance of Tyler Durden. For I believe that Ginsberg's tour de force poetic explorations of madness, *Howl* and *Kaddish*, speak powerfully—at least on the lower frequencies, if not all over the dial—to Brad Pitt's own brilliant performances of madness in *Twelve Monkeys* and *Fight Club*—with all of these texts driving their skyscraper demolition fantasies deep into the singular Ground Zero of Rockland: an excruciatingly painfully place where even the best minds can be destroyed in unfathomable and innumerable ways, and where all of their singular stories are agonizingly typed one crazy letter at a time upon what Ginsberg describes as that "dreadful typewriter" of the insane.[8] For I, too, have heard these harrowing stories though this is the first time that I have personally struck these dreadful keys.

BZN-SLC-SEA/SEA-BZN (Spring 2013)

The Captain has turned on the fasten seat belt sign, again!

But could Brad Pitt himself, especially as played through Tyler Durden, ever enter into this scatological grammar of madness itself? How much further can this mad Postscript deconstruct Brad Pitt before the words start wobbling and slipping from the page?

This plane is equipped with several emergency exits.

Believe it or not, I started going insane on the BZN-SLC-SEA flight that I took to attend an academic conference where I planned to present a paper on Brad Pitt (my first one), and this paper resulted in the second half of my Chapter 4, "Suburban Rage," in this volume. Consequently, at the same moment that I was analyzing Brad Pitt's performance of madness on a fictional plane in *Fight Club*, I was myself already beginning to go insane—on a real flight. Deconstruction often works in mysterious ways, making up its own rules as it goes.

Please take a few moments now to locate your nearest exit.

By the time that I presented my paper I had myself gone stark, raving mad, so that I presented my analysis of Pitt's performance of Tyler's madness through a mind already as mad as Tyler's own. Luckily, kind colleagues and family saw me safely(-ish) to my plane though they had no choice but to set me free, alone and mad, to pass through a nightmarish TSA version of security protocol Wipeout. With the Ramones' "I Wanna Be Sedated" blaring repeatedly in my inner ear's brain—"just put me in a wheelchair / get me on a plane; / hurry, hurry, hurry / before I go insane"—I rushed madly to my gate.[9] Only it turned out to be a false alarm; I was already too late, but luckily my flight was delayed, and this extra time allowed me to hastily encrypt notes about the three novels that I had begun writing that weekend—*Private Idaho: My Manic Mormon Childhood* (self-explanatory); *Harry Potter Goes to BYU* (about my first experience with madness); and *Elder Lithium: Zen and the Art of the Book of Mormon* (about my second)—along with a few equally coherent ideas for revising my conference paper on Pitt.

There will be slight departure delay.

It was only when I heard the intercom that I finally realized what was actually going on: the delay was probably for Him. We had been waiting for a long, long time, after all, and the lines that they kept feeding us about de-icing and inclement weather seemed implausible enough to me. So I believed, holding out hope right up until the very last moment of actually boarding the plane—only He never did show (they never do). In Rockland, they are all no-shows and false alarms. That is one of the worst parts of being crazy—all the fantastic writers and musicians and actors who you finally get to meet in Rockland, they never quite pass through the security checkpoint after your meds kick in.

> *In the event of a decompression, an oxygen mask will automatically*

But in the state of mind I was in then, even the slightest hint that Pitt might join us—on the plane—fanned the fires of my raging demented mind to hatch a second extraordinary plot. By the time that we deplaned, I was absolutely convinced— as sure as $2 + 6 = 4$ because 4 is in the middle—that the Alternative Latino band, Ozomatli, together with musicians from New Orleans (organized by my friends Chris and Rob) would imminently arrive with none other than Brad Pitt himself (most likely on my flight; hence the delay) to play a benefit concert in the ball field next to my home to raise money for Brad Pitt and myself to launch a literacy campaign across North Africa dressed in flowing jalabayas handing out four-color pens and small tablet notebooks to smiling children with outstretched hands. One, tick! By, tock! One . . . Poof!

> *In the event of an emergency, please assume the bracing position.*

Luckily for everyone, my wife greeted me at the airport bearing what the Good Book/Film describes as "your meals on a tray with a paper cup of meds."[10] It still took a week for the meds to kick in, but I passed the time throwing color-coded blue and white whiffle balls under our tree, hoping that Ozomatli's Dodger-loving musicians would catch my hints and spring the plan into action. The math was beginning to go south on me. It usually does in Rockland—for though there are plenty of genius mathematicians who are mad, the mad themselves are generally just not that good at math.

As we start our ascent, please use caution and extreme flotation devices carefully when checking under your security belt for heavy articles, life vests, or overhead bins as all personal belongings, emergency briefing decks of cards, and in-flight entertainment systems may have shifted during (or sometimes somehow even just before) turbulence.

That is, if you even make it out alive, because madness—like airline safety cards—can be your worst nightmare. But other times madness is more like some diabolical Maleficent cartoon raccoon of the mind ransacking the inner citadels of your own self, knocking over your bookshelves and spilling your books, CDs, and DVDs into your coffee spoons before scratching and sticking the whole mess up with its peanut-butter-knuckled claws—all the while a demented team of mad frenzied beavers disorganizes and chews up whatever is left into a slash pile, allowing you only a brief, exactly three-minute, reprieve to grasp a dozen items from on top before a dark or light spy dynamites the rest to kingdom come. If you keep enough copies of the Good Book/Novel around, however, then if you do somehow later end up insane on a plane, your chances are exponentially greater that Edward Norton, Brad Pitt, and Tyler Durden (or all three) will be there with you. It can just get difficult real quick when you need to decide who is going to read what book to whom for the duration of your flight.

Either way, it *will* be a rocky flight; it always is. For all flights bound for Rockland experience turbulence of one kind or another, if not outright complete and utter disaster. Think about where you are going, after all: this is where you must "bang on the catatonic piano the soul" and where you must fight against some "fascist national Golgotha" with nothing more than "police tape flutter[ing] between you and oblivion."[11] Once you get there it is not at all clear what you should do next.

Each door is equipped with an inflatable slide which may also be detached and used as a life raft.

And yet, even a hell such as this is not altogether devoid of its own peculiarly murky consolations. For not all have stood in solidarity with Allen Ginsberg and Carl Solomon in Rockland hand in hand refusing to renounce that some new day might yet dawn though we perhaps know not even if when the hospitals' "imaginary walls collapse" so that all may finally "forget our underwear, we're free."[12] I can imagine Brad Pitt, or at least Pitt as he is played by Mr. John Smith, standing in his flowing white boxer underwear amidst the fiery ruins of collapsing imaginary and not-so-imaginary walls, and such a world to me might still hold out if not promises, then at least suggestions, of certain inexplicably haunting allures.

> *To inflate the vest, pull firmly on the red cord, only when . . .*
> *If you need to refill the vest, blow into the . . .*
> *Use the whistle and light to attract . . .*

At this point only the singularity of one's own mind's eye remains. For it is *only* inside Rockland (RKL) that one can agonizingly await the Rapture of Charles Mingus as he descends from Heaven (together with Jesus Christ and Tony Kushner, of course): all just more no-shows, yet again. Consequently, it is *only* in Rockland where one can truly learn, however inarticulately and falteringly, how to DJ (or J.D.) the previously unknown beats and rhythms of the Apocalypse itself. I'd be happy to share with you that playlist. When was the last time that you discussed poetry with Pablo Neruda and Walt Whitman in the flesh on the same day, even if that flesh is perhaps not technically speaking their own? Have you really *never* tasted the erratic pleasure of playing cards with Jesus's disciple, James? He plays well, though we have both sworn never to reveal Rockland's secret in-house rules. For buried deep beneath both pain and destruction, these experiences enfold secret silver pockets within pockets holding counterintuitive consolations beyond both all justification and all calculation.

That's my Brad Pitt Studies. What's yours?

Notes

1   CFP Cultural Studies Book on Brad Pitt

Dr. Christopher Schaberg / Loyola University New Orleans contact email: schaberg@loyno.edu

Proposals are being solicited for an edited volume organized around the subject of Brad Pitt. The editors envision a book on Brad Pitt that ranges broadly across the humanities, with chapters focusing on film studies, gender & sexuality, architecture, eco-criticism & critical regionalism, and popular culture. We welcome abstracts for theoretically informed essays on topics such as: Analyses of individual Brad Pitt film roles, or comparative studies of Pitt's performances across different films; Brad Pitt as sex icon; Brad Pitt as uber-father; Brad Pitt and architecture; Brad Pitt and environment (urban, wilderness, & others); Brad Pitt and violence; Images of Brad Pitt (how they travel, what they are used for); "Brad Pitt for Mayor" (Brad Pitt in New Orleans); Brad Pitt as mainstream star; Brad Pitt as cultural rogue; Brad Pitt cameo appearances; Brad Pitt's literary personae ("The Curious Case of Benjamin Button," Legends of the Fall, Fight Club, A River Runs Through It, etc.)

Send abstracts of no more than 300 words by October 1 2011 to Christopher Schaberg at schaberg@loyno.edu. Please also include current CV. Final essays should be between 5000 and 8000 words, and will be due July 1 2012.

2   Chuck Palahniuk, *Fight Club* (New York: Henry Holt, 1996), 11.

3   *Fight Club*, directed by David Fincher (20th Century Fox, 1999).

4   Allen Ginsberg, *Howl and Other Poems* (San Francisco, CA: City Lights Books, 1959), 25.

5   *Fight Club*, directed by David Fincher (20th Century Fox, 1999).

6   Robert Bennett, *Deconstructing Post-WWII New York City: The Literature, Art, Jazz, and Architecture of an Emerging Global Capital* (New York: Routledge, 2003), 23.

7   Allen Ginsberg, *Howl and Other Poems* (San Francisco: City Lights Books, 1959), 25.9

8   Allen Ginsberg, *Howl and Other Poems* (San Francisco: City Lights Books, 1959), 24.

9   The Ramones, "I Wanna Be Sedated," *Road to Ruin* (Sire, 1978).

10 Chuck Palahniuk, *Fight Club* (New York: Henry Holt, 1996), 207.

11 Allen Ginsberg, *Howl and Other Poems* (San Francisco: City Lights Books, 1959), 25; Chuck Palahniuk, *Fight Club* (New York: Henry Holt, 1996), 193.

12 Allen Ginsberg, *Howl and Other Poems* (San Francisco: City Lights Books, 1959), 26.

BIBLIOGRAPHY

Agrawal, Arun. *Environmentality: Technologies of Government and the Making of Subjects*. Durham, NC: Duke University Press, 2005.

Babuscio, Jack. "Camp and the Gay Sensibility." In *Camp Grounds: Style and Homosexuality*. Ed. David Bergman. Amherst, MA: The University of Massachusetts Press, 1993.

Ballard, J.G. *Crash*. New York: Picador, 1973.

Barthes, Roland. "The Face of Garbo." In *Mythologies*. London: Vintage, 1993, 56–7.

Baudrillard, Jean. *Fatal Strategies*. New York: Semiotext(e), 2008.

Baudrillard, Jean. *Jean Baudrillard: Selected Writings*. Ed. Mark Poster. Stanford, CA: Stanford University Press, 2002.

Baudrillard, Jean. *Simulacra and Simulation*. Ann Arbor, MI: University of Michigan Press, 1994.

Baudrillard, Jean. *Symbolic Exchange and Death*. London: Sage, 1993.

Bell-Metereau, Rebecca. "Searching for Blobby Fissures: Slime, Sexuality, and the Grotesque." In *Infamy, Darkness, Evil, and Slime on Screen*. Ed. Murray Pomerance. Albany, NY: State University of New York Press, 2004.

Bennett, Robert. *Deconstructing Post-WWII New York City: The Literature, Art, Jazz, and Architecture of an Emerging Global Capital*. New York: Routledge, 2003.

Benshoff, Harry and Sean Griffin. *America on Film: Representing Race, Class, Gender, and Sexuality at the Movies*. Oxford: Wiley-Blackwell, 2009.

Best, Stephen. "The Commodification of Reality and the Reality of Commodification: Baudrillard, Debord, and Postmodern Theory." In *Baudrillard: A Critical Reader*. Ed. Douglas Kellner. Oxford: Blackwell, 1994.

Betterton, Rosemary. "Prima Gravida: Reconfiguring the Maternal Body in Visual Representation." *Feminist Theory* 3.3 (2002): 255–70.

Betterton, Rosemary. "Promising Monsters: Pregnant Bodies, Artistic Subjectivity, and Maternal Imagination." *Hypatia* 21.1 (2006): 85.

Braudy, Leo. *The Frenzy of Renown: Fame and its History*. New York: Oxford University Press, 1986.

Broadhurst, Susan. *Digital Practices: Aesthetic and Neuroesthetic Approaches to Performance and Technology*. New York: Palgrave, 2007.

Brown, Nathan. "Origin and Extinction, Mourning and Melancholia," *MUTE*, 9 September 2012.

Brown, Caroline. "The Representation of the Indigenous Other in *Daughters of the Dust* and *The Piano*." *NWSA Journal* 15 (2003): 1–19.

Browne, Ray B. "Popular Culture as the New Humanities." In *Popular Culture Theory and Methodology: A Basic Introduction*. Eds. Harold E. Hinds, Jr., Marilyn F. Motz, and Angela M. S. Nelson. Madison, WI: University of Wisconsin Press, 2006.

Browning, Mark. *David Fincher: Films That Scar*. Oxford: Praeger, 2010.

Browning, Mark. *George Clooney: An Actor Looking for a Role*. Westport, CT: ABC-CLIO, 2012.

Carroll, Lewis. *Through the Looking-Glass*. Seattle, WA: Madison Park, 2010.

Cook, Bernie, ed. *Thelma & Louise Live: The Cultural Afterlife of an American Film*. Austin, TX: University of Texas Press, 2007.

Cook, Paul and Suzanne Stevenson. "Automatically Identifying the Source Words of Lexical Blends in English." *Computational Linguistics* 36.1 (2010): 129–49.

Critical Art Ensemble. *The Electronic Disturbance*. New York: Autonomedia, 1994.

Currid-Halkett, Elizabeth. *Starstruck: The Business of Celebrity*. New York: Faber and Faber, 2010.

Debord, Guy. *Society of the Spectacle*. London: Rebel Press, 1977, 31–63.

Deleuze, Gilles and Félix Guattari. *Anti-Oedipus: Capitalism and Schizophrenia*. Minneapolis, MN: University of Minnesota Press, 1983.

Deleuze, Gilles and Félix Guattari. *A Thousand Plateaus: Capitalism and Schizophrenia*. Minneapolis, MN: University of Minnesota Press, 1987.

DeLillo, Don. *White Noise*. New York: Viking Penguin, 1985.

Derrida, Jacques. *Of Grammatology*. Baltimore, MD: Johns Hopkins University Press, 1976.

Derrida, Jacques. "Cogito and the History of Madness." In *Writing and Difference*. Chicago, IL: University of Chicago Press, 1978.

Derrida, Jacques. "Ulysses Grammaphone" *Acts of Literature*. New York: Routledge, 1992.

Derrida, Jacques. *Specters of Marx: The State of Debt, The Work of Mourning, and the New International*. New York: Routledge, 1994.

Derrida, Jacques. *The Gift of Death*. Chicago, IL: The University of Chicago Press, 1995.

Derrida, Jacques. "Structure, Sign, and Play in the Discourse of the Human Sciences." In *Writing and Difference*, trans. Alan Bass. London: Routledge, 2001, 278–93.

Duncan, Jody. "The Unusual Birth of Benjamin Button." *Cinefex* 116 (2009): 70–99.

Dyer, Richard. *Seven* (BFI Modern Classics). London: BFI Publishing, 1999.

Dyer, Richard. *The Matter of Images: Essays on Representation*. New York: Routledge, 2002a.

Dyer, Richard. "The White Man's Muscles." In *The Masculinity Studies Reader*. Eds. Rachel Adams and David Savran. Malden, MA: Blackwell, 2002b, 262–73.

Edwards, Gavin. *Last Night at the Viper Room: River Phoenix and the Hollywood He Left Behind*. New York: HarperCollins, 2013.

Eliot, T. S. *The Waste Land and Other Poems*. New York: Signet, 1998.

Escoffier, Jeffrey. "Gay-for-Pay: Straight Men and the Making of Gay Pornography." *Qualitative Sociology*. 26.4 (Winter 2003): 531–55.

Fiedler, Leslie. *Love and Death in the American Novel*. New York: Stein, 1966.

Fisher, Mark. *Capitalist Realism*. Winchester: Zero Books, 2009.

Fishwick, Marshall. *Probing Popular Culture: On and Off the Internet*. Binghamton, NY: Haworth, 2004.

Foucault, Michel. *Madness and Civilization?: A History of Insanity in the Age of Reason*. New York: Vintage Books, 1988.

Freud, Sigmund. *The Ego and the Id and Other Works: The Standard Edition of the Complete Psychological Works of Sigmund Freud*. Vol. 19. London: Vintage, 2001.

Frye, Northrop. *Anatomy of Criticism*. Princeton, NJ: Princeton University Press, 1957.

Frye, Northrop. *A Study of English Romanticism*. New York: Random House, 1968.

Fuchs, Cynthia. "The Buddy Politic." In *Screening the Male: Exploring Masculinities in Hollywood Cinema*. Eds. Steve Cohan and Ina Rae Hark. New York: Routledge, 1993, 194–212.

Fuqua, Joy V. "Brand Pitt: Celebrity Activism and the Make It Right Foundation in Post-Katrina New Orleans." *Celebrity Studies* 2.2 (2011): 192–208.

Giles, David. *Illusions of Immortality: A Psychology of Fame and Celebrity*. New York: St. Martin's Press, 2000.

Giles, Jeff. "Brad Pitt: The E.W. Interview." *Entertainment Weekly* September 23, 2011: 40–52.

Ginsberg, Allen. *Howl and Other Poems*. San Francisco, CA: City Lights Books, 1959.

Greven, David. "Contemporary Hollywood Masculinity and the Double-Protagonist Film." *Cinema Journal* 48.4 (2009): 22–43.

Grosz, Elizabeth. *Volatile Bodies: Toward a Corporeal Feminism*. Bloomington, IN: Indiana University Press, 1994.

Halberstam, Judith. *The Queer Art of Failure*. Durham, NC: Duke University Press, 2011.

Hammond, M. "Introduction." In *The Iliad*. London: Penguin, 1987.

Hammond, Shannon. *Brad Pitt Won't Leave Me Alone*. CreateSpace: 2011.

Harris, Cheryl and Alison Alexander (Eds.) *Theorizing Fandom: Fans, Subculture and Identity*. Cresskill, NJ: Hampton Press Inc., 1998.

Harrison, Jim. *Legends of the Fall*. New York: Delta, 1978.

Hevesi, Dennis. "Marion Dougherty, Hollywood Star-Maker, Dies at 88." *The New York Times* (December 7, 2011).

Homer. *The Iliad*. Trans. M. Hammond. London: Penguin, 2001.

Jeffords, Susan. *Hard Bodies: Hollywood Masculinity in the Reagan Era*. New Brunswick, NJ: Rutgers University Press, 1994.

Joyce, James. *Ulysses*. New York: Vintage, 1986.

Kim, Jodi. "An 'Orphan' with Two Mothers: Transnational and Transracial Adoption, the Cold War, and Contemporary Asian American Cultural Politics." *American Quarterly* 61.4 (2009): 855–80.

Lasn, Kalle. *Culture Jam*. New York: HarperCollins, 1999.

Lennard, John. *Reading Octavia E Butler: Xenogenesis/Lilith's Brood*. Penrith, UK: Humanities-Ebooks, 2007.

Leslie, Larry Z. *Celebrity in the 21st Century: A Reference Handbook*. Santa Barbara, CA: ABC-CLIO, 2011.

Maclean, Norman. *A River Runs Through It and Other Stories*. Chicago, IL: University of Chicago Press, 1976.

Martin, Aryn. "Microchimerism in the Mother(land): Blurring the Borders of Body and Nation." *Body & Society* 16.2 (2010): 23–50.

Mickey, Thomas J. *Sociodrama: An Interpretive Theory for the Practice of Public Relations*. Lanham, MD: University Press of America, 1995.

Morton, Andrew. *Angelina: An Unauthorized Biography*. New York: St. Martin's Press, 2010.

Mulvey, Laura. "Visual Pleasure and Narrative Cinema." *Screen* 16.3 (1975): 6–18.

Newman, Martin. "Art: Daniel Edwards' Brad Pitt and Angelina Jolie Sculpture." *Mirror* December 8, 2009.

Nietzsche, Friedrich. *Beyond Good and Evil*. New York: Vintage, 1989.

O'Dair, Barbara. "Preface." In *Brad Pitt*. Ed. by Holly George-Warren. New York: Little Brown, 1997.

Otnes, Cele and Elizabeth Pleck. *Cinderella Dreams: The Allure of the Lavish Wedding*. Berkeley, CA: University of California Press, 2003.

Palahniuk, Chuck. *Fight Club*. New York: Henry Holt, 1996.

Park, E. J. "Rebel Consumer." In *You Do Not Talk About* Fight Club: *I Am Jack's Completely Unauthorized Essay Collection*. Ed. Read Mercer Schuchardt. Dallas, TX: BenBella, 2008.

Pearlman, Cindy, "Brad Pitt's Seven Deadly Sins—'Sexiest Man Alive' Explains Film—and Errors of His Ways," *Chicago Sun-Times*, September 17, 1995.

People Magazine. January 30, 1995, cover.

People Magazine. November 13, 2000, cover.

Plato. "Ion". In *Criticism: Major Statements*. Fourth Edition. Charles Kaplan and William Davis Anderson, Eds. Boston, MA: Bedford St. Martin.

Robb, Brian J. *Brad Pitt: The Rise to Stardom*. London: Plexus Publishing, 1996.

Robinson, Sally. *Marked Men: White Masculinity in Crisis*. New York: Columbia University Press, 2000.

Rojek, Chris. *Celebrity*. London: Reaktion Books, 2001.

Saunders, Robert A. "Transnational Reproduction and its Discontents: The Politics of Intercountry Adoption in a Global Society." *Journal of Global Change and Governance* 1.1 (2007): 1–23.

Schaberg, Christopher. "Environmentality and Air Travel Disasters: Representing the Violence of Plane Crashes." In *Beauty, Violence, Representation*. Eds. Lisa Dickson and Maryna Romanets. New York: Routledge, 2013, 120–36.

Schickel, Richard. *Intimate Strangers: The Culture of Celebrity*. New York: Doubleday & Co., 1985.

Shome, Raka. "'Global Motherhood': The Transnational Intimacies of White Femininity." *Critical Studies in Media Communication* 28.5 (2011): 388–406.

Sloane, Judy. "David Fincher." *Film Review* (February 1996): 34–5.

Sternheimer, Karen. *Celebrity Culture and the American Dream: Stardom and Social Mobility*. New York: Routledge, 2011.

Swallow, James. *Dark Eye: The Films of David Fincher*. London: Reynaulds and Hearn, 2003.

Tasker, Yvonne. *Spectacular Bodies: Gender, Genre, and the Action Cinema*. New York: Routledge, 1993.

Taylor, Brent D. *The Creative Edge: Insights from the Lives of the World's Most Famous Outsiders*. Milton, Queensland: John Wiley, 2008.

Theweleit, Klaus. *Male Fantasies*, vol. 2. Minneapolis, MN: University of Minnesota Press, 1989.

Thoreau, Henry David. *The Maine Woods*. New York: Viking Penguin, 1988.

Thoreau, Henry David. *Walden and "Civil Disobedience."* New York: Signet, 1999.

Thurschwell, Pamela. *Sigmund Freud*. New York: Routledge, 2000.

Walker, John A. *Art and Celebrities*. London: Pluto Press, 2003.

Wallace, David Foster. "E Unibus Pluram." In *A Supposedly Fun Thing I'll Never Do Again*. New York: Back Bay, 1998.

Wallace, David Foster. *Both Flesh and Not: Essays*. New York: Little, Brown and Co., 2012.

Wicke, Jennifer. "Celebrity's Face Book." *PMLA* 126.4 (2011): 1131–9.

Wilson, James D. "Tirso, Hat, and Byron: The Emergence of Don Juan as Romantic Hero." *The South Central Bulletin* 32.4 (1972): 246–8.

Film and television work

Across the Tracks. Directed by Sandy Tung. Desert Productions, 1990.

A River Runs Through It. Directed by Robert Redford. Columbia Pictures, 1992.

The Assassination of Jesse James by the Coward Robert Ford.
    Directed by Andrew Dominik. Warner Bros, 2007.
A Stoning in Fulham County. Directed by Larry Elikann. Landsburg
    Company, 1988.
Babel. Directed by Alejandro González Iñárritu. Paramount Pictures,
    2006.
Being John Malkovich. Directed by Spike Jonze. Gramercy Pictures,
    1999.
Burn After Reading. Directed by Ethan and Joel Coen. Focus
    Features, 2008.
Confessions of a Dangerous Mind. Directed by George Clooney.
    Miramax Films, 2002.
Contact. Directed by Jonathan Darby. Chanticleer Films, 1992.
Cool World. Directed by Ralph Bakshi. Paramount Pictures, 1992.
The Counselor. Directed by Ridley Scott. Chockstone Pictures, 2013.
The Curious Case of Benjamin Button. Directed by David Fincher.
    Warner Bros, 2008.
Cutting Class. Directed by Rospo Pallenberg. April Films, 1989.
The Dark Side of the Sun. Directed by Bozidar Nikolic. Avala Film,
    1988.
Deconstructing Harry. Directed by Woody Allen. Fine Line Features,
    1997.
The Devil's Own. Directed by Alan J. Pakula. Columbia Pictures
    Corporation, 1997.
The Favor. Directed by Donald Petrie. Nelson Entertainment, 1994.
Fight Club. Directed by David Fincher. 20th Century Fox, 1999.
Fury. Directed by David Ayer. Grisbi Productions, 2014.
The Graduate. Directed by Mike Nichols. MGM, 1967.
Happy Feet Two. Directed by George Miller, Gary Eck, and David
    Peers. Warner Bros, 2011.
Happy Together. Directed by Mel Damski. Apollo Productions, 1988.
Hunk. Directed by Lawrence Bassoff. Crown International Pictures,
    1987.
Inglourious Basterds. Directed by Quentin Tarantino. Universal
    Pictures, 2009.
Interview with the Vampire. Directed by Neil Jordan. Geffen
    Pictures, 1994.
Johnny Suede. Directed by Tom DiCillo. Lions Gate, 1991.
Kalifornia. Directed by Dominic Sena. MGM, 1993.
Killing Them Softly. Directed by Andrew Dominik. Weinstein, 2012.

Legends of the Fall. Directed by Edward Zwick. TriStar, 1994.

Less Than Zero. Directed by Marek Kanievska. 20th Century Fox, 1987.

Meet Joe Black. Directed by Martin Brest. Universal, 1998.

Megamind. Directed by Tom McGrath. DreamWorks Animation, 2010.

The Mexican. Directed by Gore Verbinski. DreamWorks, 2001.

Moneyball. Directed by Bennett Miller. Columbia Picture Corporation, 2011.

Mr. & Mrs. Smith. Directed by Doug Liman. 20th Century Fox, 2005.

"Mr. & Mrs. Simpson." *The Simpsons*. Season 19, episode 5. 2007.

No Man's Land. Directed by Peter Werner. Orion Pictures Corporation, 1987.

No Way Out. Directed by Roger Donaldson. MGM, 1987.

Ocean's Eleven. Directed by Steven Soderbergh. Warner Bros, 2001.

Ocean's Thirteen. Directed by Steven Soderbergh. Warner Bros, 2007.

Ocean's Twelve. Directed by Steven Soderbergh. Warner Bros, 2004.

Seven. Directed by David Fincher. New Line Productions, 1995.

Seven Years in Tibet. Directed by Jean-Jacques Annaud. Mandalay Entertainment, 1997.

Sinbad: Legend of the Seven Seas. Directed by Patrick Gilmore and Tim Johnson. DreamWorks SKG, 2003.

Sleepers. Directed by Barry Levinson. Baltimore Pictures, 1996.

Snatch. Directed by Guy Ritchie. Columbia Pictures Corporation, 2000.

Spy Game. Directed by Tony Scott. Universal Pictures, 2001.

Thelma & Louise. Directed by Ridley Scott. Pathé Entertainment, 1991.

Today Show. August 21, 2009 [Accessed January 10, 2014]. http://www.youtube.com/watch?v=lpP2_8GH0CU.

Too Young to Die? Directed by Robert Markowitz. Frank & Bob Films II, 1990.

To Rome With Love. Directed by Woody Allen. Medusa Film, 2012.

The Tree of Life. Directed by Terrence Malick. Cottonwood Pictures, 2011.

Troy. Directed by Wolfgang Peterson. Warner Bros, 2004.

True Lies. Directed by James Cameron. 20th Century Fox, 1994.

True Romance. Directed by Tony Scott. Morgan Creek Productions, 1993.

Twelve Monkeys. Directed by Terry Gilliam. Universal Pictures, 1995.

Twelve Years a Slave. Directed by Steve McQueen. Regency Enterprises, 2013.

Voyage of Time. Directed by Terrence Malick. Sovereign Films, 2014.

World War Z. Directed by Marc Forster. Paramount Pictures, 2013.

Zabriskie Point. Directed by Michelangelo Antonioni. Warner Brothers, 1970.

Music

Benetar, Pat. "Love is a Battlefield." *Live from Earth*. Chrysalis, 1983.

Lenka. "The Show." *Lenka*. Epic, 2008.

Nelson, Ricky. "Teen Age Idol." (Imperial 5864, 1962).

The Ramones. "I Wanna Be Sedated." *Road to Ruin*. Sire, 1978.

Reynolds, Malvina. "Little Boxes." *Ear to the Ground*. Folkways, 2000.

Twain, Shania. "That Don't Impress Me Much." *Come On Over*. Mercury, 1997.

Web resources

"41 Facts from the 41st State." State Government website. http://visitmt.com/experiences/montana_extras/montana_facts/ [Accessed October 18, 2013].

Adam. "Angelina Jolie and Brad Pitt's Kids Turn Nasty." *ShowbizSpy*. Published March 17, 2011. http://www.showbizspy.com/article/228633/angelina-jolie-and-brad-pitts-kids-turn-nasty.html [Accessed December 27, 2012].

admin. "Brad Pitt Workout – The Fight Club Workout." Prove You're Alive. Published September 7, 2011. http://proveyourealive.com/brad_pitt_workout_fight_club_workout [Accessed April 24, 2013].

adoptmebrangelina. "Brangelina." *Urban Dictionary*. Published August 28, 2009. http://www.urbandictionary.com/define.php?term=brangelina [Accessed December 27, 2012].

Anderson, Lisa. "No Pit Stops for Brad." *Toronto Star*. Published August 31, 1992. LexisNexis Academic [Accessed March 30, 2013].

Anonymous. "The Brangelina family in Hello!" *Celebitchy*. Published August 9, 2007. http://www.celebitchy.com/2397/the_brangelina_family_in_hello/ [Accessed February 11, 2013].

ashley. "Brangelina to Expand its Brood?" *Hollywood Gossip*. Published December 10, 2008. http://www.thehollywoodgossip. com/2008/12/brangelina-to-expand-its-brood/ [Accessed April 5, 2013].

Bradatan, Costica. "In Praise of Failure." *Opinionator*. Published December 15, 2013. http://opinionator.blogs.nytimes. com/2013/12/15/in-praise-of-failure/ [Accessed January 2, 2014].

Brown, Nathan. "Origin and Extinction, Mourning and Melancholia." *MUTE*. Published September 9, 2012. http://www. metamute.org/editorial/articles/origin-and-extinction-mourning-and-melancholia [Accessed December 17, 2013].

Carson, Hope. "Why Justin Bieber–Selena Gomez's Love Will Last Forever." *Gather*. Published January 27, 2012 [Accessed December 30, 2012]. http://celebs.gather.com/viewArticle.action? articleId=281474981066030.

The Celebrity Stork. "The Brangelina Brood Hits New Orleans (PIC March 2011)." *Flickr*. Published March 20, 2011. http://www. flickr.com/photos/35965850@N04/5545100670/ [Accessed February 11, 2013].

"The Cultural Logic of Brad Pitt, or Does Tyler Durden Reify or Challenge Hegemonic Codes of Race, Class, Gender, or Regional and National Identities." http://acephalous.typepad.com/ acephalous/2005/05/the_cultural_lo.html. [Accessed December 3, 2013].

Cunningham III, Reginald. "BRAD AND ANGELINA SPLIT." *Weekly World News*. Published January 26, 2010. http:// weeklyworldnews.com/celebs/15324/brad-and-angelina-split/ [Accessed August 25, 2013].

Dirty Girl Gardening. "DIRTY LOVE." Published February 2012. http://dirtygirlgarden.com/2010/02/valentines-day-propagation/ [Accessed December 29, 2012].

Duganz, Patrick. "Warming Rivers May be the End of Trout Fishing." *Silverstate Post* online. Published August 31, 2011. http://ssp.stparchive.com/Archive/SSP/SSP08312011p02.php [Accessed November 8, 2013].

Dunphy, Catherine. "Ozark Lad Goes Fishin' with Redford." *Toronto Star*. Published October 9, 1992. LexisNexis Academic [Accessed September 15, 2013].

Durmann, Tina. "Brad Pitt Asked to Stand for Mayor of New Orleans." *The Mirror*. June 12, 2009. http://www.mirror.co.uk/ 3am/celebrity-news/brad-pitt-asked-to-stand-for-mayor-399532.

Franklin, Lauren. "Angelina 'planning to adopt Haitian child.'"
  Sugarscape. Published February 10, 2010. http://www.sugarscape.
  com/main-topics/celebrities/464465/angelina-planning-adopt-
  haitian-child. [Accessed December 31, 2012].

Freedman, Yacov. "Is It Real . . . or Is It Motion Capture?: The Battle
  to Redefine Animation in the Age of Digital Performance." *The
  Velvet Light Trap* 69.1 (2012): 38–49. Academic Search
  Complete, EBSCOhost [Accessed January 2, 2014].

Gabay, Jonathan as quoted in Denise Winterman. "What a Mesh."
  BBC News. Published August 3, 2006. http://news.bbc.co.uk/2/hi/
  uk_news/magazine/5239464.stm [Accessed February 22, 2013].

Gerstein, Julie. "Total Speculation: 9 Potential Reasons Heidi Klum
  & Seal Are Breaking Up." *The Frisky*. Published January 23,
  2012. http://www.thefrisky.com/2012-01-23/total-speculation-9-
  potential-reasons-heidi-klum-seal-are-breaking-up/ [Accessed
  December 30, 2012].

Green, Tom. "Unpretentious Brad Pitt." *USA Today*. October 22,
  1992. LexisNexis Academic [Accessed September 15, 2013].

Harris, Cheryl and Alison Alexander (Eds.) *Theorizing Fandom:
  Fans, Subculture and Identity*. Cresskill, NJ: Hampton Press Inc.,
  1998.

"INSIDE THE WORLD OF BRANGELINA'S BROOD." *Mirror*.
  Published March 17, 2007. http://www.mirror.co.uk/news/
  uk-news/inside-the-world-of-brangelinas-brood-459161
  [Accessed April 6, 2013].

Joe Black Crash GIF http://stream1.gifsoup.com/view2/1756535/
  brad-pitt-gets-hit-by-two-cars-o.gif [Accessed January 24, 2014].

Johns, Marjorie. "Dark Side of the Sun." *Movie Archive Reviews*.
  http://www.citizencaine.org/movies/50filmchallenge/dark-side-of-
  the-sun.shtml [Accessed January 11, 2014].

Kimball, Roger. "The Hermeneutics of Brad Pitt." Published June 10,
  2005. http://www.newcriterion.com/posts.cfm/hermeneutics-of-
  brad-pitt-3962 [Accessed November 19, 2013].

"La Logica Culturale di Brad Pitt." http://bottone.blogspot.
  com/2005/09/paperi-call-for-crazy-papers.html [Accessed
  November 19, 2013].

Lambert, Pam. "A Legend to Fall For." *People Magazine*, January 30,
  1995. http://www.people.com/people/archive/
  article/0,,20104953,00.html.

Leavitt, Mike. "Brangelina.jpg." Intuition Kitchen Productions.
  February 11, 2013.

"Lewis' 'Night' to Forget." *USA Today*. April 15, 1992. LexisNexis Academic. [Accessed September 15, 2013].

Lim, Dennis. "Don't Forget, He Acts Too." *New York Times*, December 30, 2011. www.nytimes.com/2012/01/01/movies/ awardsseason/brad-pitt-discusses-moneyball-and-tree-of-life [Accessed January 10, 2014].

"Man Photoshops Celebrities into His Holiday Party." *Buzzfeed*. February 22, 2012.

Mayes, Alison. "Emerging Star Pitt Attracted to Problem Roles." *Calgary Herald*. Published October 28 1993. Academic Search Complete, EBSCOhost. [Accessed October 1, 2012].

McMillian, Kevin. "Brad Pitt Troy Workout." Squidoo. April 24, 2013. http://www.squidoo.com/brad-pitt-troy-workout.

megsx. "Angelina 'planning to adopt Haitian child.' " *Sugarscape*. Published February 10, 2010. http://www.sugarscape.com/ main-topics/celebrities/464465/angelina-planning-adopt-haitian-child?page=1 [Accessed December 31, 2012].

Merriman, Rebecca. " 'Mr. Muscle' Brad Pitt Loves Getting His Hands Dirty." *Entertainmentwise*. Published September 17, 2012. http://www.entertainmentwise.com/news/88170/Mr-Muscle-Brad-Pitt-Loves-Getting-His-Hands-Dirty- [Accessed April 24, 2013].

Miller, Michael H. "Brad Pitt Took a Private Jet to Documenta." http://galleristny.com/2012/06/brad-pitt-took-a-private-jet-to-documenta/ [Accessed January 24, 2014].

MIMI. "SPOTTED: BRANGELINA'S BROOD." *Beauty and the Dirt*. Published March 21, 2011. http://www.beautyandthedirt. com/entertainment/gossip/spotted-brangelina-brood/ [Accessed February 11, 2013].

Mundy, Chris. "Brad Pitt." *Rolling Stone*. December 1, 1994. Academic Search Complete, EBSCOhost. October 1, 2012.

Nickerson, Norma P. "Red or Blue? An Exploration of Political Party Affiliation and Resident Attitudes toward Tourism in Montana." http://www.itrr.umt.edu/research06/2006TTRAPartya ffiliation.pdf [Accessed November 1, 2013].

Niwdenapolis. "Brad Pitt as an Art Subject." Published September 26, 2007. http://www.niwdenapolis.com/2007/09/brad_pitt_as_art_ subject. [Accessed June 30, 2012].

Paxman, Lauren. "Are Brangelina adding to their brood? The Jolie-Pitts were spotted visiting an orphanage." *Alison Jackson Online*. Published November 28, 2012. http://www.alisonjackson.

com/brangelina-adding-to-brood-brad-pitt-and-angelina-jolie-spotted-visiting-orphanage/ [Accessed February 17, 2013].

pinksugarxxx. "Angelina 'planning to adopt Haitian child.' " *Sugarscape*. Published February 10, 2010. http://www.sugarscape. com/main-topics/celebrities/464465/angelina-planning-adopt-haitian-child [Accessed December 31, 2012].

Plato. "Ion". In *Criticism: Major Statements*. Fourth Edition. Charles Kaplan and William Davis Anderson, Eds. Boston, MA: Bedford St. Martin.

Pruitt, Allie. "BAT BOY JOLIE?" *Weekly World News*. Published November 21, 2008. http://weeklyworldnews.com/mutants/4036/bat-boy-jolie/ [Accessed April 29, 2013].

PYGOD. "Brad Pitt in Fight Club." StrengthFighter.com. Published April 24, 2012. http://www.strengthfighter.com/2012/04/brad-pitt-in-fight-club.html. [Accessed April 24, 2013].

rebecca. "Brad and Angie vs. Brad and Jen!" *thinkfashion*. Published August 15, 2007. http://www.thinkfashion.com/blogs/stylosity_hollywood_hookup/archive/2007/08/15/brad-and-angie-vs-brad-and-jen.aspx [Accessed April 7, 2013].

"Robbie Williams Would Go Gay for Brad Pitt." *On Top Magazine*, December 29, 2011. http://www.ontopmag.com/article.aspx?id=1 0497&MediaType=1&Category=22 [Accessed January 11, 2014].

Rufus. "Proof that Academics Read the *National Inquirer*." Published June 7, 2005. http://gradstudentmadness.blogspot. com/2005/06/proof-that-academics-read-national.html [Accessed November 19, 2013].

Said, S. F. "It's the Thought that Counts." *The Telegraph*. Published April 19, 2003. http://www.telegraph.co.uk/culture/film/3592955/Its-the-thought-that-counts.html [Accessed November 9, 2011].

Screamname. "Angelina set to adopt another baby." *Free Republic*. Published October 27, 2006. http://www.freerepublic.com/focus/f-chat/1726790/posts [Accessed May 1, 2013].

Starpulse. "Top 10 Metrosexual Celebs." Published March 3, 2008. http://starpulse.com/news/index.php/2008/03/03/top_10_metrosexual_celebs [Accessed February 15, 2013].

Sumaray, Audie. *Bleeding Color*. Published May 28, 2009. http://bleedingcolor.com/post/114097106/guys-i-would-go-gay-for-brad-pitt [Accessed January 9, 2014].

Sunnye. "Namibia: Diamonds on the soles of my shoes, Part I." *nomadamorphose*. Published May 10, 2012. http://

nomadamorphose.blogspot.com/2012/05/namibia-diamonds-on-soles-of-my-shoes.html [Accessed December 29, 2012].

sunshine coast girl. "Angelina Jolie." *The Tyee*. December 28, 2012. http://thetyee.ca/Views/2009/06/10/Jolie/ [Accessed January 12, 2014].

"Thirteen Reasons Why Brad Pitt Should Be the Next Mayor of New Orleans." *Storyville*. Published May 2, 2009. http://www.storyvilleapparel.com/brad-pitt-for-mayor-10285.html [Accessed January 11, 2014].

Thomson, Katherine. "Brad Pitt Donates $100,000 to Fight Gay Marriage Ban." *Huffington Post*. Published September 17, 2008. http://www.huffingtonpost.com/2008/09/17/brad-pitt-donates-100000_n_127263.html [Accessed January 12, 2014].

Today Show, August 21, 2009 http://www.youtube.com/watch?v=lpP2_8GH0CU [Accessed January 10, 2014].

Ueland, John. "Congratulations, You're Man-Pregnant." *GQ*. Published February 2013. http://www.gq.com/entertainment/humor/201303/man-pregnant [Accessed December 19, 2013].

Wagaman, James Brian. "Postmodern Brad." *The Chronicle of Higher Education* on-line. https://chronicle.com/article/Postmodern-Brad/24659 [Accessed November 19, 2013].

Wikipedia. "Silent Generation." http://en.wikipedia.org/wiki/Silent_Generation. [Accessed September 27, 2012].

Wolf, Naomi. "The Power of Angelina." *Harpers Bazaar*. Published June 8, 2009. http://www.harpersbazaar.com/magazine/cover/angelina-jolie-essay-0709 [Accessed April 1, 2013].

Yahoo! Cricket News. "Will 'S-Hurleys' outnumber Brangelina brood?" *Cricket ON*. Published December 20, 2011. http://cricketon.com/uncategorized/will-s-hurleys-outnumber-brangelina-brood/ [Accessed February 11, 2013].

Zimbio, "Brangelina and Other Famous Portmanteaus." February 24, 2013. http://www.zimbio.com/Brangelina+and+Other+Famous+Portmanteaus/articles/EGHTgVLEAN6/Brangelina [Accessed January 12, 2014].

Zimmer, Benjamin. "A Perilous Portmanteau?" *Language Log*. Published November 2005. http://itre.cis.upenn.edu/~myl/languagelog/archives/2005_11.html [Accessed December 27, 2012].

LIST OF CONTRIBUTORS

Elizabeth Abele is an Associate Professor of English at SUNY Nassau Community College and former Executive Director of the Northeast Modern Language Association. She is the author of *Home Front Heroes: The Rise of a New Hollywood Archetype, 1988–99* (McFarland).

Bob Batchelor is James Pedas Professor of Communication and Executive Director of the James Pedas Communication Center at Thiel College. A noted cultural historian and biographer, Bob is the author or editor of 26 books, including *John Updike: A Critical Biography* (Praeger) and *Gatsby: A Cultural History of the Great American Novel* (Rowman & Littlefield).

Thomas M. Bayer, PhD, is an art and economic historian who formerly taught at Tulane University in New Orleans. He has published numerous scholarly papers over the past 20 years on the economics of the art market, and is the co-author (with John Page) of *The Development of the Art Market in England* (Pickering & Chatto).

Robert Bennett is an Associate Professor of English at Montana State University-Bozeman. He is the author of *Deconstructing Post-WWII New York City: The Literature, Art, Jazz, and Architecture of an Emerging Global Capital* (Routledge), as well as numerous essays on the interrelationships between post-World War II American literature, architecture, and popular music.

Nancy Bernardo is an Assistant Professor of Graphic Design at Rochester Institute of Technology.

Edmond Y. Chang is an Assistant Professor of English at Drew University in New Jersey. His areas of interest include technoculture, cultural studies, popular culture, and contemporary American literature. He has written on post-humanism, race, gender and sexuality, and in video games including *World of Warcraft* and *Bioshock*.

Andrew Horton is the Jeanne H. Smith Professor of Film and Media Studies at the University of Oklahoma, an award winning screenwriter, and the author of 30 books on film and cultural studies, the most recent of which is *Screenwriting* (Rutgers). His films include Brad Pitt's first feature film, *The Dark Side of the Sun* (1988) and *Something in Between* (1983, Dir. Srdjan Karanovic).

Rick Hudson is a literature academic and novelist based in Manchester, UK. He has published widely on a variety of subjects ranging from Medieval Literature to Marvel Comics. He lectured at Southampton Solent University from 1999–2008 and is currently based with the private sector educator Accelerate Learning and conducting research under the aegis of Bath Spa University.

Randy Laist is an Associate Professor of English at Goodwin College. He is the author of *Technology and Postmodern Subjectivity in Don DeLillo's Novels* (Peter Lang) and a recent book, *The Cinema of Simulation: Hyperreal Hollywood in the Long 1990s* (Bloomsbury). He is also the editor of *Plants and Literature: Essays in Critical Plant Studies* (Rodopi) and *Looking for Lost: Critical Essays on the Enigmatic Series* (McFarland).

Sarah Juliet Lauro is a visiting Assistant Professor of English at Clemson University, where she teaches courses on literature and film. Her interests include zombies as well as celebrities.

Her book *The Transatlantic Zombie: Slavery, Rebellion, and Living Death* (Rutgers) is in development.

Ben Leubner is a visiting Assistant Professor of English at Montana State University-Bozeman.

Fran Pheasant-Kelly is a Reader in Film and Television Studies at the University of Wolverhampton, UK. Her research centers on fantasy, 9/11, abjection, and space, which form the basis for two books, *Abject Spaces in American Cinema* (Tauris) and *Fantasy Film Post 9/11* (Palgrave).

Christopher Schaberg is an Associate Professor of English and Environment at Loyola University New Orleans. He is the author of *The Textual Life of Airports: Reading the Culture of Flight* (Bloomsbury), and founding co-editor of the book and essay series Object Lessons (published by *The Atlantic* and Bloomsbury).

Brian A. Sullivan is the Instructional and Research Technologies Librarian and Associate Professor at Loyola University New Orleans.

Michele White is an Associate Professor in the Department of Communication at Tulane University. She has published *Buy It Now: Lessons from eBay* (Duke) and *The Body and the Screen: Theories of Internet Spectatorship* (MIT). *Producing Women in Internet Sites: Traditional Femininity, Queer Engagements, and Creative Practices* is forthcoming from Routledge.

INDEX

Page references for illustrations appear in *italics*.